THE CONFEDERATION DEBATES IN THE PROVINCE OF CANADA 1865

Carleton Library Series

The Carleton Library Series, funded by Carleton University under the general editorship of the dean of the School of Graduate Studies and Research, publishes books about Canadian economics, geography, history, politics, society, and related subjects. It includes important new works as well as reprints of classics in the fields. The editorial committee welcomes manuscripts and suggestions, which should be sent to the dean of the School of Graduate Studies and Research, Carleton University.

192 The Blacks in Canada: A History
(second edition)
Robin Winks

193 A Disciplined Intelligence
Critical Inquiry and Canadian Thought in the Victorian Era
A.B. McKillop

194 Land, Power, and Economics on the Frontier of Upper Canada
John Clarke

195 The Children of Aataentsic
A History of the Huron People to 1660
Bruce G. Trigger

196 Silent Surrender
The Multinational Corporation in Canada
Kari Levitt

197 Cree Narrative
Expressing the Personal Meanings of Events
Richard J. Preston

198 The Dream of Nation
A Social and Intellectual History of Quebec
Susan Mann

199 A Great Duty
Canadian Responses to Modern Life and Mass Culture, 1939–1967
L.B. Kuffert

200 The Politics of Development
Forests, Mines, and Hydro-Electric Power in Ontario, 1849–1941
H.V. Nelles

201 Watching Quebec: Selected Essays
Ramsay Cook

202 Land of the Midnight Sun
A History of the Yukon
Ken S. Coates and William R. Morrison

203 The Canadian Quandary
Harry Johnson
(New edition)

204 Canada and the Cost of World War II
The International Operation of the Department of Finance, 1939–1947
Robert B. Bryce
Edited by Mathew Bellamy

205 Lament for a Nation
George Grant
(Anniversary edition)

206 Confederation Debates in the Province of Canada, 1865
P.B. Waite
(New edition)

The Confederation Debates in the Province of Canada 1865

A Selection Edited and Introduced by
PETER B. WAITE

With a New Introduction by
GED MARTIN

The Carleton Library Series 206

McGill-Queen's University Press
Montreal & Kingston • London • Ithaca

ISBN-13: 978-0-7735-3092-8 ISBN-10: 0-7735-3092-4 (cloth)
ISBN-13: 978-0-7735-3093-5 ISBN-10: 0-7735-3093-2 (paper)

Legal deposit second quarter 2006
Bibliothèque nationale du Québec

Printed in Canada on acid-free paper that is 100% ancient forest free (100% post-consumer recycled), processed chlorine free.

First edition published by McClelland and Stewart Limited, 1963, Carleton Library Series 2

McGill-Queen's University Press acknowledges the support of the Canada Council for the Arts for our publishing program. We also acknowledge the financial support of the Government of Canada through the Book Publishing Industry Development Program (BPIDP) for our publishing activities.

Library and Archives Canada Cataloguing in Publication

Canada. Parliament
The Confederation debates in the Province of Canada, 1865 : a selection / edited and introduced by P. B. Waite ; with a new introduction by Ged Martin.

(Carleton Library series ; 206)
First published 1963 as the second book in the original Carleton Library series.
Includes bibliographical references and index.

ISBN-13: 978-0-7735-3092-8 ISBN-10: 0-7735-3092-4 (bnd)
ISBN-13: 978-0-7735-3093-5 ISBN-10: 0-7735-3093-2 (pbk)

1. Canada—History—1841-1867—Sources. I. Waite, P. B. (Peter Busby), 1922– II. Title. III. Series: Carleton library ; 206
FC474.C24 2006 971.04'9 C2006-900455-2

Contents

Introduction to the 2006 Edition

Between 3 February and 13 March 1865, the Parliament of the Province of Canada debated the recently negotiated scheme for political union with British colonies on the Atlantic seaboard, which would create a territorial union from Newfoundland to Lake Superior. As a public information exercise, legislators decided to produce a near-verbatim account of their deliberations. Selections from the resulting thousand-page tome were published in 1963 by Peter B. Waite, whose sparkling introduction is reprinted in this new edition.[1]

In 1865, the Province of Canada was not the transcontinental nation of today but a union of the colonies of Upper and Lower Canada, sometimes referred to as Canada West and Canada East.[2] They re-emerged in 1867 as Ontario and Quebec. The Union, originally imposed by the British government after the rebellions of 1837–38, was a classic case of Canadian duality, an overarching structure that preserved the identity of the component parts. The provincial capital even alternated between Toronto and Quebec City. In 1865 Parliament was meeting in Quebec, although it would soon depart for a permanent home in Ottawa. The two sections kept their own property laws: indeed Lower Canada was in the process of codifying its civil law, thus underlining its French identity. With Upper and Lower Canada each electing sixty-five members to the Assembly, representation was equal and elected, but increasingly ineffective. The British had hoped that this artificial equality of representation would help Upper Canada representatives join with the English-speaking minority from Lower Canada to out-vote the French. In fact, Upper Canada Liberals (confusingly for modern readers called "Reformers") teamed up with French-speaking radicals, known as the "Rouges." (The modern Liberal Party has inherited its nickname, the "Grits," from those Upper Canada Reformers and its campaign colour, red, from their Lower Canadian allies.) Similarly, Upper Canadian Conservatives struck deals with Lower Canadian "Bleus," who combined adherence to traditional

Catholicism with a shrewd desire for economic development. For eight years, from 1854 to 1862, the province was governed by a precarious alliance of these two groups, a partnership symbolised by the key figures of John A. Macdonald, the moderate Conservative, and George-Etienne Cartier, the Montreal lawyer.[3]

Canada's political duality was undermined by demographic change. The 1861 census confirmed that Upper Canada, with about 1.4 million people, was forging ahead of Lower Canada, with its 1.1 million population. Some French Canadians denounced the census as a fraud, but by 1865 most people acknowledged that the gap had widened by another 100,000. The disparity was caused by the rapid settlement of the fertile lands west of the ambitious city of Toronto: in 1864, the member for the Bruce Peninsula complained that his riding contained as many people as Prince Edward Island.[4] John A. Macdonald, whose power base was Kingston, in the sluggish eastern end of Upper Canada, was unenthusiastic about recognizing this westward shift of political power but most Upper Canadian politicians were demanding representation by population ("rep. by pop.") which would give their area extra seats in the Assembly. Nowadays that sounds like a simple democratic principle. Unfortunately in the mid-nineteenth century it thinly masked the sectarian demand of English-speaking Protestants for mastery over French-speaking Catholics. In vehement editorials, George Brown of the Toronto *Globe* demanded representation by population not only because dynamic Upper Canada generated most of the provincial tax revenue but because it would weaken the power of French and Catholic interests to meddle in Upper Canadian affairs.[5] Canada, in short, was on the verge of slipping into a political culture dominated not by debate between parties and ideologies but by an unbridgeable religious confrontation, made all the sharper by Canada's linguistic divide.

Was there a way out of this looming impasse? In 1858 Cartier and Macdonald agreed to explore the possibility of a federation of all the provinces. This gained them the support of the Sherbrooke entrepreneur Alexander Galt, who argued that Canada's own sectional problems could be resolved by dividing the province into two or even three units within a wider union.[6] However the project lapsed when it became clear that the other provinces were not interested in solving Canada's internal quarrels. "We never heard another word about it," Christopher Dunkin complained during the Confederation debates.[7] When Upper Canada Reformers held a party convention in 1859, they adopted a vague policy of federalising the existing province.[8]

Although theoretically the best way forward might seem to be a union of all the provinces, D'Arcy McGee borrowed a Scots phrase to suggest that anyone who had expected a practical proposal in 1862–63 would have been "half daft."[9] Still, there is evidence of a broad measure of goodwill towards Confederation in the political background: during the 1865 debates several critics of the immediate proposal insisted that they favoured the long-term aim. The problem was that it did not look like a practical answer to pressing problems. Even as he began negotiations to enter the Great Coalition that launched Confederation in 1864, George Brown stated that "he believed that federation of all the provinces ought to come, and would come about ere long, but it had not yet been thoroughly considered by the people; and even were this otherwise ... its adoption was uncertain and remote" because so many interests would have to be squared.[10]

There was another difficulty about the union of the provinces that hindsight ignores: federation involved a division of powers between central and local legislatures, on the lines of the constitution of the United States. Reformers liked that, because they believed power should surge upwards from the people. But Conservatives had inherited the old Loyalist idea that authority should be vested in the Crown and percolate from above. They dreamed of a single government and legislature for the whole of British North America, on the model of the Parliament at Westminster that ruled England, Scotland, and Ireland. Although John A. Macdonald was politically committed to a federal solution, in 1861 he argued that the American Civil War proved that Canadians should give "to the general Government all the principles and powers of sovereignty," thus creating "a powerful Central Government, a powerful central Legislature," which would then be accompanied by a "powerful decentralized system of minor Legislatures for local purposes." When in June 1864 George Brown headed a parliamentary committee that argued for "changes in the direction of a federative system, applied either to Canada alone or to the whole British North American Provinces," Macdonald was one of a handful of politicians who refused to endorse even the principle of federation or, perhaps, a scheme associated with his most implacable political enemy. The British North America Act of 1867 would cleverly blur the distinction between centralisation and federation, but until the eve of Confederation these two forms of inter-colonial union were in competition.[11]

Into this vacuum stepped a politician who was briefly a pivotal figure, although he is largely forgotten today. J.S. Macdonald has been overshadowed by his great namesake, and even then he was known by his middle name, "Sandfield." In March 1862 he formed a ministry that ingeniously pretended that sectional difficulty did not exist. Its guiding principle was the "double majority": the government would act only when supported by a majority of members from both Upper and Lower Canada. As a practical aim this made some sense: politicians naturally sought broad-based support, and there had been major cabinet changes in 1850 and 1856 when incumbent ministries found themselves in a minority in Upper Canada. But to elevate the double majority into a principle of government was absurd, especially when the demographic shift meant that Upper Canada's basic demand – that it should be granted an increase in political power – was precisely the concession that Lower Canada refused to make. Sandfield certainly could not deliver a double majority himself. Indeed, his ministry barely commanded even a "drinking majority": his supporters were afraid to adjourn to the bar in case they missed a snap vote. He clung to office throughout 1863, surviving a vote of no confidence and an inconclusive general election. In a desperate search for new allies, he reshuffled his cabinet, dumping D'Arcy McGee, a one-time Irish revolutionary who had arrived in Montreal in 1857 after spending nine years in the United States, long enough to cure him of his enthusiasm for republican institutions. A natural orator, McGee had transmuted his dream of a free Ireland into a vision of a united British North America, perhaps headed by one of Queen Victoria's sons as its viceroy. Angry at being dumped by one Macdonald, he teamed up in fiery alliance with the other. Some of McGee's flights of fancy did not take root — he called the western prairies "British Central America" — but he contributed the element of inspiration that the Confederation project needed. Equally useful was the fact that he was one of the few public figures in the province of Canada to have personal links with leading politicians in the Maritimes.[12]

In March 1864 Sandfield Macdonald resigned, probably hoping to bounce back if his opponents failed to construct an alternative ministry. The previous Cartier-John A. Macdonald alliance became the core of a new cabinet, headed by the sixty-eight year-old Sir Etienne Taché, who had retired from active politics in 1857. Although strengthened by McGee's adherence, the Taché-John A. Macdonald ministry did not pledge itself to seek a union of British North America. Indeed, the new ministry lacked any Big Idea at all, a point which Michael Foley queried when he was offered a place in the cabinet. "Damn it, Foley," John A. cheerfully replied, "join the Government and then help to make the policy." For once, ministerial aimlessness did not matter. The focus of events had passed to George Brown's committee on the state of the province, a kind of parliamentary think-tank on Canada's future. Meeting in secret session, the committee's discussions had quickly revealed a much more flexible attitude on the part of French-Canadian members than anyone had expected. They had good reason to compromise: the anglophone population of Lower Canada was more influential than the Anglo-Quebec minority of today. Of the 65 Lower Canada seats in the Assembly, only about forty returned French-speaking representatives. There were worrying signs that in a sectional showdown some of the English-speaking members from Montreal and the Eastern Townships might give way to Upper Canadian demands for a larger share of political power. "Rep. by pop." would reduce the French to a quarrelsome minority within the united province, whereas a federal structure would at least give them continuing control over their ancestral heartland. On 14 June 1864 the committee reported, as already quoted, that the way out of the province's developing sectional deadlock was some form of federation, "applied either to Canada alone or to the whole British North American Provinces." That same day Taché's ministry lost a vote of confidence.[13]

The tough negotiations and dramatic resolution of this latest political crisis have often been recounted. In brief, George Brown and two of his Reform allies joined the cabinet, transforming a minority government into the powerful Great Coalition. Technically, the ministry was a continuation of the existing Taché-John A. Macdonald administration. This was important in two respects. First, serving under a respected senior figure – Taché had fought against the invading Americans at the battle of Chateauguay in 1813 – reduced friction over status among rival heavyweights. Second, incumbency enabled John A. Macdonald, the leader of the dwindling Upper Canada Conservatives, to keep his cabinet place. However, George Brown was the determining force in deciding policy.[14]

Nowadays the Great Coalition is remembered for launching Canada on the road to Confederation. In fact, the new government declared a dual objective and it is impossible to understand the politics of 1865 without appreciating the importance of the second element. True, ministers announced that they would immediately "address themselves, in the most earnest manner, to the negotiation for a confederation of all the British North American Provinces." But their fall-back position was equally important: if those negotiations failed, ministers pledged themselves "to legislation during the next session of Parliament for the purpose of remedying existing difficulties by introducing the federal principle for Canada alone, coupled with such provisions as will permit the Maritime Provinces and the North-Western Territory to be hereafter incorporated."[15] In summary, they committed themselves to confederation of all provinces within twelve months or to the creation of what we would now call an Ontario-Quebec federation in 1865.

There were two unresolved loopholes. Who would decide that negotiations for the wider union had definitively failed? Would the British Parliament, which was to remain Canada's ultimate constitutional arbiter until 1982, agree to federalize the Province of Canada? When news arrived of the defeat of Confederation in New Brunswick in March 1865, ministers exploited these loopholes to freeze provincial politics while they launched a mission to England. But in June 1864 it seemed that George Brown had grasped his opponents not so much by the hand as by the throat. "We are *not going to be tied to Lower Canada*, for twelve months more," the Toronto entrepreneur was heard to say. Even John A. Macdonald, whose love of procrastination would later win him the nickname "Old Tomorrow," had committed his political future to a timetable so desperately tight that it looked like a mere stay of execution. If the Maritimers proved as unenthusiastic about joining Canada in 1864–65 as they had in 1858–59, he would have made himself captive to his enemy's political triumph.[16]

As it happened, there was a window of possible opportunity, and it was slightly ajar. The provinces of Nova Scotia and New Brunswick, whose combined population was about one-fifth that of Canada, were struggling to enter the railway age. Although already burdened with debt for short and unconnected lines, their politicians dreamed of kick-starting the Maritime economy with a railway that would link Halifax with the south shore of the St Lawrence opposite Quebec City, where a connection with Canada's Grand Trunk network would link it to the heart of the continent. Unfortunately, while the proposed "Intercolonial" might eventually become an economic asset, it was unlikely to operate as a commercial success and so would require government finance.

In 1862 the three provinces had agreed on the outline of a funding package with the British government. The imperial authorities would provide a loan guarantee: Britain's Treasury would reassure British investors that their money was safe. That would enable the three provinces to raise capital at cheap interest rates – without the loan guarantee they would have been forced to borrow at danger-money rates. In a complicated formula New Brunswick and Nova Scotia agreed to become jointly responsible for seven-twelfths of the interest payments with Canada covering the other five-twelfths. The agreement remained on the table but did not take immediate effect because Sandfield Macdonald decided that the burden was not worth the benefits. Sandfield could hardly be blamed, at least not by Cartier and John A. Macdonald, since his ministry had inherited a deficit recklessly accumulated by their finance minister, Alexander Galt. Maritimers were bitter about Canadian duplicity, but their anger masked a more alarming issue: if prosperous Canada balked at five-twelfths of the interest payments, could the Maritimes possibly afford seven-twelfths?[17]

With a combined population of only 700,000 (including Prince Edward Island), the three Maritime provinces had little scope for economies of scale. One possibility was to merge the three colonies under one regional government, and their governments reluctantly decided to discuss Maritime Union at a conference planned for Charlottetown early in September 1864.[18] (Mainland politicians took the realistic view that only by going across to Prince Edward Island would they shake that tiny province into taking part at all: parochialism made Charlottetown the accidental cradle of Confederation.) Behind the scenes McGee orchestrated Canadian and Maritime timetables. He also sought to overcome Maritimers' distrust of their perfidious neighbour by organising an August tour of the Gulf provinces for a massive delegation of one hundred Canadian legislators and journalists, the first great fact-finding junket in Canadian history. Even before the formation of the Great Coalition, McGee was suggesting that the Maritime Union conference might double as a summit meeting with the Canadian ministry to re-launch the railway project. It was a short step to turning the Charlottetown meeting into a discussion of the larger project of British North American union.[19]

The high-powered Canadian delegation that descended upon the Charlottetown Conference in September had little difficulty in persuading their hosts that they might as well choose the larger over the smaller union. The crucial factor behind their sudden conversion was probably the prospect of shifting the bulk of the cost of the Intercolonial railway – which was to form a key part of the package – away from Maritime pockets and on to Canadian (nowadays we would say "central Canadian") taxpayers. At a banquet in Halifax soon after the Charlottetown Conference, Galt bluntly told his audience, "you will get the best of the bargain":[20] measured by population and wealth, the central Canadian share of the cost would double from five-twelfths to five-sixths. Unfortunately, the same arithmetic brought home to other Maritimers that they would be permanently outvoted under Confederation: Prince Edward Islanders, who had no interest in a mainland railway, dropped out of the movement altogether. But in the fall of 1864, setbacks and second thoughts were still hidden in the future. The principle of intercolonial union was endorsed at Charlottetown in September. Remarkably quickly, a more formal drafting convention met at Quebec in October and drew up an outline scheme of government, the seventy-two Quebec Resolutions. All that was now needed to approach Westminster for a new constitution was the endorsement of the provincial legislatures. The Canadian Parliament reassembled on 19 January 1865. The upper house, the Legislative Council, began a gentlemanly review of the new constitution on 3 February. The Assembly launched its set-piece debate three days later.

We should avoid thinking of the "Fathers of Confederation" as omniscient greybeards upholding their vision of a Canadian nation against narrow, unimaginative opposition.[21] Prominent supporters of Confederation spanned the whole province: Taché and the newspaper publisher J-E. Cauchon came from the Quebec City region, Cartier was a Montrealer, McGee represented Canada's Irish Catholic community, and Galt was the spokesman of Lower Canada's English-speaking Protestants. In Upper Canada, support was virtually unanimous west of Toronto, the area which would gain the greatest increase in political representation: Brown owned Toronto's leading newspaper but represented the Ingersoll district, deep in the western peninsula. By contrast, opponents clustered in the less dynamic east. Sandfield Macdonald's power base was in Glengarry County which, then as now, looked more to Montreal than to Toronto. English-speaking Lower Canadians did not all share Galt and McGee's enthusiasm for the re-creation of a French-majority province: Luther Holton, from Montreal, and Christopher Dunkin, who represented Brome County in the Townships, were shrewd critics. Rouges, such as A-A. Dorion and H-G. Joly, were unhappy at being consigned to the mercies of the dominant Bleus and so tried to portray themselves as defenders of French-Canadian rights against a sell-out. It was a strategy that was to work well twenty years later when they exploited the execution of Louis Riel but it did not succeed in 1865.

Some critics supported the idea of an eventual union of the provinces, condemning the Quebec scheme as either premature, which was Holton's view, or dangerously extravagant, the opinion of Matthew Crooks Cameron, one of the few Upper Canada Conservatives to speak in opposition. In the event, even the irreconcilables agreed to make the new system work: Sandfield Macdonald became the first premier of Ontario, with Cameron as finance minister, while Christopher Dunkin, who delivered the most devastating of all opposition speeches in 1865, entered the Dominion cabinet four years later.

Far from being greybeards (in fact, many were clean-shaven), most prominent Canadian politicians were just entering middle age. The exception was Taché, nearing seventy, but his return to active politics came at a terrible cost: on 16 February, after making a substantial speech in the Legislative Council, he suffered a stroke and died five months later. Most of the leading participants were twenty years younger, with little difference in age between supporters of Confederation and opponents. John A. Macdonald and Cartier were both fifty, Galt and Cauchon forty-seven, George Brown forty-six – but A-A. Dorion was forty-seven, Holton forty-eight, and even Dunkin and Sandfield Macdonald were hardly yesterday's men at fifty-two. We might conclude that young Canada was for Confederation given that McGee and Alexander Morris, who had been preaching the cause since 1858, were only thirty-nine, but the doubting M.C. Cameron was forty-two, and one of the most implacable critics of all, the paranoid Joseph Perrault, a bumptious twenty-six.[22] Although George Brown acknowledged that they were laying the foundations for a structure that "may not be realized in the lifetime of many who now hear me," it seems clear that most of those involved hoped to play an active part in shaping the new system – indeed, Cartier openly expected to become the first prime minister. But Perrault explained his opposition by predicting that he had "twenty years of future" in politics ahead of him, an expectation that the voters of Richelieu County cut short when they threw him out in 1867.[23]

Read from the printed page, their speeches can make them seem like two-dimensional characters acting their parts in a constitutional melodrama. But Canada's politicians were real people, and their contemporaries often filtered their own assessment of the arguments advanced through their impressions of the personalities who voiced them. John A. Macdonald in person was unforgettable. Two years later a journalist described him as "a young looking oldish man, dark hair ... a prominent nose, dark eyes, and a pliable and sagacious mouth." Macdonald's unkempt hair was almost as notable a trade mark as his famously large nose. An onlooker who saw him rushing to a crisis meeting a few weeks before the Confederation debates was amused by the "grotesque" appearance of "his hair flying in all directions like a Spanish caricature." The opinions of this workaholic lawyer-politician carried weight, not least because in the winter of 1864–65 he emerged as the key draughtsman of the new constitution. Yet, paradoxically, he was sometimes drinking so heavily that it seemed possible he would destroy himself. His political partner, the raucous and jolly Cartier, was "cast in a compact, cast-iron mould, all determination and pluck, from the tip of his foot to the topmost lock of his irongray hair." But where Macdonald always remembered that today's political foe might become tomorrow's cabinet colleague, Cartier was determined to triumph in every confrontation, however minor. The thing he most hated in the world, he remarked in his fluent but accented English, was "a comp*ee-tee*tar." It is not surprising that this small, grey-haired, combative, warm-hearted man was often likened to a terrier.[24]

Joseph Cauchon's book-length pamphlet in favour of Confederation stands out today as one of the most notable documents from the period. (He was criticised for reading from his own text under the guise of making a speech.) But Cauchon was personally unpopular, and contemporaries suspected his motives for reversing earlier opposition to the union of the provinces. On 2 March he was forced to apologise to the House after precipitating a "very unparliamentary" confrontation. A Rouge politician, Alexandre Dufresne, criticised Cauchon's business practices (seven years later Cauchon would survive a corruption charge). When Cauchon threatened to raise the subject of "a certain insurance company, an agent of which had for twenty years been robbing the public," Dufresne called him a liar and a fight broke out. The Cauchon family surname had originally been "Cochon" (pig), and many people thought it suited him. Similarly, Christopher Dunkin's formidable dissection of the Confederation scheme did not impress everybody in 1865, simply because his smug omniscience was something of a joke. "Whenever there was a hair to split," jibed D'Arcy McGee, Dunkin "never failed to have his razor at hand."[25] McGee himself traded on his appearance. Conventionally described as looking like a typical Irish peasant (he was Irish but no peasant), he exploited the stereotype in his flamboyantly informal oratorical style: his breezy speech in the Confederation debates is punctuated with the comment "(Laughter)." In two other members of the Great Coalition, appearances may have been deceptive. Galt radiated an aura of business-like efficiency that disguised his mercurial and sometimes reckless judgement, while Brown's tall form and handsome features masked an embittered streak that could lead him to be vengeful and obsessive. On the other hand, everyone agreed that with Joseph Perrault, small in stature and embarrassing in his paranoia, what you saw was what you got: "erratic," said the *Montreal Gazette*, "microscopique," chimed *La Minerve*.[26]

Public life in 1865 was male-dominated: women could neither vote nor sit in Parliament. Few married politicians subjected their wives to the parliamentary world of booze and boarding houses that supported the locker-room culture of politics. Yet some women had a ringside seat, and perhaps some indefinable degree of influence. Much depended on the dynamics of individual relationships. John A. Macdonald, a flirtatious widower, was a male chauvinist. Cartier was estranged from his wife, and it was generally assumed that his companion, the outspoken Luce Cuvillier, was also his lover – a relationship that cautions against generalisations about the stifling conservatism of French Canada.[27] Brown and Galt each supplied their absent spouses with frequent and detailed political updates. "How I do wish you had been here to advise me!," Brown wrote during the political crisis of 1864 to the wife he had married during a visit to Scotland two years earlier. Anne Brown's humanizing influence on her stern husband led one historian to nickname her the "Mother of Confederation": as a brooding bachelor, Brown would hardly have overcome his resentments to join a cabinet dominated by his enemy, Macdonald.[28] Amy Galt gobbled up political gossip so avidly that her husband had to swear her to secrecy. Formally, there was a gender barrier, but some spouses and partners participated in the political culture.[29]

Although few Canadians played baseball in those days, their government was a team of All Stars that had just hit two home runs, at Charlottetown and Quebec. Unfortunately, in politics even more than in sport, luck can change. When the game resumed in February 1865, for the first time the opposition had a chance at bat. The Great Coalition faced several challenges in securing parliamentary approval for their project. First, it was tactically necessary to persuade legislators to accept the seventy-two Quebec Resolutions as a single package, an inter-provincial treaty. As Macdonald warned, if the Canadian Parliament made unilateral amendments in the agreed terms, the other provinces would demand changes too and the whole project might vanish in a quarrelsome fog of detail.[30] For parliamentarians used to clause-by-clause scrutiny of legislation, this was hard to swallow. The imperial government, although enthusiastic about the scheme as a whole, was known to be demanding changes, and it made nonsense of self-government if on such a vital matter as the constitution, British politicians could intervene but Canada's own elected representatives had no role at all.[31]

The government's inflexibility was in curious contrast to the embarrassment of Resolution 24. The indispensable Macdonald had fallen seriously ill during the tidying-up period after the Quebec Conference. When he returned to work, he was alarmed to spot "an obvious blunder" in the authenticated version of the Resolutions: the conference had accidentally given the provincial legislatures power to fix the electoral boundaries for the central Parliament. This would mean that an Ottawa member of Parliament who quarrelled with the government of his province could find his riding gerrymandered out of existence. The Canadian ministry simply re-wrote Resolution 24 to confine the control of provincial legislatures to their own electoral boundaries. Since the discrepancy was not formally challenged until April, when the incoming anti-Confederation government in New Brunswick queried the change, it seems likely that, as they claimed, the Canadian ministers had quietly persuaded their Maritime allies to accept the laundered version. At best, the episode looked casual; at worst, distinctly high-handed. On the face of it, Resolution 24 was precisely the sort of problem that justified detailed parliamentary scrutiny. In practice, it made ministers even more determined to secure a general vote in support of the scheme, leaving future fine-tuning to inter-provincial elite accommodation.[32]

While ministers were forcing an immutable constitution down Parliament's throat, they were also embarrassingly silent about one major area of the new structure. Confederation involved the re-creation of Upper and Lower Canada as separate provinces, and as this was something for Canadians to arrange among themselves, it had not been discussed at the Quebec Conference. There were already signs that the two sections had very different ideas about local institutions. Upper Canadians expected to dominate the central government and consequently most of them wanted only cheap and simple local administration: "a sort of large municipal deliberative body," as one member put it. Although it would be a century before Quebec renamed its local Parliament the "National Assembly," French Canadians would not accept some glorified county council as the protector of their rights. In 1865 Canadians had yet to perceive the possible advantages of asymmetrical federalism. It was not even clear whether the new provinces would be governed by local responsible ministries: would the real authority shift to the Ottawa-appointed lieutenant-governors? There were fears, too, about the educational rights of minorities: would Protestant schools receive fair treatment in Lower Canada or Catholic schools be threatened by a legislature in Toronto? John A. Macdonald insisted that all this was an entirely separate and subordinate question, "for until it was settled that there was to be Confederation, it was idle to discuss what should be the constitutions of the several provinces." But the authoritative *Montreal Gazette* reported that "there are some sincere friends of union not quite content to vote for the resolutions ... until they know something of the nature and probable costliness of the local legislatures," and especially something about the educational guarantees. On one other occasion Canada has been offered a constitutional package that seemed simultaneously complicated and vague – the 1992 Charlottetown Accord – which, when put to the first-ever nationwide constitutional referendum, was thrown out.[33]

By the time the Canadian debate began, early in February 1865, the Great Coalition was coping with a new uncertainty. New Brunswick's legislature was near the end of its five-year term and the premier, Leonard Tilley, faced an awkward dilemma. If he tried to ram the Quebec scheme through the graveyard shift of the current Parliament, his enemies – and after ten years in office he had many – would probably denounce him as a traitor at the upcoming elections. After some hesitation, he decided to gamble on a direct appeal to the voters, even though there were worrying signs that New Brunswickers were wary of this sudden, huge scheme of constitutional change. So, while Canadian politicians were discussing the Quebec scheme, they had to take into account that it might falter in the Maritimes.

Whatever New Bruswick decided, the fact that it was going to the polls raised another awkward issue for the Canadian ministry. Since Confederation had not been on the agenda when Canadians had last voted in 1863, it was hard to claim that members had a mandate for so major a constitutional change. As Bruce W. Hodgins has demonstrated, the Fathers of Confederation adopted what seems to us a cavalier attitude to democracy[34] but it was still awkward that a few thousand voters in New Brunswick should be able to vote on Canada's future when this privilege was denied to Canadians themselves.

The ministerial riposte when this discrepancy was raised suggests that even if the term "spin" is a modern invention, there is nothing new about its insidious presence in politics. The argument, advanced by George Brown in this selection, was that 50 of the 130 Assembly ridings had voted their approval for the project.[35] The claim was not only brazen but, at first sight, puzzling. Death and resignations had brought about a steady trickle of by-elections, and newly appointed ministers had had to return to their constituents to seek their approval: one recruit to the Great Coalition, William McDougall, was so personally unpopular that he managed to get himself defeated. However, there had certainly not been fifty Assembly by-elections in the eight months since the formation of the ministry.

In fact, Brown's claim included votes for the Legislative Council, which had been made elective in 1856. The province was divided into forty-eight districts, one quarter of which polled every second year. Arithmetically, the forty-eight electorates for the upper house did not correspond very conveniently with the 130 Assembly ridings, making it just possible to claim that the twelve divisions where elections had been held in the fall of 1864 brought the number of ridings which had voted, in whole or part, to fifty. The problem with this imaginative claim was that members of the upper house were elected for reflective eight-year terms to allow them to give public affairs the benefit of their own Olympian judgement. When campaigning for votes, they outlined their political principles but it ran counter to the theory of an independent second chamber for them to be bound by distinct promises. One legislative councillor, the Conservative Party workhorse David L. Macpherson, boldly claimed that his Upper Canada constituents specifically endorsed his support for Confederation, but other newly elected members were not so sure about opinion in their districts. Moreover, the 1864 round of elections had coincided with the Quebec Conference, before the detailed scheme of Confederation was known. In any case, voting for the upper house never set the political world ablaze. Only one by-election, for the Assembly seat of Hamilton in mid-February, was directly relevant to the Confederation debates. The victor, Charles Magill, spoke briefly near the end of the debates to confirm what everybody already knew, that Hamiltonians supported Confederation.[36] Even if fifty ridings had endorsed the union of the provinces, this still did not explain why the other eighty should be deprived of a chance to pronounce. Ministers were on stronger ground when they pointed to the absence of petitions against the project, although, as Peter Waite amusingly recounted, in Lower Canada, J-B-E. Dorion was doing his best to manufacture them.

There is a sense in which the term "Confederation debates" is a misnomer. Parliamentary proceedings rarely equal the adversarial sparkle of a debating society. John Ross, in the upper house, was unusual in attempting a point-by-point rebuttal of James Currie's speech against the Quebec scheme. There was an undercurrent of by-play between Holton and Macdonald: Holton alleged that Macdonald did not really believe in Confederation, while Macdonald challenged his opponent to propose a better alternative. But, overall, there was relatively little verbal swordsmanship or even intelligent heckling. McGee came off second-best in an exchange with the smug Christopher Dunkin. When Dunkin doubted whether the project could be "done," McGee interjected a line from Shakespeare: "If 'twere done, 'twere well 'twere done quickly." It was a tactical blunder to quote Lady Macbeth inciting her husband to commit murder and Dunkin crushed his tormenter. When one critic in the upper house condemned the Quebec scheme as a "mongrel Constitution," neither American nor British, several members patriotically interjected that it was Canadian. When another member complained that ministers had not promised that Confederation would improve the canal system, he was told that they did not wish to throw cold water on the project.[37]

One obstacle to the free flow of debate was that, since 1848, Canada's Parliament had officially functioned in both French and English, and in those days there was no simultaneous translation. Very few English-speaking members were good linguists: John A. Macdonald, for instance, sat at his parliamentary desk openly writing letters when members spoke in French. Most of the French members, on the other hand, could understand English. Since the English-language version of the debates did not indicate which speeches had been translated, it is not always obvious which language was being used.

Cauchon and Perrault spoke in their mother tongue, but several prominent French Canadians used English. Taché, for instance, began his major speech in French but quickly agreed to switch to English, even though he complained he was "not very fluent." "I should have desired to make my remarks to the House in French," explained A-A. Dorion, "but considering the large number of honourable members who are not familiar with that language, I think it my duty to speak at the present time in English." Cartier too probably spoke mainly in English although Taché repeated part of his speech in French. A more explicitly bilingual debate might perhaps have resolved the ambiguity which A-A. Dorion exploited, that the French term "confédération" implied a much looser political association than its English counterpart – but the clarification might have revealed irreconcilable attitudes toward federalism itself.[38]

Modern-day Canadians may think it invidious that the French language should have so obviously been accorded second-class status in public life. But this suited bilingual politicians such as Cartier and Dorion, since it emphasised their role as mediators between their own community and the English-speaking world of government and business. Cartier, who was a major force in the Grand Trunk Railway, would certainly have disagreed with a later generation of Quebec nationalists who contemptuously dismissed politicians like himself as "les rois nègres," tribal leaders who sacrificed their people to imperialist masters in exchange for a few trinkets. When Henri Joly accused him of selling French Canada to secure a ministerial salary of $5,000 a year, Cartier brazenly replied: "That is not enough for me."[39]

Essentially, most members who took part in the debates were speaking for the record. As M.C. Cameron modestly put it, it was unlikely that his speech would "change in the slightest degree" the opinions of other members.[40] It is in this light that we should assess the ministerial artillery that opened the debates, speeches by Taché and his five principal lieutenants, extracts of which form one third of the text that follows. They aimed to convince, not just with individual arguments but through the cumulative battering of the message, that, from every point of view – French Canadian, Protestant, voters who wanted to get rich, voters who wanted cultural survival – there was no alternative to Confederation.[41]

John A. Macdonald, who opened in the Assembly, had the hard task of outlining "tedious details" and explaining why he had abandoned his opposition to a federal-style solution. When he spoke in Parliament, Macdonald usually adopted a conversational style. On this occasion, he locked himself away in his lodgings the previous day to prepare, puzzling his Scottish landlord who "thocht the mon was surely daft, for he's been all day alone in his room talkin' till [to] the cat." Perhaps the cat slept through the rehearsal, for Macdonald's low-key presentation was not a success. Brown thought it "a very poor speech for such an occasion" and the opposition alleged that Macdonald's heart was not really in the project. Cartier followed, "screeching" out an opinionated oration which Holton sarcastically dismissed as "perfectly characteristic." But even Holton had to acknowledge the "ease and grace" of Galt's speech. Journalists liked reporting Galt: he could fill four columns of tiny newspaper print per hour, with scarcely an error or digression. "It is in my mind, if I can get it out," Brown had written of his own contribution: out it came, fluently "piling up arguments" in favour of Confederation. Finally, McGee injected what we might now call "hype": the speech was irrelevant, jeered Holton, but it would make a fine historical essay. Ministers occupied Monday to Thursday of the first week of debate. As the Hamilton *Spectator* put it, their speeches "grouped together may form one united, entire argument in defence of the scheme of intercolonial union."[42]

How, then, did the opposition respond? Essentially, they adopted the classic ploy of counsel for the defence, denying that there was any case to answer and concentrating on procedural objections, demanding the right to move amendments, and pressing the government to call a general election. Why did they, by and large, avoid head-on debate? First, like the ministry, the opposition was a disparate coalition of disaffected individuals and rival factions, without even the bond of office to unite them. There was simply no reason for them to put forward detailed alternative proposals, not least because they denied that there was any underlying crisis in the province that merited radical surgery. Second, everyone was aware of the dual aim of the Great Coalition. If the push for a wider union should falter, the ministry might break up. Another ministerial crisis might open the way to fresh combinations and new deals, and so opposition figures like Holton and Dorion avoided commitment to specific policies. Hence the most detailed refutation of the case for Confederation came from Dunkin, the least likely team player in Canadian public life.

Above all, Canada's Confederation debates were overshadowed by the elections in New Brunswick, which might well bring the Confederation movement to a dead halt. John Ross insisted that Tilley was unbeatable, but since nobody in Canada knew much about Maritime politics, the New Brunswick situation provided a third reason for opposition caution. Tilley's opponents were reported to "seize upon every unguarded word uttered in Canada."[43] In fact Maritime newspapers showed relatively little interest in the Canadian debates, but critics of Confederation were wise to be cautious. To attack the

Intercolonial railway as a bad deal for which Canada would pay for the benefit of Maritimers might have convinced New Brunswickers to vote in its favour.

Early in March, as the debate ran its course, the anti-Confederates defeated Tilley by a landslide. "The news from New Brunswick made the faces of the Opposition radiant last night," reported one newspaper. Sandfield Macdonald, who had so far kept a low profile, proposed a day of thanksgiving and joined Dorion in challenging the coalition to deliver on its Plan B, federal reconstruction confined to the province of Canada. Could the coalition team survive such a major shift in its policy? George Brown was ready "to go on with our scheme for Canada alone," but John A. Macdonald insisted that the setback in the Maritimes made it all the more vital for the Canadian Parliament to pronounce emphatically in favour of Confederation. In the early hours of 11 March, the Assembly voted to endorse the Quebec resolutions by a massive 91 votes to 33. Peter Waite analyses the division to show that there were majorities from Upper and Lower Canada, as well as majorities of both English- and French-speaking members – "in fact," remarked the *Globe*, "every sort of majority that politicians have been in the habit of looking for and desiring."[44]

Sandfield Macdonald had failed to deliver his double majority; now Confederation had secured the unbelievable triumph of a quadruple majority, from both sections and both language groups.[45] A last-ditch call for a general election was rejected on Monday, 13 March, after which a ministerial delegation prepared to sail for England to ask the British government to put pressure on New Brunswick. Beyond sending stern despatches to Fredericton, it was never clear just what the British were expected to do, but the mission bought some useful time. The emphatic vote for Confederation thus postponed the moment, openly demanded by the *Globe* on 6 March, when the wider union would have to be abandoned and a purely Canadian federation attempted instead.

Allowing for some abridged reports, around 900,000 words were uttered during the Confederation debates in the Canadian Parliament, about ten percent more than the entire text of the King James Bible – an impressive oratorical output. What can we say of the quality and impact of this verbal torrent? Writing in 1963, when Canada's politicians were still treated with elaborate respect, Peter Waite condemned many of the speeches as "drivel" and "twaddle." There is a huge difference between his impish mockery and the visceral contempt with which many Canadians treat their politicians today. A very different verdict came from another great Canadian historian, W.L. Morton, who favourably compared the debates to the *Federalist Papers*, the work of the American giants Hamilton, Jay and Madison back in 1787–88, who mixed federalist theory with propaganda for the new United States constitution. No doubt it was true that "a few of the leading members on both sides have read up extensively for the occasion": one member cited the contemporary English political theorist John Stuart Mill, but called him "Mr Mills." Some members parroted Shakespeare, others appealed to the authority of ultimate wisdom and quoted themselves. Many speeches included machine-gun bursts of statistics, which were not always obviously relevant. Still, on the whole, the debates impress as being what we might call indirect intellectual discourse. That is to say, the participants knew the difference between a delegate and a representative, a federation and a legislative union, even if they could not have supplied the footnote references for a political science seminar paper.[46]

In assessing their arguments, we need to distinguish between those reasons for (or against) Confederation that had convinced the politicians and those that they hoped might sway the public, and here there is a fine line between consensus-building and outright hypocrisy. Take, for instance, two arguments advanced by Taché. Strikingly, he claimed that without Confederation, the provinces would be placed "upon an inclined plane" that would end with annexation to the United States – an image that particularly irritated several opposition speakers. If anything, Taché's use of what the *Globe* once called the "Annexation boogaboo" proves only that the thought of transferring Canada from "beloved Britain to hated Yankeedom" (as Oliver Mowat put it) was so unpopular that it made tactical sense to portray Confederation as its antidote. Similarly, Taché claimed that in June 1864 the province "was bordering on civil strife." This directly contradicted his own remarks at a banquet a few months earlier, where he had reassuringly commented that Canada's "political difficulties ... were not so great." Later, John A. Macdonald cynically denied that Taché had threatened civil war. "An election is civil strife, and a lawsuit is civil strife, but warfare is a most uncivil strife."[47]

Taché had emphatically adopted a different position nine years earlier, during his previous term as premier, when he had denounced as "ill-timed, and uncalled-for" a proposal in the Legislative Council for the union of the provinces. Probably thinking in French, he had declared that "Constitutions political were not things to be put on and put off like a suit of clothes." As for the argument that it would improve Canada's defences, "a union with the other Provinces would give us no help even if we were in danger. Before we could reach them or they us, we must have a railway, and until then to talk of a political alliance was, to say the least, to lose time." Of course, Taché was entitled to have changed his mind since 1856.[48] Whether he was justified in using misleading and alarmist arguments in 1865 is another question.

John A. Macdonald can also be convicted of inconsistency. He assured the Assembly that, despite his theoretical preference for legislative union, federation was "the only scheme practicable," simply because each province had its own local laws. But in attempting to win over M.C. Cameron, Macdonald had predicted that they would "live to see both Local Parliaments and Governments absorbed in the General Power." Although Macdonald acknowledged that "it does not do to adopt this point of view in discussing the subject in Lower Canada," this isolated glimpse of his private thoughts does not justify the demonology that claims that Macdonald aimed to drown Quebec's autonomy in constitutional small print: it is more likely that he was sweet-talking the reluctant Cameron rather than lying to Parliament.[49]

Politicians undoubtedly shaped their arguments in different ways to different audiences. Speaking in the Assembly, J-B-E. Dorion stressed the threat of the centralizing elements in the scheme to local autonomy, but in an anti-Confederation diatribe at Drummondville, he was much more explicit. Dorion used "Anglais" for anyone who spoke English, regardless of national origin, and to translate this by the sterilised term "anglophone" would miss his angry note of contempt. In the old days in Lower Canada, he said, every French Canadian found an "Anglais" in front of him, blocking his path. After the union with Upper Canada in 1841, there was one in front and another one behind. Now, with Confederation, he told his audience, you will have an "Anglais" in front of you, another behind, one on either side and maybe one standing on your head as well.[50] Dorion's remarks were hardly parliamentary, but they captured his fear of cultural obliteration.

It is difficult to measure the impact of the six-week debate on public opinion. The telegraph and the steam printing press made possible the wide diffusion of parliamentary proceedings. An editor rejoiced that "speeches which are made in the House of Assembly after midnight, nearly two hundred miles [320 kilometres] away, appear in the *Montreal Gazette* the next morning," but how diligently those long columns of small type were studied in the front parlours and back kitchens of Victorian Canada, we simply do not know. It is perhaps significant that major newspapers devoted few leading articles to individual speeches. Indeed, by the end of February, even journalists were complaining about the interminable discussion. The arguments now addressed to near-empty benches were either stale or bizarre: one member combined originality with absurdity when he compared

Canada to "the Roman Empire when near its fall." Although recognising that the speeches were "tedious," the *Globe* thought that as an exercise in public information the debate was "on the whole, well worthy of a great occasion." But that begged the basic question: was it true, as some alleged, that press and parliamentary controversies over the proposed constitution "excite no interest whatever" in the public mind? Here the *Globe* could offer one clinching argument: if Confederation had been unacceptable to the voters, the debate would have provoked protest meetings and petitions against the scheme. "In a country where the people are so intelligent as they are in Canada, the political quiet, which some journals choose to call indifference, is the best possible proof that the union scheme is acceptable to the country." Certainly, despite the setback in New Brunswick, ministers felt that the outcome entitled them to press the scheme forward.[51]

Peter Waite's selections remain a fair reflection of the discussions of eighty years earlier. Indeed, the mood of confident nationalism of 1865 would have been recognisable to Canadians of 1963. However, since then, the country has faced serious challenges from within and without: should these affect the way in which we read the Confederation debates? Patriotic political scientists sometimes urge a return to the ideas of Canada's founders; more cautious historians would warn against reading modern concerns into mid-Victorian controversies.

In January 1865, *La Minerve*, a Montreal newspaper close to Cartier, remarked that every French Canadian schoolboy had dreamed of an independent Lower Canada but no adult had ever campaigned for such an aim. It is hardly surprising that adolescent hero-worship for the *Patriotes* of 1837 did not translate into political action. Even if they could have extricated themselves from the British empire, one million French Canadians had little chance of establishing a viable state alongside the rampant United States, where the census of 1870 would count over 38 million people. Quebec separatism thus belongs to the second century of Confederation, not the first. The French Canadians of 1865 used the vocabulary of independence and cultural survival, but usually in relation to provincial autonomy within a British North American structure.[52]

For some despairing Canadians, the decision in 1988 to accept continental free trade fatally weakened the project of building a second North American nation truly separate from the United States. In 1865 the equation was reversed: thanks to the Reciprocity Treaty of 1854, British North America already enjoyed partial free trade – in natural products but not manufactured – but the United States was about to abrogate the agreement. Because the massive consumption needs of the

Northern armies had distorted American demands for Canadian products, nobody really knew how far the Treaty itself had benefited the provinces. Congress chose St Patrick's Day, 17 March, a week after the close of the debates, to deliver the threatened twelve months' notice that Reciprocity would come to an end. Even so, there remained hopes that an alternative agreement might be concluded: indeed, George Brown resigned from the ministry in December 1865 in protest against the alleged mishandling of the negotiations. There was some talk of seeking alternative markets in the Maritimes, but did anyone take this seriously? New Brunswick and Nova Scotia represented very small pickings compared with the United States, their economies were very similar to Canada's, and, as Henri Joly pointed out, it would be perfectly possible to have British North American free trade without political union.[53] From the point of view of modern political debate, with its perennial emphasis on growth, the parliamentarians of 1865 seem almost naïve in apparently ignoring the economic dimension. Certainly we cannot draw any direct line between the Confederation debates and the National Policy of tariff protection that Macdonald launched fourteen years later, in his second incarnation as Dominion prime minister. Perhaps there is some consolation here for the wounded nationalists of 1988: in the first decade of Confederation, Canadians worked energetically for an east-west political union but still hankered after a north-south economic orientation.

The most drawn-out constitutional saga in twentieth-century Canada was the project to remove control of the British North America Act from Westminster. It was an anomaly that a parliament across an ocean remained the ultimate arbiter of Canada's constitution, but the difficulty lay in agreeing how to amend the document once it was "patriated": who would have the right to veto unpalatable changes? Except through resounding silence, the debates of 1865 give us no help on these questions. Everyone took it for granted that the new constitution would require imperial legislation. Even Christopher Dunkin, in his encyclopaedic nit-picking, did not query the absence of an amending formula.[54]

Other issues that loom large in twenty-first century Canada were not even a blip on the radar screen of 1865. In the settled areas of eastern British North America, most "Indians," as they were called, seemed to be adopting a quasi-European life-style, which did not call for specific political recognition. Questions of Native title and Aboriginal sovereignty simply did not arise, although the new Dominion would quickly find itself confronting the first on the prairies and denying the second in British Columbia. Nor, for the obvious reason that the debaters of 1865 came from what is now Ontario and Quebec, can we trace the origins of the alienation so often voiced today from Winnipeg to the Pacific. Sensitive westerners may regard the debates as a typically narcissistic discussion of central Canada's own interests: when William McGiverin urged that the vast territories beyond Lake Superior "should be placed in precisely the same position as regards Canada that the Western States occupy in relation to the Eastern," he was talking about sharing resources rather than power. Equally, since representation by population was a key principle of Confederation and a redistribution of ridings would take place after every census, there was no reason why political power should not eventually flow to the West – even though no specific provision was made to create new provinces on the prairies. In 1865, "western Canada" referred to the territory between Toronto and Sarnia, and this "western Canada" felt alienated. Confederation was its way of "wanting in."[55]

In 1987, Canadians embarked on a five-year period of the most intense discussion of constitutional review since the mid-1860s. Ironically, nothing actually changed: the saga that began with the Meech Lake Accord of 1987 ended with the rejection of its successor, the Charlottetown Accord, in 1992. It is tempting to read Macdonald and his colleagues of 1865 through the filter of Mulroney and his allies a century and a quarter later. Some of the criticism of Meech Lake was directed at "process," the way in which the prime minister and provincial premiers, "eleven white males," struck a deal behind closed doors. In many respects, the Quebec Conference of 1864 was a more transparent exercise. Although it also met in secret – in 1864, unlike 1987, journalists did at least demand admission[56] – there had already been wide public discussion of its purpose, unlike the 1987 Accord, which came as a bolt from the blue. Although white and male, the delegations at Quebec were more inclusive: Canada was represented by a coalition ministry and participants from the other provinces included prominent opposition politicians. In some cases, bipartisanship did not last long but, with the exception of the Lower Canada Liberals, no major group was totally excluded from the deliberations of 1864.

The most controversial element in the Meech Lake Accord was its description of the province of Quebec as a "distinct society within Canada" – although those last two words are not always emphasised. The Quebec Resolutions did not use any such formula, because they did not need to: Lower Canada – Quebec after 1867 – was guaranteed its own legal system and was the only province where the use of both languages was specified in courtroom and legislature. The other controversial provision of the Meech Lake Accord, the "opting-out" clause, hardly applied in 1864, since governments did not operate welfare programs. Of course, government was important in running school systems, and the Confederation package embodied a general "opting-out" element by devolving *all* educational matters to the provinces. Rather than see 1864 as a move to a unitary state and 1987 as a countervailing corrective, it is perhaps best to see both the Quebec Resolutions and the Meech Lake Accord as attempts to weave centralist and federalist themes into a peculiarly Canadian mix. However, it was the opting-out provision that explains the very different stance taken by the smaller provinces. In 1864–67, they feared loss of autonomy to a distant central government, but in 1987–90 they foresaw the fatal weakening of Ottawa's ability to support them, as larger provinces siphoned off funding and ran their own programs.

The contrasting role played by the smaller provinces in the two episodes highlights another key point. In 1990 Manitoba and Newfoundland blocked ratification of the Meech Lake Accord and, two years later, voters in the smaller provinces were prominent in rejecting its successor. In 1864–66, the smaller provinces were simply not permitted to obstruct the road to Confederation. It is here that we should seek the true significance of the Confederation debates in the province of Canada. When, in March 1865, it became clear that the voters of New Brunswick rejected the scheme, the Canadian ministry used the votes of its own legislature, after considered and exhaustive discussion, to interpret the setback not as a veto but as a challenge.

NOTES

Thanks are due to Colin Coates, Mélanie Desmeules, and Andrew Smith for help in the preparation of this Introduction, and to Peter Waite for his generous guidance on the Macdonald Papers.

1 The full version was published as *Parliamentary Debates on the Subject of the Confederation of the British North American Provinces, 3rd Session, 8th Provincial Parliament of Canada* (Quebec: Hunter, Rose & Co, 1865). A facsimile edition was issued in 1951 (Ottawa: Edmond Cloutier, King's Printer). References to the full edition are given as *CD*.

2 At the time of the Union, in 1841, the former colonies of Upper and Lower Canada were renamed Canada West and Canada East. When Peter Waite wrote in 1963, historians used these names for the whole period from 1841 to 1867 to distinguish it from the earlier colonial phase and the later Dominion. However, the old names continued in general use and, in 1849, Parliament officially re-adopted them. Geographical echoes survived in the offices of Attorney General East (in 1865 held by Cartier) and Attorney General West (John A. Macdonald). During the debates, Alexander

Mackenzie was a rare exception in speaking of "Canada West," perhaps because he came from Sarnia. But, in his full speech, even Mackenzie referred to "Upper Canada" as often as he did to "Canada West," while he used "Canada East" just once but "Lower Canada" or "Lower Canadians" twenty-two times. Politicians were starting to look beyond the boundaries of the province, and Mackenzie's clumsy expression of hope that there would be "another colony to the westward of Canada West" helps to explain why the term was falling out of use. However, confusingly, almost everybody called the Maritimes the "Lower Provinces," although some, like Macdonald, used both terms interchangeably. One other point of terminology should be noted. As Peter Waite's Introduction (xl) shows, variants of the word "Québécois" were occasionally imported into English, but always to describe francophone residents of the city of Quebec. It is an anachronism to use the term to refer to nineteenth-century French Canada, whose people called themselves "canadiens" or French Canadians. Margaret A. Banks, "Upper and Lower Canada or Canada West and East?" *Canadian Historical Review* 54 (1973): 473–80; *CD*, 421–34.

3 For general accounts, see J.M.S. Careless, *The Union of the Canadas: The Growth of Canadian Institutions 1841–1857* (Toronto: McClelland and Stewart, 1967) and W.L. Morton, *The Critical Years: The Union of British North America 1857–1873* (Toronto: McClelland and Stewart, 1964).

4 The member, James Dickson, was lampooned as a Bruce Peninsula secessionist. *Montreal Gazette*, 17 March, 23 May 1864.

5 The *Globe* praised the United States, where Irish Catholic immigrants were "put between the upper and nether mill-stones of the Bible and the Common School and ground out Protestants in a very short time." Representation by population and non-sectarian schools were the means by which "the deep schemes of Romish Priestcraft are to be baffled." *Globe*, 12 January, 4 February 1856.

6 The idea of splitting the province into three units (i.e. partitioning Lower Canada on language lines) was briefly revived in 1865 by James O'Halloran, who represented Missisquoi in the Eastern Townships. *CD*, 793.

7 Reviewing the five years from 1859, Dunkin claimed that "we quarrelled and fought about almost everything, but did not waste a thought or a word upon this gigantic question of the Confederation of these provinces." *CD*, 485.

8 J.M.S. Careless, *Brown of the Globe: I, The Voice of Upper Canada 1818–1859* (Toronto: Macmillan of Canada, 1959), 311–22; Elwood H. Jones, "Ephemeral Compromise: The Great Reform Convention Revisited," *Journal of Canadian Studies* 3 (1968): 21–8.

9 *CD*, 126.

10 Ministerial explanations of 22 June 1864, Joseph Pope, *Memoirs of the Right Honourable Sir John Alexander Macdonald G.C.B., First Prime Minister of the Dominion of Canada,* 2 vols, (Ottawa: J. Durie and Son, 1894), I: 346.

11 For Macdonald's 1861 speech, Pope, *Memoirs,* I, 229. Even in this emphatic endorsement of centralisation, Macdonald accepted a role for subordinate local legislatures. For Brown's 1864 committee, see J.M.S. Careless, *Brown of the Globe: II, Statesman of Confederation 1860–1880* (Toronto: Macmillan of Canada, 1963), 126–9.

12 Bruce W. Hodgins, *John Sandfield Macdonald 1812–1872* (Toronto: University of Toronto Press, 1971), esp. 56–74. For the story of the "drinking majority," J. Young, *Public Men and Public Life in Canada: The Story of the Canadian Confederacy,* 2 vols, (Toronto: William Briggs, 1912), I: 197–8. McGee called the North-West "British Central America" in a speech at Ottawa in 1863. T. D'Arcy McGee, *Speeches and Addresses Chiefly on the Subject of British-American Union* (London: Chapman and Hall, 1865), 53.

13 For Foley (who joined the Taché-Macdonald ministry, but was dropped from the Great Coalition), see Young, *Public Men and Public Life in Canada,* I: 201. Joseph Cauchon warned that the Lower Canada British might switch sides over representation by population. J. Cauchon, *L'Union des Provinces de l'Amérique Britannique du Nord* (Quebec: A. Côté et Cie, 1865), 18. The *Montreal Gazette* openly threatened their defection on 2 September 1864.

14 The classic account of the formation of the Great Coalition remains Donald Creighton, *The Road to Confederation: The Emergence of Canada 1863–1867* (Toronto, Macmillan of Canada, 1964), 39–69. Two recent studies attempt to view the politics of coalition without the retrospective glow of nation-building: Ged Martin, *Faction and Fiction in Canada's Great Coalition of 1864* (Sackville, New Brunswick: Mount Allison University Centre for Canadian Studies, 1993) and Christopher Moore, *1867: How the Fathers Made a Deal* (Toronto: McClelland and Stewart, 1997), 1–31.

15 Pope, *Memoirs*, I: 347.

16 J.K. Chapman, *The Career of Arthur Hamilton Gordon First Lord Stanmore 1829–1912* (Toronto: University of Toronto Press, 1964), 28. Oliver Mowat had warned the Reform Convention in 1859 that the British government might not automatically accept constitutional change. C.R.W. Biggar, *Sir Oliver Mowat,* 2 vols, (Toronto: Warwick Brothers and Rutter, 1905), I: 93.

17 For the Intercolonial Railway negotiations, see Morton, *Critical Years*, 120–5. Although often referred to as a railway from Halifax to Quebec, the Intercolonial would link with the Grand Trunk system at Rivière-du-Loup, on the south shore of the St Lawrence, providing a direct connection to Lévis, opposite Quebec, but not into the city itself. Quebec City's own ambitions aimed at becoming the Atlantic terminus for a transcontinental railway. Brian J. Young, *Promoters and Politicians: The North-Shore Railways in the History of Quebec 1854–85* (Toronto: University of Toronto Press, 1978).

18 The seaboard provinces were like rejected suitors on the rebound: in 1863, Canada was very unpopular, Creighton, *Road to Confederation*, 24–5. The

Halifax *Morning Chronicle* (27 October 1863) argued for "consolidation upon a smaller scale" since British North American union "is no longer a project which men of the present generation can hope to see accomplished." Interestingly, the Toronto *Globe* (25 November 1863) reproved such talk. "The union of all British America is not a question of gain with us; it is one of *prestige* and of nationality. It is favourably viewed by our population. We look forward to it as our destiny; but it is not a scheme which we feel ourselves compelled to undertake at once by any pressing necessity."

19 For the August 1864 Canadian tour of the Maritimes, P.B. Waite, *The Life and Times of Confederation 1864–1867: Politics, Newspapers and the Union of British North America* (Toronto: University of Toronto Press, 1962), 66–72. The tour was referred to during the Confederation debates, e.g. *CD*, pp. 135, 152, 171, 227. Waite regards it as a success, but one New Brunswick legislator objected to being ruled by "such men as we have lately had travelling through this country from Canada." Janet Ajzenstat, Paul Romney, Ian Gentles, and William D. Gairdner, eds, *Canada's Founding Debates* (Toronto: Stoddart, 1999), 74. For McGee's comment, see University of New Brunswick, Harriet Irving Library, S.L. Tilley Papers, McGee to Tilley, 1 April, 9 May 1864.

20 Edward Whelan, *The Union of the British Provinces,* ed. D.C. Harvey (Gardenvale, Quebec: Garden City Press, 1927), 51.

21 The opponents of Confederation were not stupid: Ged Martin, "The Case Against Canadian Confederation," in Ged Martin, ed., *The Causes of Canadian Confederation* (Fredericton: Acadiensis Press, 1990), 19–49.

22 The great biography associated with Confederation remains the two-volume study of Macdonald by Donald Creighton, especially *John A. Macdonald: The Young Politician* (Toronto: University of Toronto Press, 1952), although it is rivalled by Careless, *Brown of the Globe: II, The Statesman of Confederation 1860–1880*). The best starting point for information about the participants is the multi-volume *Dictionary of Canadian Biography*, in which entries are arranged by the decade of death. McGee and Taché appear in Volume IX (1861–70), Brown, Cartier, Holton, Sandfield Macdonald, and Morris in Volume X (1871–80), Matthew Cameron, Cauchon, and Dunkin in Volume XI (1881–90), Dorion, Galt, and John A. Macdonald in Volume XII (1891–1900), Joly and Perrault in Volume XIII (1901–10). The essay on John A. Macdonald, by J.K. Johnson and Peter Waite, is especially recommended.

23 *CD*, 86 (Brown) and 626 (Perrault). For Perrault's defeat in 1867, see A.I. Silver, *The French-Canadian Idea of Confederation 1864–1900* (Toronto: University of Toronto Press, 2nd ed., 1997), 27. For Cartier's ambitions, *CD*, 500. As Canada's prime minister from 1873 to 1878, Alexander Mackenzie is often represented as a politician of limited vision, but in 1865 he hoped to become "before I die, a citizen of an immense empire built up on our part of the North American continent." *CD*, 433.

24 For Macdonald and Cartier, *Montreal Gazette*, 11 November 1867 and W.L. Morton, ed, *Monck Letters and Journals 1863–1868: Canada from Government House at Confederation* (Toronto: McClelland and Stewart, 1970), 158–9, 183, 250.

25 For Cauchon, see this volume, 126, and *Canadian News* (London), 23 March 1865, 177. For McGee on Dunkin, see McGee, *Speeches and Addresses*, 206. McGee enjoyed baiting Dunkin: during the Confederation debates, he admitted that "we ought to aim at perfection, but who has ever attained it, except perhaps the hon. Member for Brome." (*CD*, 136). Of Dunkin's subsequent term as a Dominion cabinet minister, Macdonald wrote that he "was most painstaking and conscientious, but really threw himself away on detail." Joseph Pope, ed., *Correspondence of Sir John Macdonald* (Garden City, NY: Doubleday, Page and Company, 1921), 149.

26 For McGee, Morton, ed, *Monck Letters and Journals*, 80; for Perrault, *Montreal Gazette*, 2 January 1864, *La Minerve*, 22 March 1864.

27 Brian Young, *George-Etienne Cartier: Montreal Bourgeois* (Montreal: McGill-Queen's University Press, 1981), 32–8.

28 Careless, *Brown of the Globe: II, Statesman of Confederation*, 138; J.M.S. Careless, "George Brown and the Mother of Confederation," Canadian Historical Association *Report* (1960): 57–73.

29 For Galt's letters to his wife, see O.D. Skelton, *Life and Times of Sir Alexander Tilloch Galt*, ed. G. MacLean (Toronto, McClelland and Stewart, 1966), 163–72, 186–7, 189–94. Occasionally, a woman might make a decisive intervention: in 1887 Margaret Blake bluntly told the reluctant Wilfrid Laurier that he must take over as Liberal leader from her ailing husband. Within hours of Macdonald's death in 1891, his formidable second wife unsuccessfully lobbied the governor-general to appoint Tupper as prime minister.

30 Macdonald's fears were probably justified, as may be seen from the later movement for political union in Australia. When a federal constitution was drafted in 1897, five of the six colonial legislatures demanded changes. New South Wales proposed ninety-eight amendments, while even tiny Tasmania, which was keen to join, came up with eighty-four. One historian has concluded that "a coherent document could never have been assembled from the pieces." John M. Williams, *The Australian Constitution: A Documentary History* (Melbourne: Melbourne University Press, 2005), 666–704; J.A. La Nauze, *The Making of the Australian Constitution* (Melbourne: Melbourne University Press, 1972), 162.

31 The despatch containing the British government's criticisms had been published. G. P. Browne, ed., *Documents on the Confederation of British North America* (Toronto: McClelland and Stewart, 1969), 168–71; *CD*, 119–20.

32 Pope, ed., *Correspondence*, 15; Browne, ed., *Documents on the Confederation of British North America*, 175–8. The cavalier treatment of Resolution 24 is barely noticed in the standard texts.

33 *CD*, 207; Silver, *French-Canadian Idea of Confederation*, 32–45. For Macdonald, *CD*, 18 and see *Montreal Gazette*, 15 February 1865. Local structures for what would become Ontario and Quebec (the names were not chosen until early in 1867) were eventually unveiled in July 1866. Then Macdonald announced that it was not necessary "to discuss them at length ... since their subject had been more or less under discussion during the general debate on Confederation." *Montreal Gazette*, 14 July 1866.

34 Bruce W. Hodgins, "Democracy and the Ontario Fathers of Confederation," in Bruce W. Hodgins and Robert Page, eds, *Canadian History Since Confederation: Essays and Interpretations* (Georgetown, Ont.: Irwin-Dorsey, 2nd ed., 1979), 19–28. Macdonald dismissed the idea of a referendum on Confederation as "unconstitutional and anti-British." Creighton, *John A. Macdonald: The Young Politician*, 387. Brown's argument (this volume, 76) that ministers knew they had public support so they had no reason to risk losing an election sounds positively totalitarian. In 1887, a journalist claimed that Cartier had told him that there was no popular vote on Confederation because the people of Lower Canada would have rejected it. (Library and Archives Canada, Macdonald Papers, vol. 44, cutting from the *London Advertiser*, 16 July 1887.) "The natural inference is that the politicians were not sure they had the people with them," commented Goldwin Smith in 1891: *Canada and the Canadian Question*, ed. Carl Berger (Toronto: University of Toronto Press, 1971 ed.), 114. But, then as now, a majority of voters in Lower Canada/Quebec is not the same as a majority of French Canadians. J.W. Dawson, principal of McGill, believed that "scarcely any one among the English of Lower Canada desires Confederation" and that, of the French, "nearly one half are against the Scheme." Waite, *Life and Times of Confederation*, 135. If Dawson's assessment was accurate, then a popular vote in Lower Canada could have been swung by the non-francophone minority against the wishes of the majority of French Canadians – as happened, in the other direction, in the 1995 referendum on secession.

35 For Brown's "fifty ridings" claim, see this volume, 76.

36 For Macpherson, who represented the Bruce peninsula, *CD*, 149. John Simpson and James Skead, elected in 1864 for the Whitby and Ottawa areas, both denied that they had pledged themselves on Confederation. James Aikins, elected for the Burlington-Brampton district, reported that "a very large proportion" of his constituents had "no fixed and definite opinions" about Confederation, and might reject it if it proved expensive. *CD*, pp. 231, 242, 158. In short, the claim that the Legislative Council elections constituted a back-door mandate was absurd. Charles Magill was declared elected for Hamilton on 19 February, and spoke briefly on 13 March, after the main vote had been taken. *CD*, 997–8.

37 For Ross, *CD*, 71–80; for Macdonald versus Holton, *CD*, 147–8, 704–30 ; "cold water," *CD 50;* "Canadian, " *CD* 205. For McGee's unwise quotation

from *Macbeth*, this volume, 112. The Canadian Assembly was not the ideal arena for witty repartee. An angry journalist dismissed many members as "half-informed or wholly uneducated boors ... men with the manners of the stable yard." A lady in the governor-general's entourage was similarly scandalised: "they have no *manners*." *Montreal Gazette*, 3 June 1864; Morton, ed., *Monck Letters and Journals*, 65.

38 J.K. Johnson, ed., *"Affectionately Yours": The Letters of Sir John A. Macdonald and His Family* (Toronto: Macmillan of Canada, 1969), 79. For Taché, *CD*, 6, 9, 235; for Dorion, *CD* 245. Henry Best challenged Waite's view that Cartier repeated his entire speech in French, pointing out that *La Minerve* grumbled that it had to publish its report 24 hours after the *Montreal Gazette* because of the need to translate Cartier's remarks. (Henry B.M. Best, "George-Etienne Cartier", PhD thesis, 1969, Université Laval, 329–31.) Cauchon complained of the pressures that translation placed upon Canada's francophone journalists. This restricted the flow of news and was one reason most French-language papers appeared only tri-weekly. Hence Cartier could assume that it would take several days for his speech to circulate in his own section anyway. In speaking in English, he was perhaps bidding to be Taché's successor as premier. Waite, *Life and Times of Confederation*, 135, and see 142 for Dorion's widely reported exploitation of the ambiguity of "confédération."

C.B. de Niverville complained that unilingual French-Canadian members were condemned by the predominantly English atmosphere of parliament "to hold our tongues, to listen, and to understand if we can." But François Bourassa was said to have admitted that he could only tolerate sitting in parliament at all because most of the time he had no idea what was going on. *CD*, 950; Roger le Moine, *Napoléon Bourassa: l'homme et l'artiste* (Ottawa: Les Presses de l'Université d'Ottawa, 1974), 15.

39 This volume, 97.

40 In 1980, when Quebec's separatist government put its referendum legislation before the provincial legislature, Parti Québécois strategist Claude Charron marshalled the caucus to unleash a similar barrage of focused argument to portray independence as inevitable and out-gun the opposition. L. Ian MacDonald, *From Bourassa to Bourassa: A Pivotal Decade in Canadian History* (Montreal: Harvest House, 1984), 143.

41 *CD*, 448. One member, Louis Archambeault, announced that his opinion had been changed by the debate: he voted for Confederation. *CD*, 544.

42 E.B. Biggar, *Anecdotal Life of Sir John Macdonald* (Montreal: John Lovell, 1891), 225. For Brown's comment on the speeches of Macdonald and Cartier, Creighton, *Road to Confederation*, 236; for Holton, *CD*, 147; for Galt, *Quebec Morning Chronicle*, 4 March 1865; for Brown's own speech, Careless, *Brown of the Globe: II, The Statesman of Confederation*, 182; for McGee's interjection, *CD*, 147; for Hamilton *Spectator*, Creighton, *Road to Confederation*, 237.

43 *CD*, 72; *Canadian News* (London), 16 March 1865, 171.

44 *Montreal Gazette*, 7 March 1865; CD, 648–57; Careless, *Brown of the Globe: II, Statesman of Confederation*, 190 and *Globe*, 13 March 1865.

45 Equally remarkable was the size of the division. Apart from the Speaker, only five members missed the key vote in the night hours of 11 March. J.J.C. Abbott, Macdonald's eventual successor as prime minister in 1891, was away on legal business. Dunkin was exhausted after his mighty speech. Two other Lower Canada members abstained, and one was keeping a low profile while facing fraud charges.

46 Waite's "Introduction" to this edition, ix-xi; W.L. Morton, ed., *The Shield of Achilles: Aspects of Canada in the Victorian Age* (Toronto: McClelland and Stewart, 1968), 316. Allusions to the *Federalist Papers* were surprisingly few, e.g. *CD*, 219, 675. For "Mills", *CD*, 339, but John Stuart Mill was quoted more accurately at 334, 439. By coincidence, the first Canadian to contribute a theoretical analysis of federation *was* called Mills: David Mills had studied the subject at the University of Michigan Law School, making him one of the few politicians with a college education – but he did not enter parliament until 1867. He is the central figure in Vipond's *Liberty and Community*, cited below. One limitation on theoretical debate was the problem of access to sources in mid-Victorian Canada. When Dunkin was caught out misquoting an article in the most recent issue of the influential *Edinburgh Review*, he pleaded that there had been only one copy available, presumably in the Parliamentary Library, and that as a result his transcription had been hasty. *CD*, 538. Ideological elements in the approach of both Reformers and Conservatives to Confederation are stressed by Robert C. Vipond, *Liberty and Community: Canadian Federalism and the Failure of the Constitution* (Albany: State University of New York Press, 1991), 15–45 and Peter J. Smith, "The Ideological Origins of Canadian Confederation," in Janet Ajzenstat and Peter J. Smith, eds, *Canada's Origins: Liberal, Tory or Republican* (Ottawa: Carleton University Press, 1995), 47–78.

47 For Taché's reference to the "inclined plane," see this volume, 21, and *CD*, 46, 124, 155 for opposition annoyance. For the unpopularity of annexation, *Globe*, 18 November 1856, and Biggar, *Sir Oliver Mowat*, I, 143. For Taché's October 1864 speech, Whelan, ed. Harvey, *Union of the British Provinces*, 83 and *CD*, 1001 for Macdonald.

48 *Montreal Gazette*, 14 March 1856. The sole vote in favour of British North American union in this unnoticed debate came from the 77–year-old James Crooks, who argued that Canada needed "new blood." For another abortive attempt to raise Confederation in 1856, *CD*, 915.

49 Contrast Macdonald on the impossibility of complete unification in *CD*, 29 with his indiscreet letter to Matthew Cameron, in Waite, *Life and Times of Confederation*, 123, and see also his comments to a Montreal editor, Library

and Archives Canada, Brown Chamberlin Papers, Vol. 3/35, Macdonald to Chamberlin, private, 26 October 1868.

50 For J-B-E. Dorion's speech, *CD*, 856–71, and compare Jean-Paul Bernard, *Les Rouges: libéralisme, nationalisme et anticléricalisme au milieu du XIXe siècle* (Montreal: Les Presses de l'Université du Québec, 1971), 284: "Avant l'Union nous avions un Anglais devant nous; avec l'Union nous en avons un en avant et un en arrière; avec la Confédération nous en aurons un en avant, un en arrière, un de chaque côté et peur-être sur la tête."

51 *Montreal Gazette*, 8 February 1865. *CD*, 948 for the Roman Empire, and *Globe*, 1, 13 March 1865 on the debate. What became of the 11,500 copies of the printed debates? Some were distributed as offprints. The binding of the original edition of 1865 was not robust and many probably disintegrated. The Confederation debates did not become a major focus in later constitutional discussion. For two references in 1870, see Peter Oliver, ed., *The Conventional Man: The Diaries of Ontario Chief Justice Robert A. Harrison, 1856–1878* (Toronto: University of Toronto Press, 2003), 378, and *Montreal Gazette*, 10 September 1870. In 1891, Goldwin Smith dismissed the 1,032–page debate as mainly "mere assertion and counter-assertion," although he praised Dunkin – a generous act, since Dunkin had been critical of his own views on colonial relations. Goldwin Smith, ed. C. Berger, *Canada and the Canadian Question*, 113–14.

52 *La Minerve*, 5 January 1865, analysed by Silver, *French-Canadian Idea of Confederation*, 45–6. As an intellectual game, the origins of René Lévesque's theory of "sovereignty association" might be traced back to Sandfield Macdonald's "double majority" – but in 1865 the double majority system was generally regarded as a failure.

53 For Brown's resignation, Careless, *Brown of the Globe: II, The Statesman of Confederation*, 211–20. For Joly on free trade with the Maritimes, *CD*, 356, echoed by A-A. Dorion, 528. However, one counter-argument was the commitment of New Brunswick and Nova Scotia to meet seven-twelfths of the interest on an Intercolonial loan, if terms could ever be agreed: the Maritimes simply could not afford to sacrifice tariff revenue. W.M. Whitelaw, *The Maritimes and Canada before Confederation*, ed. P.B. Waite (Toronto: Oxford University Press, 1966 ed.,), 165.

54 The lack of an amending formula was raised by Nova Scotian opponents, Martin, "Case Against Canadian Confederation," 30, and see Ajzenstat et al., eds, *Canada's Founding Debates*, 273. In a rare explicit statement on the subject, Macdonald assured the governor-general in 1873 that only the Dominion parliament could request Westminster legislation to amend the British North America Act: the Ottawa government alone had no right "to assume the power of asking the Imperial Parliament to alter our Constitution." Pope, ed., *Correspondence*, 218. Macdonald evidently assumed that governments could not dictate parliamentary approval, as

would become the case with tighter party discipline in modern times. Failure to confront the issue of an amending formula probably reflects confidence that constitutional change would only occur by consensus.

55 For McGiverin, *CD*, 469. For south-western Ontario as "Western Canada," Pope, *Memoirs of Sir John Macdonald*, I, 281. "In the 1860s, western alienation began at Yonge Street." Moore, *1867: How the Fathers Made a Deal*, 1.

56 Representatives of the *Montreal Gazette* and the Toronto *Leader* sought admission to the Quebec Conference in a sarcastic missive which claimed that press access had been allowed "in cases where an European Congress holds the peace of the world and the fate of nations in its hands." The initiative was directed against their rival, the *Globe*, which had insider status through George Brown's role as a delegate. The request was denied. J. Pope, ed., *Confederation* (Ottawa: Carswell, 1895), 7–8, 10–11.

Introduction to the First Edition

A selection is both better and worse than the original, better because it may pick out salient points otherwise unobserved, worse because it is a distortion. It is idle to pretend that the 1032 pages of the *Confederation Debates* can be cut to one-twelfth without serious loss of range and coherence. This selection is rather an introduction to the *Debates* than a substitute for them. (The full debates are at present available in reprint from the Queen's Printer, Ottawa.)

The selection has been made on the basis of intrinsic merit; I have preferred force, relevance, shrewdness, and wit. Thus no apology is needed for giving George Brown and Christopher Dunkin the largest amount of space, with John A. Macdonald and A. A. Dorion next. Although I should like to have included more from minor figures in the debate, I have tried to include all major points of view. Selections are grouped under the Legislative Council and the Assembly respectively; otherwise they follow the same order as the original *Debates*. The *Debates* are almost devoid of paragraphing, and where it seemed clearly to be required I have inserted paragraphs. Occasionally I have indulged a wish to give something of the spirit of the Assembly, I hope at not too great a cost.

The *Debates* have been collated with contemporary newspaper reports, the best of which were in the Quebec *Morning Chronicle*. While the official *Debates* were nearly always more comprehensive, in a few instances the Quebec *Morning Chronicle* was, and when it was, I have used it. Of course the newspapers reported the session as a whole, not just the Confederation debate. These reports I have used in the following attempt to suggest the setting and character of the Confederation debate as well as the immediate circumstances of Confederation.*

* I should like to thank the Canada Council for its assistance toward the research for the Introduction to this selection from the *Confederation Debates*.

I

It was cold at Quebec that January of 1865. Snow stretched away across the long valleys and mottled the dark precipices along the St Lawrence; in the river was forming the strongest ice bridge in several years. A bright Saturday just at the beginning of the session of Parliament brought people out by the hundreds to skate on patches of ice cleared of snow. "Little houses are built here and there on the ice, from which flags are gaily flying. Roads out in all directions, from shore to shore, are crowded with sleighs and pedestrians. . . . The whole scene is animated and brilliant, and the Quebecoise may be truly said to be enjoying a gala day. . . ."[1]

On Thursday, January 19, 1865, Lord Monck opened the Parliament of the Province of Canada. A four-horse sleigh, elaborately accoutred, brought the Governor General from Spencer Wood to the unprepossessing brick Parliament Buildings at 3 p.m., and he was duly installed on the Throne in the Legislative Council chamber. Gentleman Usher of the Black Rod, all black and lace, stepped forward and after elaborate bows made off to bring the Assembly, who shortly came trooping in to the Bar of the Legislative Council. Then Lord Monck took a huge scroll, "with a powerful effort raised his cocked hat an inch and a half, trembled under the shock when it fell again to its place, cleared his throat and commenced reading. . . ."[2]

To Lord Monck it was not just another session. He spoke with marked deliberation; it was obvious from the pitch of his voice and the emphasis of his words that he wanted to impress his audience with the gravity of the occasion. And he succeeded. He was heard amid "profound silence and breathless interest" from the entire assemblage.

A careful consideration of the general position of British North America induced the conviction that the circumstances of the times afforded the opportunity not merely for the settlement of a question of Provincial politics, but also for the simultaneous creation of a new Nationality. . . . With the public men of British North America it now rests to decide whether the vast tract of country which they inhabit shall be consolidated into a State, combining within its area all the elements of national greatness. . . .[3]

II

One of the prevalent assumptions that bespeaks the central Canadian orientation of our history is that the Confederation debates in the

Canadian legislature were *the* Confederation debates. It is sometimes forgotten that there were others in other provinces. Confederation was debated in Newfoundland, in Prince Edward Island, and in Nova Scotia in both the 1865 and the 1866 sessions in substance, if not in form, as it was in Canada. New Brunswick had elections in both these years with Confederation the main issue. Confederation was more controversial in the four Atlantic provinces than it was in the Province of Canada. It was not just the choice between a British North American nationality and old provincial loyalties, though there was plenty of talk about that. It was a natural concern with Maritime interests in Confederation: whether the federal system was good or bad; whether the Maritime provinces would be bled white by tariffs and taxation basically determined elsewhere (and on which columns of agitated arithmetic were spent); whether, for example, Nova Scotia, a careful man doing a snug business, should be tempted into partnership with a "wild speculator" like Canada.[4]

In the Province of Canada Confederation had a different purpose and quite a different effect. Its purpose was to cure political difficulties that had hampered, at times hamstrung, the government for at least six years; it was to remedy long-standing and well-articulated grievances in Canada West and at the same time to give French Canadians reasonable security that their rights would be preserved as well under a new system as under the old. It would end a state of affairs that a majority believed pernicious, and which young Richard Cartwright described in the *Confederation Debates* in this way:

> *. . . three changes of Ministry within the space of a single twelve month; the fate of cabinets dependant on the vote of a single capricious or unprincipled individual, in a House of 130 members; a deficient revenue and a sinking credit; all useful legislation at a standstill. . . . I speak of facts patent and known to all, when I say that the position of parties in this province, the bitterness and virulence of party feeling, and the narrowness and acrimony to which those feelings gave rise, were degrading and demoralizing to us all. . . .*[5]

Hitherto Confederation had been a dream that had floated in the Canadian imagination; it had appeared in the past, sometimes after a bout of bad times, sometimes during fitful politics, but always it faded when reality touched it. It seemed impossible to bring to the light of day. Galt's address in 1858 had barely a hearing. Back Canadians went, with relief it seemed, to "the petty strifes and contentions which formed the staple product of our political warfare. . . ."[6] Finally in June, 1864, came George Brown's forthright offer to the Conservatives to make a coalition that would deal with Canada's difficulties once and for all.

It was this coalition of June, 1864 that made Confederation a reality. It united the Conservatives with the Reformers, the western wing of the Liberal party, thus joining together three of the four major political groups in the province. It revolutionized Canadian politics. First and foremost in the minds of Canadians, Confederation would settle the Canadian problem by federation of the two sections of the old Province of Canada; and the inclusion of the Maritime colonies would balance ancient antipathies in Canada and at the same time establish the nucleus of a whole new British North American nationality. By means of Canadian energy, determination, and not a little luck, this program not only succeeded in Canada but in a matter of months had also drastically altered the complexion of politics in the Maritime colonies.

The driving force for Confederation came from Canada West. And the Reform party's agitation for representation by population was the vital part of that force. There is no doubt that "rep. by pop.," as it was called, was a major issue. But Alexander Mackenzie believed, perhaps rightly, that it merely disguised the real nature of the conflict between Canada West and Canada East. Mackenzie said frankly that "rep. by pop." alone would not satisfy Canada West, and George Brown agreed with him.[7] Probably the great bulk of the Reform party would have said that Canada West wanted an end to French-Canadian influence (or interference) in her internal affairs: nothing less, in fact, than the separation that would be realized in a separate province of Ontario, and yet without the disadvantages of a complete dissolution of the Canadian union. For views like these, Confederation was not only *an* answer, it was probably the *only* answer. On the other hand there is much evidence in the *Debates* that many English Canadians in Canada East felt the necessity of the two nationalities continuing to live as before, in the same constitutional habitation. Difficult it was; quarrels there were; but the old way was still, in their view, the best way. The existing union of the Province of Canada did make Canadians, French and English, get along somehow; and its continuance was better than splitting Canada into separate provinces. If the two nationalities were to go their separate and doubtless antagonistic ways, it would leave an important group of English in Canada East under French-Canadian control.

As for the French Canadians, they had sought at first to resist, then to control the force from Canada West. Most preferred the *status quo*; some of them, notably the Liberals (or Rouges as the French-Canadian Liberal wing was sometimes called), had recognized for six years and more, that some concessions to Canada West might be desirable, perhaps inevitable. But the Conservative party of Canada East, both French and English wings, had resolutely resisted any concessions. Then suddenly in June, 1864, these Conservatives embraced the Reform party of Canada West, Confederation, and "rep. by pop." in the coalition. This left the Liberals of Canada East nowhere. They who had been the first in Canada East to recognize the grievances of Canada West and to suggest, tentatively to be sure, some means of alleviating them, were now left altogether outside of the coalition and, inevitably, of Confederation. At the same time the French-Canadian Conservatives (or Bleus), led by George Cartier, who had for years past set their faces against "rep. by pop." in any form, had now to justify themselves to a surprised and bewildered electorate. Cartier, the Attorney General East, gambled his political life, and won. His power over French Canadians, which even his opponents acknowledged,[8] enabled him, with the tacit though not yet overt assistance of the Church, to carry a narrow majority of French-Canadian members with him. What the electorate thought is uncertain: Cartier had no intention of calling an election to find out. The Rouges stormed, threatened, agitated: but Cartier, strongly entrenched as a French Conservative, the superintendent (as Attorney General East) of the forthcoming *Code Civile*, was able effectively to pose as the champion of the French Canadians. He swore that Confederation was necessary, and that it would not in any way weaken French-Canadian privileges. With him he carried a small but influential middle group who, though manifestly uncomfortable about the breakup of the *status quo*, believed the time had come to recognize necessity.

Here relations with the United States exercised a powerful influence. The crisis in American affairs in late 1864, culminating in December with the dismissal of the St Albans raiders by the Montreal magistrate, C. J. Coursol, had produced wild recriminations in the American press, unwelcome action by the State Department in demanding passports for British North American travellers, and threats in Congress to end both the bonding privileges for Canadian goods going to Portland and the Reciprocity Treaty. This is what McGee meant when he spoke of "events stronger than advocacy, events stronger than men."[9] In the circumstances that led to Confederation some Canadians discerned the hand of God: the June coalition uniting men long bitterly opposed, the accident of the Charlottetown Conference, coming, it appeared, at so opportune a moment, the dazzling success of Canadians at Charlottetown and at Quebec, and all when the American union seemed broken in the holocaust of war. There were not a few in Parliament who avowed beliefs about divine influence in Confederation.

The Opposition were inclined to attribute Confederation to less exalted causes. They believed Confederation was a conspiracy engineered by Conservatives with a taste for office and naïve, well-meaning Reformers. Conservatives wanted power, Reformers wanted "rep. by pop.": a bargain was struck. "Who could have thought," wrote one bitter Reformer, "we would have come to this pass."[10] Yet such was the power of Confederation that even this Reformer, Dr T. S. Parker, member for North Wellington, finally voted for it. For him, as for so many Upper Canadians, "the *status quo* is impossible."[11] In Canada East the Opposition were not now so concerned about the problems of Canada West: they wanted to keep the old Union and not attempt something that was, they alleged, crude and dangerous. To say that Canada was now at the parting of the ways, that her future had to be determined now or never, was nonsense. What was worse, it was tendentious: it was trying to make men forswear criticism for the sake of a spurious belief in a great destiny. The old Union would still work; all that was needed was more forbearance, less personal recrimination, and some scheme for amelioration of present difficulties within the existing system. It was a new theory of settling a domestic quarrel to join with the establishments (and the quarrels) of the neighbours. Why should Canada unite with the Maritime colonies in order to solve Canadian problems?

The Opposition's difficulty was that it was heterogeneous. Its core was the Liberals of Canada East, French and English, held together by common experience and Liberal principles rather than by common interests. To the Liberals were joined some dissentient Conservatives from Canada East – English-speaking – who feared a separate province of Quebec; a few French Conservatives who disliked the idea of Confederation; some Conservatives from Canada West who hated Reformers; and a group of Reformers who hated Conservatives, and who rallied behind a little group led by Sandfield Macdonald. Such a motley Opposition did not have much of a chance, and they probably knew they had not; but their comments on Confederation are by no means without point. The scheme was not perfect – even its supporters admitted that. Some members both of the Government and of the Opposition said it could be improved with more work; generally the Opposition said Confederation should be abandoned altogether. The Opposition failed to stop Confederation. In their attempt they made irrelevant criticisms and drew absurd conclusions; they failed, one suspects, to dent the complacency of the Government: but they illuminated, often with disconcerting brilliance, the origins of Confederation, and they picked out, at times with uncanny accuracy, flaws and inconsistencies in the constitution that we have discovered since 1867 by painful experience.

III

That there were official *Debates* at all appears to have been an accident. The Government originally seem to have had no intention of publishing debates. Canada was not in the habit of doing so. Some colonies, Prince Edward Island and Nova Scotia, did; New Brunswick started and stopped according to the power of various groups who supported or opposed it. Newfoundland did not, nor did Vancouver Island or British Columbia. The newspapers of the time published regular reports as a matter of course, but rarely in full, and often much abbreviated.

It was not until the debates on Confederation had started in the Legislative Council that the question of their being officially published was raised in the Assembly. It was M. C. Cameron, independent Conservative, member for North Ontario,[12] to whom we probably owe the *Debates*. He raised the matter just before Macdonald's opening speech in the debate, on February 6. Macdonald replied that the Government had made no special arrangements for printing the debates on Confederation, but if the House wanted to publish them, the Government would afford every facility. M. C. Cameron moved the matter go to the House Committee on Printing, and two days later the Committee through its spokesman, Alexander Mackenzie, reported back that the project would cost about $2,200. W. F. Powell, Conservative member for Carleton, asked how on earth anyone could estimate cost. "We should be deluged with speeches which we should not otherwise [have] had. (Hear, hear.) The member for Brome (Mr. Dunkin) would speak at least forty-five times. (Laughter.) The project might probably cost twenty thousand dollars."[13] No one believed that figure, or anything like it; but Powell was far nearer the mark than Alexander Mackenzie was. The *Confederation Debates* actually cost $14,490.65.[14]

They were published in French (four thousand copies) and English (seventy-five hundred copies), with each member allowed fifty copies of his own speech in either language. Members were to receive copies as they were set up in print. But it became more and more difficult for the printers to keep up with the spate of words and the slowness of members' corrections; by the end of the debate on Confederation the printing was a month behind the speeches, and according to J. H. Pope two-thirds of the members heartily regretted ever having had the debates printed at all.[15]

It need not be assumed that publishing an official version of the debates was necessarily a good thing. The fact that debates were being reported fully, and officially, encouraged quantities of plain drivel.

Moreover members could correct their speeches before they were printed; this meant that speeches were dressed up for public consumption. There are interesting differences between the pungency of a remark on the floor of the House and the pomposity preferred by a member in the "corrected" version of his speech.

The House was by no means without humour, though it favoured a style characterized more by spirit than by intellect. The House was not a place for delicacy or fine-spun argument; Cartier's vulgar irrelevancies during Dunkin's closely argued speech illustrate the short-run capacity for following close analysis enjoyed by some of the members. Personalities were often the mainspring of debate. Here is Cartier hitting at Luther Holton in the debate on the resolutions from Committee of Supply:

> *the hon. gentleman was a great water drinker. . . if there is one fluid less likely than another to produce ascerbity* [sic] *and bitterness in any body or substance, it was water. (Renewed laughter and cheers.) . . . he did not know what process the water went through after Hon. Mr. Holton drank it, as it appeared to come up all turned to vinegar in his constitution. (Roars of laughter.) Then he went on to advise the vinegar manufacturers present to hire that hon. gentleman to drink water for them. . . . (Great laughter, cheers and counter-cheers.)*[16]

There were periodic and unedifying squabbles over precedence in the Confederation debate, among which Cauchon's was about the worst, and since it serves to illustrate some aspects of the character of the debates, it is worth telling. Cauchon had with some reluctance yielded the floor for February 27 to Christopher Dunkin. Dunkin could not finish his speech that night; sick anyway, and exhausted after four hours, he sat down at 11:30 quite unable to continue. Then followed an unpleasant discussion – unreported in the *Confederation Debates* – about what should happen next. Colonel Haultain, member for Peterborough, said that Dunkin's speech had been such "an intellectual treat" that he should be given the floor for the next evening in order to finish.[17] To this proceeding Cauchon strenuously objected. Finally Cauchon grumblingly consented to postpone his speech till March 1. But on the afternoon of March 1 Cauchon got into a violent argument with Dufresne, member for Iberville, behind the Speaker's chair, during which, Dufresne alleged, he had been struck in the face. This quarrel carried the House through the supper adjournment. Cauchon, without supper, and more important, without notes, was in no position to speak just then, and was obliged to postpone his speech still another day. Finally, on Thursday, March 2, Cauchon's great speech was made.

Its mode of delivery was regrettably symptomatic of others. Cauchon appeared with a pile of manuscript on the desk in front of him and began to read his speech. It was even said that it had already been in type for two days. Cauchon had a considerable following of friends and compatriots in the public gallery who followed him like *claqueurs* at an Italian opera, cheering him and laughing at his hits, but there were only thirty or forty members in the House.[18] It was a dreary speech. He repeated most of what he had said in his newspaper – *Le Journal de Québec* – on Confederation, and spent much time attempting to show why he had had a change of mind since 1858.[19]

Cauchon's speech in favour of Confederation points up another feature of the debate. The best French-Canadian speeches were not, generally speaking, by those who supported Confederation. The French-Canadian ministers and their supporters were on the defensive: they were trying to show the necessity for Confederation and that it would not harm the institutions of French Canada. Cartier gave two long speeches, one in English, the other in French, virtual repetitions of one another; Langevin and other ministers spoke; but the best speech of this type was that of the Premier, Sir Etienne Taché, who by his years, graciousness, tolerance, and common sense, as well as by his brevity, was persuasive. One is inclined toward even the partisan opinion of the ministerial Quebec *Morning Chronicle*: "Let every man in Canada who has a doubt about Confederation read this unanswerable speech."[20]

But there were too many speeches of the Cauchon type and not all so well delivered. The printing of the debates had the effect that had been feared: members would speak for the record. They could not simply give, as they used to say, "a silent vote on the great question." So the amount of twaddle grew as the days went heavily on. Newspapers from one end of the country to the other complained of the monumental dullness of the debate. "It is very certain," opined the waspish Toronto *Leader* when the debate started, "that not one half of the members can throw the least light on the question, and if they all speak, one half will repeat what the other half says."[21] Three weeks later the *Leader* said its worst suspicions were realized, and it was no wonder that members turned away from "this standing dish of unrelieved dullness, to the superior excitement which a small railroad bill can be made to yield. . . ."[22] On February 23, for example, when J. H. Bellerose got up, there was "a general rush for the doors," and before long there was even doubt about a quorum. When the count-out was ordered and the Clerk was calling the roll, Paul Denis hopefully told the House – such was Bellerose's fearsome reputation for dullness – that Christopher Dunkin was in the lobby keeping the members back! Notwithstanding

Dunkin's efforts, nineteen members responded, who with the Speaker made the quorum of twenty. So Bellerose wagged on.[23]

The tedium of the debate seems to have set in early. The ministerial speeches of the first week were delivered to a half-empty House. Macdonald spoke to empty benches. Galt drew a better crowd for a short and excellent speech. "But even in his case," wrote the correspondent of the Hamilton *Spectator*, "the number of empty seats was a curious commentary upon the professed interest which is felt in this subject. I cannot help feeling that the number of members who have given the subject any serious consideration at all is very small, and that members are drifting into this new state of political existence with a blind reliance upon the soundness of their leaders. . . ."[24]

One ought not to place more weight upon newspaper opinion that it can properly sustain; the newspapers liked their politics hot and heavy. "This is the third day of the session," wrote the *Leader*'s correspondent on January 21, "and we haven't had a fight yet."[25] And sometimes newspaper correspondents were not above complaining of dullness when the truth was that they simply lacked the discernment to understand the debate fully. But in general they were right. It is perhaps natural to assume that the greatness of the issue aroused men's spirits and elevated their minds; for some this was undoubtedly true – George Brown, for example. Some knew their own capacities and concentrated on matters whereof they could speak: James Ferrier, Alexander Mackenzie, Walter Shanly, to name just three. Such speeches often threw a vivid light on Canadian politics for the ten years past and more, and in perspectives such as these the causes of Confederation become discernible. There were others also who were genuinely attracted by Confederation, but who had not the intelligence for dealing with it. But for others, too many others, the debate was an opportunity for windy dilations for the edification of constituents and posterity, while they themselves preferred the really important questions of personalities and local legislation.

The method of presenting Confederation to the Canadian Parliament also helped to militate against effective debate. The Government decided to carry the Quebec Resolutions *per saltum*, one of Macdonald's favourite techniques. "One fell swoop" is a less elegant way of putting it. Not only would there be no consideration of the Resolutions individually, but there would be no entertainment of amendments either. The Government took the lofty position that the Resolutions were by way of being a treaty which would if amended return Confederation to the limbo of negotiation once more. Members could talk as they pleased, but the Government, with nearly the whole power of the Reform party now behind them, was strong enough to insist that any amendment that was passed was tantamount to defeating the scheme. The Government afforded considerable opportunity for debate; it suspended the ordinary rules and followed ones which allowed every person to speak as often as he pleased; but without being able to change the scheme by criticism or argument, Parliament was being told by the Government: talk all you please, what matters is how you vote.

IV

Parliament was asked to approve an Address to the Queen praying that she "may be graciously pleased to cause a measure to be submitted to the Imperial Parliament for the purpose of uniting the Colonies of Canada, Nova Scotia, New Brunswick, Newfoundland, Prince Edward Island, in one Government, with provisions based on the following Resolutions. . . ." Here follow the seventy-two Quebec Resolutions.

Discussion on the question had of course begun before the Address was formally proposed. The reference in the Speech from the Throne to the creation of "a new Nationality" produced a clever motion by the Leader of the Opposition, A. A. Dorion: that the people of Canada, "fully appreciating the blessings of their political relations with the Great Empire of which they form a part, neither wish nor seek to create a new nationality."[26] That this motion was so decisively defeated (64–25) was a body blow to the Opposition. Up to that point the Opposition had counted on a majority of members from Canada East, at least, voting against the motion, and the result seemed to discourage them. "Elle [l'opposition] a montré sa faiblesse sans autre avantage. . . . Elle croyait embarrasser les députés bas canadiens et elle s'est prise dans son propre piège."[27] After the passage of the Alien Bill on February 2, with the chill of impending crisis in American relations helping to persuade the Government and its supporters,[28] the Confederation debate was opened on February 3 in the Legislative Council by the Premier, Sir Etienne Taché. The debate in the Legislative Council was interesting, for that House had a fair sprinkling of talent, and tended to be more critical than the Assembly with its heavy Government majority. The Legislative Council concentrated a good deal of attention on the future Senate, and, as one might expect, on the method of appointment of Senators. One major difficulty for the existing Legislative Council was that it was a House of sixty members, of whom only forty-eight (twenty-four for Quebec and twenty-four for Ontario) would be appointed to the Senate. In this game of senatorial musical chairs twelve would be out. Hence the amendment proposed on February 9, that all present members of the Canadian Legislative Council be retained in the future Senate, with ten additional members being given to the Maritime provinces. This was defeated a week later, 41–18.

Several attempts were made in the Legislative Council to postpone further debate. It was argued that the Government had given no indication how the Province of Canada was to be split up, as by Confederation it would be; there were no local constitutions brought down for the new provinces of Ontario and Quebec, no indication of how the liabilities and assets of the old province would be reckoned up between the two new ones. Then it was urged that there should be no final commitment to Confederation until the people had had a chance to vote upon the question, either by a general election – which seemed to some in the Legislative Council rather presumptuous – or by a referendum. All such attempts were defeated. On February 20, two and a half weeks after the debate had started, the Address to the Queen passed the Legislative Council, 45–15.

In the Assembly the debate was much more protracted. The Government did not at first seem to be in a hurry. The session began on January 19, but the correspondence was only tabled on January 27, and the Confederation Address was not moved in the Assembly until February 6. Macdonald's illness, together with the tactical advantage of pressing the Alien Bill first, were probably the reasons why the House met for hardly more than an hour a day for the first ten days.

There was much discussion on the mode of proceeding with the debate on Confederation. Macdonald proposed that it go on every evening after the supper recess. J. H. Cameron suggested that the debate should be opened by the Government, then adjourned a week to allow the public an opportunity to make representations. This the Government agreed to; after the first five ministerial speeches – Macdonald, Cartier, Galt, Brown, and McGee – the debate was adjourned on Thursday, February 9, for a week. On February 16 the Opposition opened up.

After the initial speeches, the Opposition developed the tactic of prolonging the debate by talk. Joseph Perrault's speech lasted over five hours – outside of Christopher Dunkin's speech (which took two nights) the longest speech in the debate – and it incorporated chunks of Garneau's *Histoire du Canada*, which Perrault obligingly read to the House. While this was going on, petitions were being circulated in the French constituencies against Confederation, and these were duly tabled later. The Government tried, with some success, to discredit such petitions; Cartier read out a private letter from J. B. E. Dorion (member for Drummond and Arthabaska) to one of the agents: "Sir – Be kind enough to have the enclosed petition signed as soon as possible by men, women and children. Yours very truly, J. B. E. Dorion." Amid loud ministerial laughter, Macdonald said it reminded him of Fag, in Sheridan's *The Rivals*, who said he had no objection to lying a little, but it hurt him to be found out."[29] But however bland the Government may have appeared, they were well aware that any successful agitation of French Canadians, by whatever means, could have serious effects. The final French-Canadian vote on Confederation was close enough.

By the end of February, with the debate dragging on and on, the Government decided to make the Confederation debate the first order of the day in the afternoons as well as in the evenings. Motions for this purpose were carried at the end of every evening's debate from March 2 on.

The weekend of Saturday, March 4, produced a sensation: the first results of the New Brunswick general election. On Friday, March 3, Tilley was defeated in Saint John City. This defeat was followed by other defeats as the two-week-long voting in New Brunswick continued, and they made the Canadian Opposition jubilant. Sandfield Macdonald wore an air of triumph when he announced Tilley's defeat to the House early on Saturday morning, March 4. All that weekend rumours circulated, emanating doubtless from Opposition sources, that Confederation would now have to be abandoned, that the Administration itself might break up.[30] And the Government was not in an easy position. The members of the Coalition had pledged themselves, back in June, 1864, to press for Confederation of all the provinces, but failing that, federation of the two Canadas. The New Brunswick government was now defeated; as far as anyone could see Confederation was finished in New Brunswick for some time to come, and if so, it was impossible for Nova Scotia. So Confederation was at a standstill. Was the Government to proceed with that Reform scheme that Conservatives hated, federation of the Canadas alone? And the defeat of Confederation went further even than that. "Many of the advocates of Confederation in Parliament," wrote the *Prescott Telegraph*, "blundered exceedingly when they argued that, unless the grand scheme for the union of the North American Provinces should carry, Canada would inevitably drift into annexation with the United States."[31] If the alternatives before Canada were Confederation or annexation, what of annexation now?

In these circumstances the Government determined to act promptly and decisively.[32] On Monday, March 6, they announced their determination to carry Confederation in the Assembly as soon as possible, to prorogue Parliament, and to send a delegation to England to concert measures for Confederation and for defence. This forthright policy put heart into Government supporters, for whom the uncertainties of the weekend past had been disconcerting. And the next day, Tuesday March 7, Macdonald moved the previous question in the Confederation debate. This important technical motion extinguished even attempts at amendments.

As the defeat of Confederation in New Brunswick had given the Opposition heart, so Macdonald's moving the previous question gave it animus. The debate that had been growing insufferable was now enlivened by strong speeches from Holton, the two Dorions, and others. These in turn provoked John A. Macdonald into his best speech in the whole debate.[33]

Although the prorogation of the session appeared to come as the result of events in New Brunswick, an adjournment had been decided on some three weeks before.[34] What was new was that the adjournment became a prorogation. The reason for the change was simple, if unedifying. Each member received a sessional indemnity of $600. The business of Parliament was still unfinished, and another meeting was necessary. Prorogation thus meant a new session, so each member would now get another $600. This sop, so it was said, allayed discontent over the choking off of the debate and ameliorated the unhappy prospect of a summer meeting of Parliament.[35]

But $600 could not alter the fact that Confederation, even if passed in Canada, was nowhere. As the last stage of the debate developed a consciousness seemed to grow up on all sides of this impasse in Canadian affairs. As the *Quebec Daily News* put it:

> *Our position just now is far from agreeable. We were in a state of transition, but that is suddenly checked, and we must remain for some time with our hands tied up, inert, passive. We cannot go back to the old condition of parties which existed prior to the coalition; nor can we advance till New Brunswick changes her present attitude.*[36]

It was not surprising that the Canadian ministers had to act with determination, or that, while they were in England, annexation sentiment began to develop in Canada.[37]

A violent snow storm descended upon Quebec during the last days of the debate. The final day was March 10, and the debate went on into the small hours of the morning of Saturday, March 11. A vast lobby of members were waiting to vote; unable to endure any more Confederation talk, they had eaten and drunk everything the House restaurant and bar could supply, and were lying about the ante-rooms and corridors of the House, impatient for the division bell. It rang at last at 4:15 a.m., and the members crowded into the chamber. The division on the main motion was 91–33. It was a huge vote: of a House of

130 members, 124 responded. Of 62 members from Canada West that were present, 54 voted for Confederation; of 62 from Canada East, 37 did so. Of the 48 French-Canadian members present, 27 voted for, 21 against.[38]

As the Speaker left the chair members ingloriously indulged themselves in raucous cheering and singing; then, upon the early dawn of a clear, quiet morning, they trooped wearily home to their lodgings. The convent bell across the St Charles River was ringing five o'clock.[39]

A week later, on Saturday, March 18, 1865, Parliament was prorogued.

P. B. WAITE
Dalhousie University,
March, 1963.

NOTES

1 Toronto *Leader*, Jan. 25, 1865, report from Quebec of Jan. 21, signed "Citadel."
2 Ibid., Jan. 24, 1865, report from Quebec of Jan. 20, signed "Citadel."
3 Province of Canada, Assembly, *Journals*, 1865 (1st Session), p. 9.
4 The metaphor is Joseph Howe's in his "Botheration Letter No. 10," Halifax *Morning Chronicle*, Feb. 8, 1865.
5 Province of Canada, Legislature, *Parliamentary Debates on the Subject of the Confederation of the British North American Provinces*, 1865 (hereafter *Confederation Debates*), p. 821.
6 Belleville *Intelligencer*, Oct. 14, 1864. This paper was Conservative, and was edited by Mackenzie Bowell.
7 *Confederation Debates*, p. 422–23; see below, p. 102.
8 Joly, for example, *ibid.*, p. 358; see below, p. 96.
9 Ibid., p. 127; see below, p. 80.
10 T. S. Parker to Charles Clarke, June 23, 1864, Clarke Papers, Public Archives of Ontario.
11 *Confederation Debates*, p. 936.
12 Matthew Crooks Cameron (1822–1887), not to be confused with Malcolm "Coon" Cameron (1808–1876), a Reformer who was at this time Queen's Printer, or Malcolm Colin Cameron (1832–1898), who was "Coon" Cameron's son.
13 Quebec *Morning Chronicle*, Feb. 10, 1865, reporting debates of Feb. 9.
14 Province of Canada, Assembly, *Journals*, 1865 (2nd Session), Appendix 2.
15 Quebec *Morning Chronicle*, March 14, 1865, reporting debates of March 13.
16 Ibid., Feb 18. 1865, reporting debates of Feb. 17.

17 Ibid., Feb. 28, 1865, reporting debates of Feb. 27.
18 Toronto *Leader*, March 3, 1865, telegraphic report of March 2.
19 Cauchon was opposed to Confederation in 1858, and published his views in a pamphlet: he did the same with his changed stand in 1865.
20 Quebec *Morning Chronicle*, Feb. 6, 1865.
21 Toronto *Leader*, Feb. 4, 1865.
22 Ibid., Feb. 28, 1865.
23 Ibid., Feb. 25, 1865, report of Feb. 24 from Quebec; also Quebec *Morning Chronicle*, Feb. 25, 1865, report of Feb. 24.
24 Hamilton *Spectator*, Feb. 13, 1865, report from Quebec of Feb. 8.
25 Toronto *Leader*, Jan. 25, 1865, report from Quebec of Jan. 21, signed "Citadel."
26 Province of Canada, Assembly, *Journals*, 1865. (1st Session), p. 17, (Jan. 23).
27 Quebec *Le Canadien*, 27 jan. 1865.
28 For accounts of these circumstances see R. W. Winks, *Canada and the United States: The Civil War Years* (Baltimore, 1961), pp. 326–31; P. B. Waite, *The Life and Times of Confederation, 1864–1867* (Toronto, 1962), pp. 150–52.
29 Quebec *Morning Chronicle*, March 8, 1865, reporting debates of March 7. This particular debate on petitions is not in the *Confederation Debates*, though there are later references in the *Debates* to Dorion's letter and to Cartier's reading of it (see *Confederation Debates*, pp. 873, 927).
For Macdonald's reference to Fag, see *The Rivals*, Act II, scene 1.
30 Hamilton *Spectator*, March 11, 1865, report from Quebec of March 7.
31 *Prescott Telegraph*, March 29, 1865.
32 George Brown to Anne Brown, March 6, 1865, Brown Papers, Public Archives of Canada.
33 *Confederation Debates*, pp. 728–30; see below, p. 146.
34 George Brown to Anne Brown, Feb. 24, 1865, Brown Papers, Public Archives of Canada.
35 Toronto *Leader*, March 7, 1865, report from Quebec of March 6.
36 *Quebec Daily News*, March 8, 1865.
37 See P. B. Waite, *Life and Times of Confederation*, pp. 157–59.
38 Province of Canada, Assembly, *Journals*, 1865 (1st Session), p. 192; *Confederation Debates*, p. 962. See also analysis in P. G. Cornell, *The Alignment of Political Groups in Canada, 1841–1867* (Toronto, 1962). pp. 58–59, and Table 19.
The *Debates* record further discussion on Monday, March 13, when Macdonald moved for a committee to draft the address to the Queen. Several amendments were proposed but all were decisively voted down by the Government majority.
39 *Stratford Beacon*, March 17, 1865, report of March 11.

The Legislative Council

FRIDAY / FEBRUARY 3, 1865.

Hon. Sir Etienne-Pascal Taché (Premier, Receiver-General, Minister of Militia) [Life member]:

HON. SIR E.P. TACHÉ then said that in moving the resolution he felt it his duty first to make a few preliminary remarks, and to give fully and thoroughly the reasons which had induced him to assume the grave responsibility of laying this measure before the House and the country. The reasons were two-fold. They related first to the intrinsic merits of the scheme itself, divested of all other considerations, and next, to the settlement of the domestic difficulties which for some years had distracted the country, and the means we might and ought to employ to restore good feeling, harmony and concord therein. He would, then, first address himself to what he considered the intrinsic merits of the scheme of Confederation, and he would therefore say that if [we] were anxious to continue our connection with the British Empire, and to preserve intact our institutions, our laws, and even our remembrances of the past, we must sustain the measure. If the opportunity which now presented itself were allowed to pass by unimproved, whether we would or would not, we would be forced into the American Union by violence, and if not by violence, would be placed upon an inclined plane which would carry us there insensibly. In either case the result would be the same. In our present condition we would not long continue to exist as a British colony. . . .

The honorable member then referred to the artificial communications of the country, viz., our Canals, which, he said, were on a scale unequalled in America, or, indeed, in the world. Our Railway system too, in proportion to our means and population, was as extensive as could be found anywhere else; yet with all these advantages, natural and acquired, he was bound to say we could not become a great nation. We labored under a drawback or disadvantage which would effectually prevent that, and he would defy any one to take a map of the world and point to any great nation which had not seaports of its own open at all times of the year. Canada did not possess those advantages, but was shut up in a prison, as it were, for five months of the year in fields of ice, which all the steam engineering apparatus of human ingenuity could not overcome, and so long as this state of things continued, we must consent to be a small people, who could, at any moment, be assailed and invaded by a people better situated in that respect than we were. Canada was, in fact, just like a farmer who might stand upon an elevated spot on his property, from which he could look around upon fertile fields, meandering streams, wood and all else that was necessary to his domestic wants, but who had no outlet to the highway. To be sure he might have an easy, good-natured neighbor, who had such an outlet, and this neighbor might say to him, "Don't be uneasy about that, for I will allow you to pass on to the highway, through my cross road, and we shall both profit by the arrangement." So long as this obliging neighbor was in good humor everything would go on pleasantly, but the very best natured people would sometimes get out of temper, or grow capricious, or circumstances might arise to cause irritation. And so it might come to pass that the excellent neighbor would get dissatisfied. For instance, he might be involved in a tedious and expensive law suit with some one else; it might be a serious affair – in fact, an affair of life or death, and he might come to the isolated farmer and say to him, "I understand that you and your family are all sympathising with my adversary; I don't like it at all, and I am determined you will find some other outlet to the highway than my cross road, for henceforth my gate will be shut against you." In such a case what is the farmer to do? There is the air left, but until the aerostatic science is more practically developed, he can hardly try ballooning without the risk of breaking his neck. (Laughter.) Well, that was precisely our position in reference to the United States. . . . The people of the Northern States believed that Canadians sympathized with the South much more than they really did, and the consequences of this misapprehension were: first, that we had been threatened with the abolition of the transit system; then the Reciprocity Treaty was to be discontinued; then a passport system was inaugurated, which was almost equivalent to a prohibition of intercourse, and the only thing which really remained to be done was to shut down the gate altogether and prevent passage through their territory. Would any one say that such a state of things was one desirable for Canada to be placed in? Will a great people in embryo, as he believed we were, coolly and tranquilly cross their arms and wait for what might come next? . . .

On the whole, he thought that the Confederation of all the Provinces had become an absolute necessity, and that it was for us a question of to be or not to be. If we desired to remain British and monarchial, and if we desired to pass to our children these advantages, this measure, he repeated, was a necessity. But there were other motives and other reasons which should induce us to agree to the scheme. Every honorable gentleman in the House knew the political position of the country, and were acquainted with the feelings of irritation which have prevailed for many years. They knew it happily not by their experience in this House, but by the tone of the public press, and by the discussions in another place where taunts and menaces were freely flung across the floor by contending parties. They knew what human passions were, and how, when bitter feelings continued for a long time, the distance between exasperation and actual conflict was not very great. They had now before their own eyes an example of the effects of such disagreements. It was persistently believed by many that the rival interests would never come to a rupture, but for three years they had been waging a conflict which had desolated and ruined the fairest portion of the country, and in the course of which acts of barbarity had been committed which were only equalled by the darkest ages. We in Canada were not more perfect, and the time had arrived when, as he believed, all the patriotic men in the country ought to unite in providing a remedy for the troubles we had to contend with. It might be said that the remedy proposed was not required, but he would like to know what other could be proposed. Legislation in Canada for the last two years had come almost to a stand still, and if any one would refer to the Statute Book since 1862, he would find that the only public measures there inscribed had been passed simply by the permission of the Opposition. This was the condition of things for two years, and if this were an evil there was another not less to be deplored; he referred to the administration of public affairs during the same period. From the 21st May, 1862, to the end of June, 1864, there had been no less than five different Governments in charge of the business of the country. . . .

Lower Canada had constantly refused the demand of Upper Canada for representation according to population, and for the good reason that, as the union between them was legislative, a preponderance to one of the sections would have placed the other at its mercy. It would not be so in a Federal Union, for all questions of a general nature would be reserved for the General Government, and those of a local character to the local governments, who would have the power to manage their domestic affairs as they deemed best. If a Federal Union were obtained it would be tantamount to a separation of the provinces, and Lower Canada would thereby preserve its autonomy together with all the institutions it held so dear, and over which they could exercise the watchfulness and surveillance necessary to preserve them unimpaired. [The honorable member repeated this portion of his speech in French, for the express purpose of conveying his meaning in the clearest and most forcible manner to his fellow-members for Lower Canada, who might not have apprehended so well the English.] But there might be a portion of the inhabitants of Lower Canada who might at a first glance have greater reason to complain than the French Roman Catholics, and these were the English Protestants. And why? Because they were in a minority; but he thought that if they took the trouble fully to consider the subject, they would be reassured and satisfied with the scheme. First a great event had taken place; the law of Lower Canada had been consolidated, and the English-speaking people residing in that section had got reconciled to it; in fact they were well satisfied therewith. In this respect, then, they were secure. But they might say that the majority in the Local Legislature might hereafter be unjust to them, but he thought that, on looking at the past, their fears might be allayed. Before the union of the provinces, when the large majority of members in the Legislature were French, the English inhabitants had never found cause of complaint against them. In no instance had injustice been attempted. The difficulty was that the minority wanted to rule and wanted to possess the whole power of the state in their hands. That the people of Lower Canada always acted towards the English with liberality was best exemplified by facts. Before the union while the constituencies were almost exclusively French, English Protestant gentlemen were frequently returned to Parliament, and he had now opposite to him an honorable member who had for twenty years represented an entirely French and Roman Catholic county. He doubted if in the course of those twenty years that honorable member had ever been asked whether he were Scotch or Protestant. They took the man for his sterling worth. It was even a fact that the French had elected members with extraordinary names, and as everybody knew, there was sometimes a good deal in a name. (Hear, hear.) Now if there was one name which French Canadians disliked more than another, it was that of Luther. (Hear, hear, and laughter.) Yet they had elected a gentleman bearing that significant appellation. He was glad they had, and he had no doubt he had been elected because of his personal worth; but it unquestionably showed a great deal of liberal feeling on the part of the electors. (Hear, hear.) But if an English Protestant was bad in the eyes of a French Canadian, a French Protestant was infinitely worse, and yet the county of Lotbinière had elected a French-Canadian Protestant without even questioning his religion. That gentleman was a most worthy, able and well educated person, and every way well qualified for the important trust. But again, quite lately, in a division in Lower Canada numbering over fifty thousand souls, of which only one thousand four hundred were English, an election of a member to this Chamber had taken place, the candidates being a French Roman Catholic gentleman, long and well known, and an English Protestant – and with what result? Why, that the English Protestant had beaten the French-Canadian Roman Catholic by one thousand votes. (Hear.) Could any greater proof of a tolerant and liberal feeling be exhibited? These examples should show, as he thought, that the Protestants of Lower Canada were sure to meet with not justice simply, but with the largest toleration. It might perhaps be said that MR. PRICE, who had been elected for the division of which he spoke [Laurentides], being a large merchant doing business in Chicoutimi, had used the influence which his position gave him over many electors who were in his debt to obtain success; but whatever might be said of Chicoutimi, it could not be said of the county of Charlevoix, where he had no such business relations, and yet he obtained a majority there too. The fact was, the result might be considered not only as a mark of confidence in MR. PRICE, the son elected, but as a token of respect and gratitude to MR. PRICE, senior, who had by his energy and enterprise opened up the Saguenay country, and who, in a certain sense, might be said to be the father of that region. Much had been said on the war of races, but that war was extinguished on the day the British Government granted Canada Responsible Government, by which all its inhabitants, without distinction of race or creed, were placed on a footing of equality. (Hear, hear.) The war of races found its grave in the resolutions of the 3rd September, 1841, and he hoped never to hear of it again. We were so situated that there must needs be mutual forbearance. This life was one of compromise. Not only was forbearance needed in public life, but in domestic life. If one member in a family insists upon having all his own way, there will be trouble, and so through all possible relations of humanity. He believed the French Canadians would do all in their power to render justice to their fellow-subjects of English origin, and it should not be forgotten that if the former were in a majority in Lower Canada, the English would be in a majority in the General Government, and that no act of real injustice could take place, even if there were a disposition to perpetrate it, without its being reversed there. He had now given to the House the motives which had led him to take the responsibility of introducing this important measure, and he trusted they would be viewed as sufficient. . . .

WEDNESDAY / FEBRUARY 8, 1865.

Hon. John Ross [Life member]:

. . . I will say that if the delegates who met at Quebec and prepared that instrument were incompetent for the task, I do not know where others can be found to do it better. . . .

I will honestly say, as many others have said before me, that if it could have been attained, I would have preferred a Legislative union, but it is well understood that Lower Canada would never have agreed to it.

Hon. Sir E. P. Taché – Nor the Lower Provinces.

Hon. Mr. Ross – Nor, as my honorable and gallant friend the Premier states, would the Lower Provinces have consented to it. He may well be supposed to know, for he was in the Conference, presiding over its deliberations, and had the very best opportunity of ascertaining the opinions of the delegates. (Hear.) But coming down to later times – the times so well described by the hon. Premier in his excellent speech – when difficulties between Upper and Lower Canada began to thicken, the HON. MR. GALT brought up the scheme of Colonial Federation as the best mode of overcoming those difficulties, and made a most able speech on the subject in his place in Parliament. Subsequently, in 1858, that honorable minister entered the Government with the express understanding that the question would be dealt with. It is well known that he carried his point so far, that the subject was alluded to at the close of the session of 1858, in the Speech of SIR. E. READ, the Governor General, and communication with the Imperial Government for permission to negotiate with the Lower Provinces on the subject was then undertaken. Shortly after this, three members of the Government, viz., HON. MESSRS. CARTIER, GALT, and myself, went to England, and on the 25th of October, 1858, we laid our request before the Secretary of State for the Colonies, SIR E.B. LYTTON, but difficulties, not of our creation, intervened and caused delay – LORD DERBY'S Government was defeated, and the matter continued in abeyance. To say, in the face of the facts I have stated, that the project is unknown and has taken the country by surprise, is to say what is not the case. Even last year it was distinctly referred to in His Excellency's Speech at the close of the session, and HON. MESSRS. BROWN, MCDOUGALL and MOWAT entered the Government with the express understanding that negotiations were to ensue to bring about the proposed Federation. HON. MESSRS. BROWN and MOWAT went back to their constituents and were re-elected by acclamation, and although HON. MR. MCDOUGALL was defeated, he too was subsequently elected for another constituency by acclamation. These gentlemen, instead of being decried and assailed for the part they have acted, should be honored for their patriotism. There has been no such thing as surprise. The resolutions were sent to all the members of the Legislature shortly after they were fully settled upon, and even before that the plan was published in all the newspapers of the province, and I am at a loss to know how it could have been made more public.

THURSDAY / FEBRUARY 9, 1865.

Hon. George William Allan [York]:

. . . In this Confederation scheme he believed that a golden opportunity was offered to us of remedying the evils under which we were now suffering, and of opening out a new and prosperous career for this country, if we would avail ourselves of it. He believed that it might be said of nations as of individuals:

There is a tide in the affairs of man
Which, taken at the flood, leads on to fortune;
Omitted, all the voyage of their life is spent
In shallows and miseries.
On such a full sea are we now afloat,
And we must take the current as it flows,
Or lose our venture.

He would urge then upon the House, not to allow the opportunity to pass – even should it be at the sacrifice of individual opinions – of forming a strong, powerful and prosperous Confederation, and thus ensure for ourselves, and our children's children, a national existence as British North Americans, which may endure for many ages to come. (Cheers.)

FRIDAY / FEBRUARY 10, 1865.

Hon. James Cox Aikins [Home]:

. . . It is said that the public is well acquainted with the nature of the scheme. I demur to that statement *in toto*. The public is not acquainted with it in all its bearings, and if there is one thing I regret, it is this, that it has not been made a party measure. (Hear, hear.) I regret this because, although perhaps no party could have carried it as a party measure through this Legislature, it would have been better if proposed as a party scheme, for then its merits would have been more thoroughly canvassed and its demerits more thoroughly exposed. Our public men would have ranged themselves on either side; some would have favored it, and others would have opposed it; they would have pointed out its defects as well as its good points; the whole subject would have been fully ventilated, and the result would have been that, if passed at all, the scheme would have been as perfect as it was possible to have made it. But what do you find now? You scarcely see a newspaper from one end of the country to the other that is not full of laudations of the scheme. And why? Because the leading public men of the country have thought proper to make a fusion; the leading daily journals on both sides applaud the step and the scheme that followed, and the small papers throughout the province, as in duty bound, follow in their wake.

Hon. Mr. Campbell – They only express public opinion.

Hon. Mr. Aikins – Public opinion, the honorable gentleman says. I say that public opinion has not sufficiently weighed this scheme, and that we should be influenced here by our own matured opinion in regard to it. (Hear, hear.) As I have already stated, I am in favor of the confederation of these provinces, framed on a proper basis; and all I desire is that we should have the opportunity of examining all these resolutions, and if we object to any of them, finding them imperfect or unsuitable, that we should have power to amend them. (Hear, hear.) . .

MONDAY / FEBRUARY 13, 1865.

Hon. David Reesor [King's]:

. . . I hope we shall be some day a great British North American Confederacy, but that is the greater reason why the terms of the agreement should be of such a character that we can all, or nearly all, approve of them. We must bear in mind, also, that one reason why those who were heretofore the exponents of the views of two great political parties are all on one side at the present time, arises from the very peculiar circumstances in which the country has been placed for the last eight or ten years. Those who support this measure have given as reasons for it that we have had so many political crises, and the changes have been so varied, that it becomes necessary for some great constitutional change to be made. . . . Each party desired to rule, but neither was able. Out of political adversity grew political desperation. It was called by some a political millennium, and perhaps it was; but matters were just in that shape to induce parties to take up almost any new scheme, as in this case, in which I think they have gone on quite too rapidly. They have not deliberated sufficiently to propose a measure of that mature character which the country had a right to expect. Perhaps as good a measure has been brought out as could have been, considering the short time that has elapsed, and the disadvantages under which they labored during the discussion of the scheme. But it must be admitted that when this measure was agreed to by our Government, they adopted a hasty course. The country heard only one side of the question. (Hear.) They had the great daily newspapers, the chief organs of public opinion of both political parties, all on their side, and there was only a small portion of the country press, and that not widely circulated, that gave the opposite side of the question. And so it has been going on up to the present time; and now we have the scheme brought before us in its present shape. I consider that, under these circumstances, it is our duty to give very serious attention to the question, before we adopt it as it is. (Hear, hear.) I further think, and I know many others agree with me, that these resolutions may be amended in some points, and yet without in the slightest degree endangering the whole scheme. But the Government say, "you must take the whole measure, or no part of it." I very much fear that the determination of the Government in this respect is, if I may so speak, father to their wish. That they have fallen in love with their scheme. It is their pet measure – their bantling – and they wish to get it through, without any amendment, just as it is. . . .

MONDAY / FEBRUARY 13, 1865.

Hon. Louis Auguste Olivier [De Lanaudière]:

. . . My opinion is, that as much power as possible should have been entrusted to the local governments, and as little as is consistent with the functions it will have to discharge to the Central Government, and my reason for entertaining this opinion is, that the Supreme Government, with its power of purse and its control of the armies, will always be more disposed to stretch its prerogatives and to trench upon the domain of the local governments than to narrow down and retain its authority. The scheme then, in my opinion, is defective in that it inverts this order and gives to the General Government too much power and to the local governments too little. As it is now, if the scheme goes into operation, the local governments will be in danger of being crushed (écrasés) by the General Government. The tendency of the whole scheme seems to be one of political retrogression instead of advancement. . . .

TUESDAY / FEBRUARY 14, 1865.

Hon. Sir Narcisse Fortunat Belleau [Life member]:

. . . The first point to which I directed my attention was to ascertain what guarantees Lower Canada would find in Confederation for its laws, its religion and its autonomy. I find the guarantee of all these things in that article of the scheme which gives to Lower Canada the local government of its affairs, and the control of all matters relating to its institutions, to its laws, to its religion, its manufactures and its autonomy. Are you not all prepared, hon. gentlemen, and you especially members from Lower Canada, to make some few sacrifices in order to have the control of all those things to which I have just referred, and which are all to be within the jurisdiction of the local governments? Are you not ready to make some few sacrifices to see an end put to those struggles which have been constantly recurring during the last few years, to the imminent peril of Lower Canada and of its institutions – dangers which still exist and which might even now become only too apparent were the friends who have sustained the combat to grow weary, or to give way and leave the field to their adversaries? If we persist in striving to obtain too much, if we are unwilling to make any sacrifice, we may lose the whole result of these struggles and the advantages now offered for our acceptance. For my part the consideration that we shall have the control of our local affairs in Lower Canada, under the Confederation, is a sufficient inducement to vote in favor of the scheme now submitted to us, even although it offered us no other advantage.

. . . The Government will be responsible to the Legislature. Let us never lose sight of the fact, that our national representatives will always see that Lower Canada shall have in the Federal Government one, or perhaps two, representatives – the number is not of importance. What is of importance is, that such one, or such two members, should represent in her Executive Council the national representation, which will be composed of 65 members, in the Federal Legislature. And this, forsooth, is called a clique! I insist somewhat at length upon this point, because the operation of the principle of responsible government in the Federal Legislature is lost sight of. I beg to call the attention of Lower Canada members to this. Suppose it were proposed to adopt a law in the Federal Legislature calculated to injure Lower Canada, our 65 representatives in the House of Commons discuss the law, and decide that they must oppose it; they at once communicate with the members of the Government representing Lower Canada, and inform them that they cannot accept the measure, and that if it be passed, they will coalesce with the minority, which always exists under responsible government, and that they will overthrow the Ministry. Such is the weight of our influence in the Federal Government; and if this were not lost sight of, there would be no grounds for fear. The influence of Lower Canada will enable her to make and unmake governments at pleasure, when her interests shall be at stake or threatened. . . .

WEDNESDAY / FEBRUARY 15, 1865.

Hon. James Ferrier [Life member]:

. . . In past years there were two great questions which had agitated both Eastern and Western Canada. The one was the Seigniorial question in Lower Canada; the other was the Clergy Reserve question in Western Canada. These two questions, for many years, occupied the attention of the Legislature and of the statesmen conducting successive governments. At last a settlement of these important questions was arrived at – I believe satisfactory to the majority of the people. Since that time no great questions of public interest have occupied the minds of the people, or have been urged either by the Government of the day or by the leaders of the Opposition. The consequence has been that a political warfare has been waged in Canada for many years, of a nature calculated almost to destroy all correct political and moral principle, both in the Legislature and out of it. Has it not been the fact that any man who, through life, had sustained a good character, either as a private individual or a professional man, no sooner accepted office in the Government than the Opposition and the Opposition papers would attack him at once as having joined a very doubtful company? Or, when a man of plain sense came and visited the Legislature, and took his seat in the galleries to listen to the debates, did he not hear so frequently the charges of political crime, bribery and corruption, that he left the House with very different views from those with which he entered it? Every member of Parliament has felt this demoralizing influence, and it has met him at the polls, and nothing but money, in some cases, could secure his election. (Hear, hear.) I come now to the period of 1863–64, when we find two political parties nearly equal in strength, with a majority supporting the Government of only two or three. That Government found it necessary to appeal to the country by a general election. After that election the Government of the honorable and gallant Knight

(HON. SIR E.P. TACHÉ) was formed. It existed only a very short time, and on the 14th of June of last year came what has been called the deadlock. Then, honorable gentlemen, there was, for eight or ten days, a breathing time for the parties who had been engaged in this political strife. It was a breathing time to them, as it were, to reflect upon the past and to endeavor to look forward to the future. It had been thought by many that the spirit of patriotism in the hearts of our statesmen was a dead principle. In their strife they seemed to have forgotten the best interests of Canada. But, during these ten days, the spirit of patriotism revived. This was a memorable period in the history of Canada. The leader of the Opposition, the HON. GEORGE BROWN – I speak it to his honor – was the first to declare what he was ready to do, and what he proposed was so reasonable that very soon the acceptance of his propositions was brought about. I have pleasing recollections in referring to that period, particularly as having had an opportunity of giving a word of advice on the evening of the day these propositions were made. I may refer to it, as the name of the gentleman I allude to, MR. MORRIS, a member of the Legislative Assembly, was incorporated in the documents that were submitted to this honorable House, when the result of the resolutions was laid before us. Meeting MR. MORRIS one evening, he informed me of what the HON. MR. BROWN had proposed. I thought it was so reasonable, and looked so like a deliverance from the dilemma we were in, that I recommended him at once to communicate it to the leading members of the Government, and I accompanied him to a member of the Government, who is also a member of this House, now present. He told that honorable gentleman what HON. MR. BROWN had communicated to him, and he (MR. MORRIS) was authorized to make an arrangement for the other members of the Government to meet HON. MR. BROWN. We all very well remember the time I am speaking of, and the astonishment of many that a reconciliation could have taken place between gentlemen who had been so long opposed to each other. I do not know that I ought to repeat what was the on-dit of the day with reference to it. But, I think I can remember this being said, that, when HON. MR. GALT met HON. MR. BROWN, he received him with that manly, open frankness, which characterizes him; and that, when HON. MR. CARTIER met HON. MR. BROWN, he looked carefully to see that his two *Rouge* friends were not behind him – (laughter) – and that when he was satisfied they were not, he embraced him with open arms and swore eternal friendship – (laughter and cheers) – and that HON. MR. MACDONALD, at a very quick glance, saw there was an opportunity.

Hon. Mr. Seymour – Saw his advantage.

Hon. Mr. Ferrier – That HON. MR. MACDONALD saw there was an opportunity of forming a great and powerful dependency of the British

Empire; that the gallant Knight, the Premier of the Government, with his liberal, cautious, and comprehensive mind, did not object; and that the Commissioner of Crown Lands, with his usual courtesy, his vigorous and acute mind, agreed. (Hear, hear.) To the best of my recollection, that was the way in which it was said out of doors the propositions of HON. MR. BROWN were received by the gentlemen composing the Government of that day. You all remember how delighted we were to find that political bitterness had ceased. We all thought, in fact, that a political millennium had arrived – and the Opposition was nowhere. (Laughter.) The business of the session progressed very rapidly, and we were soon relieved from our responsible duties here. Immediately after the close of the session, the agreement entered into was fully carried out. HON. MR. BROWN and the other two honorable gentlemen who entered the Government with him, were added to it, according to the agreement. These honorable gentlemen went to the country, and they were all returned, except one, and he very soon afterwards found a place. The Government thus formed, had, I believe, a majority of two-thirds of the population of Canada in their favor; and, so far as my observation has gone, two-thirds of the press also, have supported them in this scheme of union. The Government, thus sustained, soon began to act, and their first movement was to take the provincial steamer and go off to Prince Edward Island. I remember well standing on the bank of the river at Rivière du Loup, seeing the steamer pass down, and I wished them God-speed. They went to the Conference at Charlottetown, and I have no doubt they acted in a manner worthy of gentlemen going to propose a union. We know too that they were well received. There had been a growing love in these provinces towards Canada for some time. This was manifested when they gave an invitation to this Legislature to visit them, after the close of last session. And I only regret that the Legislature – every member of it – did not accept that invitation. Those who did, came back much better informed than when they went there. We had the satisfaction of seeing those who probably are going to be our partners in this union. And I do assure you, that for one, I can speak of the people of the Lower Provinces, as an energetic, active, industrious people, quite equal to ourselves. (Hear, hear.) And, as regards the resources of these provinces, I had no idea of them approaching the reality, before I paid that visit. We saw farms there on the banks of the River St. John, quite equal to any farms in our western peninsula, which is called the garden of Canada. . . .

Then the Intercolonial Railway has been referred to. That road has become, I think, even at present a necessity. It should have been made some years ago, and it would have been made but for the political incapacity of the Government of that day, which prevented it. (Hear, hear.)

Hon. Mr. James Currie [Niagara] – Let me remind my honorable friend that two members of that Government – HON. MESSRS. MCDOUGALL and HOWLAND – are in the present Government.

Hon. Mr. Ferrier – It is fortunate that some men see the error of their ways, and do better, and I trust it has been so in the present case. (Hear, hear, and laughter.) If we had had this road to the sea-board at the present time, it is very likely the Reciprocity Treaty would not have been repealed. (Hear, hear.) We want the road at the present moment for the business of the country. * Some honorable gentlemen say that, if the road were made to-day, we would have nothing to send over it. The fact is, these honorable gentlemen, when they make such a statement, shew that they have not taken the trouble to enquire what the position of the trade of the country is. For the last ten days we have had about 100 cars standing loaded at Point St. Charles, and no way of getting them off. These cars are full of produce for Boston and New York, and the two roads leading to these cities have so much to do, that they are unable to do the business of their own country and of ours too. And, while these cars are thus detained, they are wanted for Western Canada, where the people are evermore crying for cars, and we cannot get rid of the produce we have.

Hon. Mr. John Simpson [Queen's] – Will my honorable friend state what kind of produce these cars are loaded with, and where it came from?

Hon. Mr. Ferrier – The whole, I believe, is the produce of Canada. (Hear, hear.) One portion of it is for the supply of New York and Boston, or for shipment there; and another portion is to be distributed along the routes by which these railways run. I was so particular as to make these enquiries of MR. BRYDGES the day before yesterday.

Hon. Mr. Simpson – I saw MR. BRYDGES too.

Hon. Mr. Ferrier – We have also a large accumulation of cars standing full of produce at Portland, and no ships to take it away. Such is the present state of the Grand Trunk Railway, and it is a very awkward position to be placed in. As the gallant Knight (HON. SIR E.P. TACHÉ) told us the other day, it is just as if a neighbor's farm stood between us and the highway. That is the position of the United States, they stand between Canada and the sea-board, and they have now been pleased to say, "we will not allow you to pass through our farm" – because, although the Reciprocity Treaty is not yet repealed, they have put a check on intercourse by this passport system, and by the way in which

* James Ferrier had been a director of the Grand Trunk Railway since 1857.

they work the present law with reference to the produce we are taking along. For instance, if pork is sent on, an affidavit must be put in that that pork is the produce of Canada. Now, it is a difficult thing to make such an affidavit. At this season of the year loads of pork come from all quarters, and after it is all packed into a barrel, it is almost impossible for any man to make an affidavit where it was raised. (Hear, hear.) It is the same with flour. A miller frequently mixes flour brought in from the United States, and how is an affidavit to be made whether that flour is mixed or not? There may be four-fifths of it the produce of Canada, and yet the other fifth prevents it from going. Hence, the trade is so hampered by all these obstructions put in the way by the United States Government, that it is very seriously interfered with. And, that being the position of our trade, I beg to ask whether the Intercolonial Railroad is not now wanted? . . .

THURSDAY / FEBRUARY 16, 1865.

Hon. William McMaster [Midland]:

. . . whatever may be said in favor of the Intercolonial road in a military point of view, or however it may be urged as a necessity in order to furnish easy and convenient intercourse between the provinces in the event of their being united, I hold that as a commercial speculation it will prove an entire failure, which must necessarily add greatly to our already large unproductive investments. (Hear.) And how the honorable gentleman from Toronto (HON. MR. ROSS) could say as he did the other day, that Upper Canada alone had better build the Intercolonial Railway than be without it, is what I cannot comprehend.

Hon. Mr. Ross – I say so again.

Hon. Mr. McMaster – Well, if the honorable gentleman would resign his seat and present himself to any constituency west of Kingston, giving the views he has enunciated about this railroad a prominent place in his address to the electors, I fear this House would be deprived of his valuable services. (Laughter.) . . .

THURSDAY / FEBRUARY 16, 1865.

Hon. John Simpson [Queen's]:

. . . As to the Intercolonial Railway, we have no information from the government respecting the route to be followed or the length or cost of the road; but from figures I have been able to obtain, the following may be taken to be nearly correct:

	Miles built	*To be built*
From Halifax to Truro	65	
From Truro to Shediac		90
From Shediac to St. John	108	
From St. John to St. Andrews (under contract)		75
From St. Andrews to Woodstock	50	
From Woodstock to Rivière du Loup		160
Totals	223	325

The total length of road from Rivière du Loup is 548 miles; add from Riviere du Loup to Quebec, 120 miles; Quebec to Montreal, 170 miles; Montreal to Toronto, about 330 miles; so that we have a total of 1,168 miles over which it is gravely proposed to send flour and other heavy produce during the winter months. (Hear, hear.) As has been already stated, before a barrel of flour could reach Halifax from Toronto, it would be nearly eaten up in expenses. [An honorable member – there would be nothing left but the hoops. (Laughter.)] It has been urged that under Confederation an active trade would spring up between Canada and the Maritime Provinces. A trade in what? What have we to send them excepting flour and the coarser grains? The former, as has been shown, cannot be sent, and the latter they do not require. The principal articles of export from the Lower Provinces are fish, timber and ships. We can take a moderate quantity of fish; but our forests supply us with an abundance of timber, and the ship yards of Quebec turn out some of the finest sailing ships in the world. The true markets for the principal staples of export for these provinces are New York and Boston. Small vessels from thirty to fifty tons, laden with fish, run from the Maritime Provinces to these ports, where they dispose of their cargoes and purchase with the proceeds, corn meal, flour, pork, molasses and other necessaries. But it has been left for our Canadian statesmen to propose new political alliances in order to divert trade and commerce from their natural channels.

FRIDAY / FEBRUARY 17, 1865.

Hon. Alexander Campbell (Commissioner of Crown Lands) [Cataraqui]:

. . . Do you desire to have a union of all the British American Provinces, or do you desire to remain as you are? That is the issue. . . . If the scheme is postponed now, it is postponed indefinitely. For years past the effort has been making to get the Lower Provinces to assent to a union with Canada, and, if the question is now postponed, there is no knowing whether we shall ever be able to get their assent to it again or not. Action in the parliaments of Nova Scotia, Newfoundland, and Prince Edward Island, is now hanging upon the proceedings in this House. If you pass an amendment, it will indicate to them that the people of Canada are not warmly in favor of the scheme. Honorable gentlemen, are you ready to take the responsibility of declaring that the people of Canada are opposed to Confederation? There is no knowing when circumstances will allow of its being brought to this forward stage again. Those of you who know what difficulties and objections were met with – the selfish interests of the various sections of this and of the other provinces, which we had to overcome – must feel that a very great advance was made when the measure was brought to the present forward stage. When again will it be likely to happen that the representatives of the various provinces will be brought together to consider the question? When will it again happen that the governments of the several provinces concerned will be able to lay upon the table or their respective legislatures a scheme so complete in all its details as this is? It is impossible to say when that happy coincidence of circumstances will again occur. . . . This Confederation has been sought after for years, but never until now has it approached so near a consummation – never was it a possibility as it is now a possibility. After years of anxiety, after years of difficulty, after troubles here and divisions there, the scheme is found possible, and I will not put it away from me because I object to this point or to that. If this harness of the Confederation of the country is to be put on, we cannot but expect that it will chafe here and chafe there; but time will give relief and provide the remedy, as it has done in other circumstances before. It was so in regard to the union of 1840. The Lower Canadians had a grievance in the French language being excluded from the Provincial Parliament. That chafed, as was to be expected, and provoked remonstrance. And what was the result? The injustice complained of was done away with, and both languages were thereafter permitted to be used. Then it was the desire of the people that the elective system should be introduced into this House. I believe myself that it was a mistake, but a change was desired, and a change was brought about. And so it will be in this case. If change is seriously desired, it will be had. It would be unwise and unstatesmanlike, in my opinion, to declare that because we cannot have our way on this point or on that point – that because the scheme in all its features is not exactly what we would like it to be – we will not have it at all. Where, honorable gentlemen, is the union effected between any two countries, or any two individuals even, which has lasted for any length of time without mutual forbearance and mutual concessions? Let those honorable gentlemen who have had the good fortune of forming unions, and who can therefore speak from experience, say whether any union can be formed either happy or lasting without forbearance on both sides. (Hear, hear, and laughter.) You must give up all thoughts of union unless you are willing to give and take, and cease persisting for everything you think best. Nobody ever did effect a union upon such terms, and nobody ever will. . . .

The Legislative Assembly

MONDAY / FEBRUARY 6, 1865.

Hon. John Alexander Macdonald (Attorney General West) [Kingston]:

. . . only three modes that were at all suggested, by which the dead-lock in our affairs, the anarchy we dreaded, and the evils which retarded our prosperity, could be met or averted. One was the dissolution of the union between Upper and Lower Canada, leaving them as they were before the union of 1841. I believe that that proposition, by itself had no supporters. It was felt by everyone that, although it was a course that would do away with the sectional difficulties which existed, – though it would remove the pressure on the part of the people of Upper Canada for the representation based upon population, – and the jealousy of the people of Lower Canada lest their institutions should be attacked and prejudiced by that principle in our representation; yet it was felt by every thinking man in the province that it would be a retrograde step, which would throw back the country to nearly the same position as it occupied before the union, – that it would lower the credit enjoyed by United Canada, – that it would be the breaking up of the connection which had existed for nearly a quarter of a century, and, under which, although it had not been completely successful, and had not allayed altogether the local jealousies that had their root in circumstances which arose before the union, our province, as a whole, had nevertheless prospered and increased. It was felt that a dissolution of the union would have destroyed all the credit that we had gained by being a united province, and would have left us two weak and ineffective governments, instead of one powerful and united people. (Hear, hear.) The next mode suggested, was the granting of representation by population. Now, we all know the manner in which that question was and is regarded by Lower Canada; that while in Upper Canada the desire and cry for it was daily augmenting, the resistance to it in Lower Canada was proportionably increasing in strength. Still, if some such means of relieving us from the sectional jealousies which existed between the two Canadas, if some such solution of the difficulties as Confederation had not been found, the representation by population must eventually have been carried; no matter though it might have been felt in Lower Canada, as being a breach of the Treaty of Union, no matter how much it might have been felt by the Lower Canadians that it would sacrifice their local interests, it is certain that in the progress of events representation by population would have been carried; and, had it been carried – I speak here my own individual sentiments – I do not think it would have been for the interest of Upper Canada. For though Upper Canada would have felt that it had received what it claimed as a right, and had succeeded in establishing its right, yet it would have left the Lower Province with a sullen feeling of injury and injustice. The Lower Canadians would not have worked cheerfully under such a change of system, but would have ceased to be what they are now – a nationality, with representatives in Parliament, governed by general principles, and dividing according to their political opinions – and would have been in great danger of becoming a faction, forgetful of national obligations, and only actuated by a desire to defend their own sectional interests, their own laws, and their own institutions. (Hear, hear.) The third and only means of solution for our difficulties was the junction of the provinces either in a Federal or a Legislative union. Now, as regards the comparative advantages of a Legislative and a Federal union, I have never hesitated to state my own opinions. I have again and again stated in the House, that, if practicable, I thought a Legislative union would be preferable. (Hear, hear.) I have always contended that if we could agree to have one government and one parliament, legislating for the whole of these peoples, it would be the best, the cheapest, the most vigorous, and the strongest system of government we could adopt. (Hear, hear.) But, on looking at the subject in the Conference, and discussing the matter as we did, most unreservedly, and with a desire to arrive at a satisfactory conclusion, we found that such a system was impracticable. In the first place, it would not meet the assent of the people of Lower Canada, because they felt that in their peculiar position – being in a minority, with a different language, nationality and religion from the majority, – in case of a junction with the other provinces, their institutions and their laws might be assailed, and their ancestral associations, on which they prided themselves, attacked and prejudiced; it was found that any proposition which involved the absorption of the individuality of Lower Canada – if I may use the expression – would not be received with favor by her people. We found too, that though their people speak the same language and enjoy the same system of law as the people of Upper Canada, a system founded on the common law of England, there was as great a disinclination on the part of the various Maritime Provinces to lose their individuality, as separate political organizations, as we observed in the case of Lower Canada herself. (Hear, hear.) Therefore, we were forced to the conclusion that we must either abandon the idea of Union altogether, or devise a system of union in which the separate provincial organizations would be in some degree preserved. So that those who were, like myself, in favor of a Legislative union, were obliged to modify their views and accept the project of a Federal union as the only scheme practicable, even for the Maritime Provinces. Because, although the law of those provinces is founded on the common law of England, yet every one of them has a large amount of law of its own – colonial law framed by itself, and affecting every relation of life, such as the laws of property, municipal and assessment laws; laws relating to the liberty of the subject, and to all the great interests contemplated in legislation; we found, in short, that the statutory law of the different provinces was so varied and diversified that it was almost impossible to weld them into a Legislative union at once. Why, sir, if you only consider the innumerable subjects of legislation peculiar to new countries, and that every one of those five colonies had particular laws of its own, to which its people have been accustomed and are attached, you will see the difficulty of effecting and working a Legislative union, and bringing about an assimilation of the local as well as general laws of the whole of the provinces. (Hear, hear.) We in Upper Canada understand from the nature and operation of our peculiar municipal law, of which we know the value, the difficulty of framing a general system of legislation on local matters which would meet the wishes and fulfil the requirements of the several provinces. Even the laws considered the least important, respecting private rights in timber, roads, fencing, and innumerable other matters, small in themselves, but in the aggregate of great interest to the agricultural class, who form the great body of the people, are regarded as of great value by the portion of the community affected by them. And when we consider that every one of the colonies has a body of law of this kind, and that it will take years before those laws can be assimilated, it was felt that at first, at all events, any united legislation would be almost impossible. I am happy to state – and indeed it appears on the face of the resolutions themselves – that as regards the Lower Provinces, a great desire was evinced for the final assimilation of our laws. One of the resolutions provides that an attempt shall be made to assimilate the laws of the Maritime Provinces and those of Upper Canada, for the purpose of eventually establishing one body of statutory law, founded on the common law of England, the parent of the laws of all those provinces. . . .

As I stated in the preliminary discussion, we must consider this scheme in the light of a treaty. By a happy coincidence of circumstances, just when an Administration had been formed in Canada for the purpose of attempting a solution of the difficulties under which we labored, at the same time the Lower Provinces, actuated by a similar feeling, appointed a Conference with a view to a union among themselves, without being cognizant of the position the government was taking in Canada. If it had not been for this fortunate coincidence of events, never, perhaps, for a long series of years would we have been able to bring this scheme to a practical conclusion. But we did succeed. We made the arrangement, agreed upon the scheme, and the deputations from the several governments represented at the Conference went back pledged to lay it before their governments, and to ask the legislatures and people of their respective provinces to assent to it. I trust the scheme will be assented to as a whole. I am sure this House will not seek to alter it in its unimportant details; and, if altered in any important provisions, the result must be that the whole will be set aside, and we must begin *de novo*. If any important changes are made, every one of the colonies will feel itself absolved from the implied obligation to deal with it as a Treaty, each province will feel itself at liberty to amend it *ad libitum* so as to suit its own views and interests; in fact, the whole of our labors will have been for nought, and we will have to renew our negotiations with all the colonies for the purpose of establishing some new scheme. I hope the House will not adopt any such a course as will postpone, perhaps for ever, or at all events for a long period, all chances of union. All the statesmen and public men who have written or spoken on the subject admit the advantages of a union, if it were practicable: and now when it is proved to be practicable, if we do not embrace this opportunity the present favorable time will pass away, and we may never have it again. Because, just so surely as this scheme is defeated, will be revived the original proposition for a union of the Maritime Provinces, irrespective of Canada; they will not remain as they are now, powerless, scattered, helpless communities; they will form themselves into a power, which, though not so strong as if united with Canada, will, nevertheless, be a powerful and considerable community, and it will be then too late for us to attempt to strengthen ourselves by this scheme, which, in the words of the resolution, "is for the best interests, and present and future prosperity of British North America." If we are not blind to our present position, we must see the hazardous situation in which all the great interests of Canada stand in respect to the United States. I am no alarmist. I do not believe in the prospect of immediate war. I believe that the common sense of the two nations will prevent a war; still we cannot trust to probabilities. . . .

The Conference having come to the conclusion that a Legislative union, pure and simple, was impracticable, our next attempt was to form a government upon federal principles, which would give to the General Government the strength of a legislative and administrative union, while at the same time it preserved that liberty of action for the different sections which is allowed by a Federal union. And I am strong in the belief – that we have hit upon the happy medium in those resolutions, and that we have formed a scheme of government which unites the advantages of both, giving us the strength of a Legislative union and the sectional freedom of a Federal union, with protection to local interests. In doing so we had the advantage of the experience of the United States. It is the fashion now to enlarge on the defects of the Constitution of the United States, but I am not one of those who look upon it as a failure. (Hear, hear.) I think and believe that it is one of the most skilful works which human intelligence ever created; is one of the most perfect organizations that ever governed a free people. To say that it has some defects is but to say that it is not the work of Omniscience, but of human intellects. We are happily situated in having had the opportunity of watching its operation, seeing its working from its infancy till now. It was in the main formed on the model of the Constitution of Great Britain, adapted to the circumstances of a new country, and was perhaps the only practicable system that could have been adopted 'under the circumstances existing at the time of its formation. We can now take advantage of the experience of the last seventy-eight years, during which that Constitution has existed, and I am strongly of the belief that we have, in a great measure, avoided in this system which we propose for the adoption of the people of Canada, the defects which time and events have shown to exist in the American Constitution. . . . They commenced, in fact, at the wrong end. They declared by their Constitution that each state was a sovereignty in itself, and that all the powers incident to a sovereignty belonged to each state, except those powers which, by the Constitution, were conferred upon the General Government and Congress. Here we have adopted a different system. We have strengthened the General Government. We have given the General Legislature all the great subjects of legislation. We have conferred on them, not only specifically and in detail, all the powers which are incident to sovereignty, but we have expressly declared that all subjects of general interest not distinctly and exclusively conferred upon the local governments and local legislatures, shall be conferred upon the General Government and Legislature. – We have thus avoided that great source of weakness which has been the cause of the disruption of the United States. We have avoided all conflict of jurisdiction and authority, and if this Constitution is carried out, as it will be in full detail in the Imperial Act to be passed if the colonies adopt the scheme, we will have in fact, as I said before, all the advantages of a legislative union under one administration, with, at the same time, the guarantees for local institutions and for local laws, which are insisted upon by so many in the provinces now, I hope, to be united. . . .

As may be well conceived, great difference of opinion at first existed as to the constitution of the Legislative Council. In Canada the elective principle prevailed; in the Lower Provinces, with the exception of Prince Edward Island, the nominative principle was the rule. We found a general disinclination on the part of the Lower Provinces to adopt the elective principle; indeed, I do not think there was a dissenting voice in the Conference against the adoption of the nominative principle, except from Prince Edward Island. The delegates from New Brunswick, Nova Scotia and Newfoundland, as one man, were in favor of nomination by the Crown. And nomination by the Crown is of course the system which is most in accordance with the British Constitution. We resolved then, that the constitution of the Upper House should be in accordance with the British system as nearly as circumstances would allow. An hereditary Upper House is impracticable in this young country. Here we have none of the elements for the formation of a landlord aristocracy – no men of large territorial positions – no class separated from the mass of the people. An hereditary body is altogether unsuited to our state of society, and would soon dwindle into nothing. . . .

I shall not detain the House by entering into a consideration at any length of the different powers conferred upon the General Parliament as contradistinguished from those reserved to the local legislatures; but any honorable member on examining the list of different subjects which are to be assigned to the general and local legislatures respectively, will see that all the great questions which affect the general interests of the Confederacy as a whole, are confided to the Federal Parliament, while the local interests and local laws of each section are preserved intact, and entrusted to the care of the local bodies. As a matter of course, the General Parliament must have the power of dealing with the public debt and property of the Confederation. Of course, too, it must have the regulation of trade and commerce, of customs and excise. The Federal Parliament must have the sovereign power of raising money from such sources and by such means as the representatives of the people will allow. It will be seen that the local legislatures have the control of all local works; and it is a matter of great importance, and one of the chief advantages of the Federal union and of local legislatures, that each province will have the power and means of developing its own resources and aiding its own progress after its own fashion and in its own way. Therefore all the local improvements, all local enterprises or undertakings of any kind, have been left to the care and management of the local legislatures of each province. (Cheers.) . . .

One of the great advantages of Confederation is, that we shall have a united, a concerted, and uniform system of defence. (Hear.) We are at this moment with a different militia system in each colony – in some of the colonies with an utter want of any system of defence. We have a number of separate staff establishments, without any arrangement between the colonies as to the means, either of defence or offence. But, under the union, we will have one system of defence and one system of militia organization. In the event of the Lower Provinces being threatened, we can send the large militia forces of Upper Canada to their rescue. Should we have to fight on our lakes against a foreign foe, we will have the hardy seamen of the Lower Provinces coming to our assistance and manning our vessels. (Hear, hear.) We will have one system of defence and be one people, acting together alike in peace and in war. (Cheers.) The criminal law too – the determination of what is a crime and what is not and how crime shall be punished – is left to the General Government. This is a matter almost of necessity. It is of great importance that we should have the same criminal law throughout these provinces – that what is a crime in one part of British America, should be a crime in every part – that there should be the same protection of life and property as in another. It is one of the defects in the United States system, that each separate state has or may have a criminal code of its own – that what may be a capital offence in one state, may be a venial offence, punishable slightly, in another. But under our Constitution we shall have one body of criminal law, based on the criminal law of England, and operating equally throughout British America, so that a British American, belonging to what province he may, or going to any other part of the Confederation, knows what his rights are in that respect, and what his punishment will be if an offender against the criminal laws of the land. I think this is one of the most marked instances in which we take advantage of the experience derived from our observations of the defects in the Constitution of the neighboring republic. (Hear, hear.) The 33rd provision is of very great importance to the future well-being of these colonies. It commits to the General Parliament the "rendering uniform all or any of the laws relative to property and civil rights in Upper Canada, Nova Scotia, New

Brunswick, Newfoundland and Prince Edward Island, and rendering uniform the procedure of all or any of the courts in these provinces." The great principles which govern the laws of all the provinces, with the single exception of Lower Canada, are the same, although there may be a divergence in details; and it is gratifying to find, on the part of the Lower Provinces, a general desire to join together with Upper Canada in this matter, and to procure, as soon as possible, an assimilation of the statutory laws and the procedure in the courts, of all these provinces. At present there is a good deal of diversity. In one of the colonies, for instance, they have no municipal system at all. In another, the municipal system is merely permissive, and has not been adopted to any extent. Although, therefore, a legislative union was found to be almost impracticable, it was understood, so far as we could influence the future, that the first act of the Confederate Government should be to procure an assimilation of the statutory law of all those provinces, which has, as its root and foundation, the common law of England. But to prevent local interests from being over-ridden, the same section makes provision, that, while power is given to the General Legislature to deal with this subject, no change in this respect should have the force and authority of law in any province until sanctioned by the Legislature of that province. (Hear, hear.) The General Legislature is to have power to establish a general Court of Appeal for the Federated Provinces. Although the Canadian Legislature has always had the power to establish a Court of Appeal, to which appeals may be made from the courts of Upper and Lower Canada, we have never availed ourselves of the power. Upper Canada has its own Court of Appeal, so has Lower Canada. And this system will continue until a General Court of Appeal shall be established by the General Legislature. The Constitution does not provide that such a court shall be established. There are many arguments for and against the establishment of such a court. But it was thought wise and expedient to put into the Constitution a power to the General Legislature, that, if after full consideration they think it advisable to establish a General Court of Appeal from all the Superior Courts of all the provinces, they may do so. (Hear, hear.) I shall not go over the other powers that are conferred on the General Parliament. Most of them refer to matters of financial and commercial interest, and I leave those subjects in other and better hands. Besides all the powers that are specifically given in the 37th and last item of this portion of the Constitution, [it] confers on the General Legislature the general mass of sovereign legislation, the power to legislate on "all matters of a general character, not specially and exclusively reserved for the local governments and legislatures." This is precisely the provision which is wanting in the Constitution of the United States. It is here that we find the weakness of the American system – the point where the American Constitution breaks down. (Hear, hear.) It is in itself a wise and necessary provision. We thereby strengthen the Central Parliament, and make the Confederation one people and one government, instead of five peoples and five governments, with merely a point of authority connecting us to a limited and insufficient extent. . . .

There are numerous subjects which belong, of right, both to the Local and the General Parliaments. In all these cases it is provided, in order to prevent a conflict of authority, that where there is concurrent jurisdiction in the General and Local Parliaments, the same rule should apply as now applies in cases where there is concurrent jurisdiction in the Imperial and in the Provincial Parliaments, and that when the legislation of the one is adverse to or contradictory of the legislation of the other, in all such cases the action of the General Parliament must overrule, ex-necessitate, the action of the Local Legislature. (Hear, hear.) . . .

In conclusion, I would again implore the House not to let this opportunity to pass. It is an opportunity that may never recur. At the risk ot repeating myself, I would say, it was only by a happy concurrence of circumstances, that we were enabled to bring this great question to its present position. If we do not take advantage of the time, if we show ourselves unequal to the occasion, it may never return, and we shall hereafter bitterly and unavailingly regret having failed to embrace the happy opportunity now offered of founding a great nation under the fostering care of Great Britain, and our Sovereign Lady, Queen Victoria. (Loud cheers, amidst which the honorable gentleman resumed his seat.)

The House, at eleven P.M., adjourned.

TUESDAY / FEBRUARY 7, 1865.

Hon. George Etienne Cartier (Attorney General East) [Montreal East]:

. . . Every one who knew anything of his past public course was aware that he was opposed to the principle of representation by population while Upper and Lower Canada were under one government. He did not regret his opposition. If such a measure had been passed, what would have been the consequence? There would have been constant political warfare between Upper and Lower Canada. True it was that the members from Upper Canada, being in the majority, it might have been imagined they would have carried everything before them; but as far as justice to Lower Canada was concerned, such might not have been the case. The consequence of representation by population would have been that one territory would have governed another, and this fact would have presented itself session after session in the House, and day after day in the public prints. (Hear, hear.) The moment this principle had been conceded as the governing element, it would have initiated between the two provinces a warfare which would have been unremitting. (Hear, hear.) . . .

In 1858 he first saw that representation by population, though unsuited for application as a governing principle as between the two provinces, would not involve the same objection if other partners were drawn in by a federation. In a struggle between two – one a weak, and the other a strong party – the weaker could not but be overcome; but if three parties were concerned, the stronger would not have the same advantage; as when it was seen by the third that there was too much strength on one side, the third would club with the weaker combatant to resist the big fighter. (Cheers and laughter.) He did not oppose the principle of representation by population from an unwillingness to do justice to Upper Canada. He took this ground, however, that when justice was done to Upper Canada, it was his duty to see that no injustice was done to Lower Canada. He did not entertain the slightest apprehension that Lower Canada's rights were in the least jeopardized by the provision that in the General Legislature the French Canadians of Lower Canada would have a smaller number of representatives than all the other origins combined. . . .

Confederation was, as it were, at this moment almost forced upon us. We could not shut our eyes to what was going on beyond the lines, where a great struggle was going on between two Confederacies, at one time forming but one Confederacy. We saw that a government, established not more than 80 years ago, had not been able to keep together the family of states which had broken up four or five years since. We could not deny that the struggle now in progress must necessarily influence our political existence. We did not know what would be the result of that great war – whether it would end in the establishment of two Confederacies or in one as before. However, we had to do with five colonies, inhabited by men of the same sympathies and interests, and in order to become a great nation they required only to be brought together under one General Government. The matter resolved itself into this, either we must obtain British American Confederation or be absorbed in an American Confederation. (Hear, hear, and dissent.) . . .

The question for us to ask ourselves was this: Shall we be content to remain separate – shall we be content to maintain a mere provincial existence, when, by combining together, we could become a great nation? It had never yet been the good fortune of any group of communities to secure national greatness with such facility. In past ages, warriors had struggled for years for the addition to their country of a single province. . . . Here, in British North America, we had five different communities inhabiting five separate colonies. We had the same sympathies, and we all desired to live under the British Crown. We had our commercial interests besides. It was of no use whatever that New Brunswick, Nova Scotia and Newfoundland should have their several custom houses against our trade, or that we should have custom houses against the trade of those provinces. In ancient times, the manner in which a nation grew up was different from that of the present day. Then the first weak settlement increased into a village, which, by turns, became a town and a city, and the nucleus of a nation. It was not so in modern times. Nations were now formed by the agglomeration of communities having kindred interests and sympathies. Such was our case at the present moment. Objection had been taken to the scheme now under consideration, because of the words "new nationality." Now, when we were united together, if union were attained, we would form a political nationality with which neither the national origin, nor the religion of any individual, would interfere. It was lamented by some that we had this diversity of races, and hopes were expressed that this distinctive feature would cease. The idea of unity of races was utopian – it was impossible. Distinctions of this kind would always exist. Dissimilarity, in fact, appeared to be the order of the physical world and of the moral world, as well as of the political world. But with regard to the objection based on this fact, to the effect that a great nation could not be formed because Lower Canada was in great part French and Catholic, and Upper Canada was British and Protestant, and the Lower Provinces were mixed, it was futile and worthless in the extreme. Look, for instance, at the United Kingdom, inhabited as it was by three great races. (Hear, hear.) Had the diversity of race impeded the glory, the progress, the wealth of England? Had they not rather each contributed their share to the greatness of the Empire? Of the glories of the senate, the field, and the ocean, of the successes of trade and commerce, how much was contributed by the combined talents, energy and courage of the three races together? (Cheers.) In our own Federation we should have Catholic and Protestant, English, French, Irish and Scotch, and each by his efforts and his success would increase the prosperity and glory of the new Confederacy. (Hear, hear.) He viewed the diversity of races in British North America in this way: we were of different races, not for the purpose of warring against each other, but in order to compete and emulate for the general welfare. (Cheers.) We could not do away with the distinctions of race. We could not legislate for the disappearance of the French Canadians from American soil, but British and French Canadians alike could appreciate and understand their position relative to each other. They were placed like great families beside each other, and their contact produced a healthy spirit of emulation. It was a benefit rather than otherwise that we had a diversity of races. . ."

This scheme, he repeated, met with the approval of all moderate men. The extreme men, the socialists, democrats and annexationists were opposed to it. The French Canadian opponents of the project were, it appeared, afraid that their religious rights would suffer under the new arrangement. Fancy the celebrated *Institut Canadien*, of Montreal, under the lead of citizen BLANCHET, taking religion under their protection! (Laughter.) MR. DOUGALL [of the Montreal *Witness*] loudly proclaimed that the British Protestant minority would be entirely placed at the mercy of the French Canadians. He (HON. MR. CARTIER) thought the arguments of the young French gentlemen belonging to the national democratic party who cried out that their religion and nationality would be destroyed, ought in all reason to be sufficient to satisfy the scruples and calm the fears of MR. DOUGALL. The *True Witness*, which was also one of the enemies of the scheme, said that if it were adopted the French Canadians were doomed; while his brother in violence, the *Witness*, said that the Protestants were doomed. (Hear, hear, and laughter.) At a meeting recently held in Montreal on the subject, he (HON. MR. CARTIER) observed that MR. CHERRIER had enrolled himself among the enemies of the project. Well, this fine, quiet, old gentleman announced that he had come out of his political retirement for the purpose of opposing Federation. All he (HON. MR. CARTIER) could say was that he never knew MR. CHERRIER was a strong politician. However, it appeared that he had come out once more on the political stage for the purpose of opposing this villainous scheme, which was intended to destroy the nationality and religion of the French Canadians – all brought about by that confounded CARTIER! (Laughter and cheers.) Allusion had been made to the opinion of the clergy. Well, he would say that the opinion of the clergy was for Confederation. (Hear, hear.) Those who were high in authority, as well as those who occupied more humble positions, were in favor of Federation, not only because they saw in it so much security for all they held dear, but because it was just to their Protestant fellow-subjects as well, because they were opposed to political bickering and strife. This opposition to a state of political dissension and trouble was the general feeling of the clergy, and because they saw in Confederation a solution of those difficulties which had existed for some time, due regard being had to just rights, they were favorable to the project. – The fact, however, was that when we saw such extreme opponents as MR. CLERK, of the

True Witness, MR. DOUGALL, of the *Witness*, and the young gentlemen of the *Institut Canadien* combined to resist Confederation, because each party argued it would produce the most widely different results – we might look upon this fact, he repeated, as one of the strongest arguments in favor of Confederation. (Hear.) We had, on the other hand, , all the moderate men, all that was respectable and intelligent, including the clergy, favorable to Federation. (Hear, hear, and oh, oh.) He did not, of course, mean to say that there were not respectable opponents to the project – what he did mean, however, was that it met general approval from the classes referred to. He was opposed, he might as well state most distinctly, to the democratic system which obtained in the United States. In this country of British North America we should have a distinct form of government, the characteristic of which would be to possess the monarchical element. When we had Confederation secured, there was not the least doubt but that our Government would be more respectable – that it would have more prestige, and command more respect from our neighbors. . . .

TUESDAY / FEBRUARY 7, 1865.

Hon. Alexander Tilloch Galt (Minister of Finance) [Sherbrooke]:

. . . I now propose, sir, to refer to the means which will be at the disposal of the several local governments to enable them to administer the various matters of public policy which it is proposed to entrust to them, and it is evident that unless ample provision is made in the arrangements, great danger will arise that the machinery whereby the local wants of the people are intended to be met will speedily become impaired, causing complaint on the part of the inhabitants of the respective localities, and involving considerable danger to the whole machinery of government. (Hear, hear.) In the case of Canada it will be remembered that the sum of nearly five millions of the public debt has to be borne by Upper and Lower Canada. It will hereafter be for the House to decide how this sum shall be apportioned, but the probability is that the Government will recommend that it shall be divided on the basis of population. (Hear, hear.) It must be remembered that Canada will have at its disposal a large amount of the local assets, including especially the sums due to the municipal loan fund, which will produce an income for the support of their local institutions. As a matter of account between Upper and Lower Canada and the General Government, they will be charged with the interest on their respective proportions of the five millions against the subsidy which it is proposed shall be given to them, while they themselves will collect from the municipalities and other local sources all the revenue and amounts which now enter into the general revenue of the Province of Canada. The question of the sub-division of the local assets of Canada is not, however, before the House. What we have now to consider is whether the bargain as between Canada as a whole and the Lower Provinces ought to be assented to. If it be assented to the question will arise, how shall we deal with the local matters between Upper and Lower Canada? and a proposition will be brought down which I hope and believe will satisfy both sections, and do them substantial justice. . . .

We may. . . place just confidence in the development of our resources, and repose in the belief that we shall find in our territorial domain, our valuable mines and our fertile lands, additional sources of revenue far beyond the requirements of the public service. If, nevertheless, the local revenues become inadequate, it will be necessary for the local governments to have resort to direct taxation; and I do not hesitate to say that one of the wisest provisions in the proposed Constitution, and that which affords the surest guarantee that the people will take a healthy interest in their own affairs and see that no extravagance is committed by those placed in power over them, is to be found in the fact that those who are called upon to administer public affairs will feel, when they resort to direct taxation, that a solemn responsibility rests upon them, and that that responsibility will be exacted by the people in the most peremptory manner. (Hear, hear.) If the men in power find that they are required, by means of direct taxation, to procure the funds necessary to administer the local affairs, for which abundant provision is made in the scheme, they will pause before they enter upon any career of extravagance. . . .

The House must now, sir, consider the means whereby these local expenditures have to be met. I have already explained that, in the case of Canada, and also in that of the Lower Provinces, certain sources of revenue are set aside as being of a purely local character and available to meet the local expenditure; but I have been obliged in my explanations with regard to Canada to advert to the fact that it is contemplated to give a subsidy of 80 cents per head to each of the provinces. In transferring to the General Government all the large sources of revenue, and in placing in their hand with a single exception, that of direct taxation, all the means whereby the industry of the people may be made to contribute to the wants of the state, it must be evident to every one that some portion of the resources thus placed at the disposal of the General Government must in some form or other be available to supply the hiatus that would otherwise take place between the sources of local revenue and the demands of local expenditure. The members of the

Conference considered this question with the most earnest desire to reduce to the lowest possible limits the sum that was thus required, and I think the figures that I have already given to the House afford the best possible evidence that no disposition existed, at any rate on the part of our friends from the Lower Provinces, to take from the public exchequer one shilling more than the necessities of their respective communities absolutely demanded. (Hear, hear.) In the case of Canada, perhaps it will be said that a smaller sum would have met our immediate wants, but it was felt that it would be impossible to justify any distinction being drawn between subjects of the same country. And if in Canada we receive perhaps a somewhat larger amount than we absolutely require, it ought rather to be a subject of gratification to this House that it will possess the means of giving greater encouragement to our educational system, and greater development to those interests which are peculiarly entrusted to the charge of the local governments, and this, too, without making any greater demand than is at this time made upon the resources of the people. (Hear, hear.) A subsidy of 80 cents per head was provided, based upon the population according to the census of 1861. The amount, if taken upon the basis of the present population, would undoubtedly be considerably less; and it must be observed that the agreement does not contemplate any future extension of this amount. It is hoped that being in itself fixed and permanent in its character, the local governments will see the importance – I may say the necessity – of their exercising a rigid and proper control over the expenditure of their several provinces. We thus obtain one of the greatest securities that can be offered to us that those influences which, in such a Legislature as we now possess in Canada, are brought to bear for the purpose of swelling the public expenditure, will not exist in the local legislatures, but will meet with such a resistance, from the mere fact of the inability of the local governments to obey them, as to produce a very considerable saving in the general expense of the whole country. (Hear, hear.) . . .

On the one hand we shall be free from the empty parade of small Courts entailed by our present system on each of these provinces, keeping up a pretence of regal show when the reality is wanting; we shall have the legislation of the General Government restricted to those great questions which may properly occupy the attention of the first men in the country; we shall not have our time frittered away in considering the merits of petty local bills, and therefore we may reasonably hope that the expenses of the General Legislature will be considerably less than even those of the Legislature of Canada at the present moment, – while, on the other hand, the local legislatures having to deal rather with municipal than great general questions, will be able to dispose of them in a manner more satisfactory to the people, and at infinitely less expense than now. I believe, therefore, the simple cost of the Government of the country will not be in reality any greater under the new than under the old system; but there are other items of expenditure for great public objects, the absence of which from the estimates of any country is an indication rather of weakness and of dependence than a subject that ought to form a source of satisfaction. If such items are not now found in the public expenditure, either of Canada or the Lower Provinces, it is the best proof that could be given that our position is one of inferiority, and that we do not possess either the power or the means to undertake such works as make such items necessary. Let me give one or two points as examples of my meaning; and first I will instance the great question of defence – (hear, hear) – the absence of items of expenditure for which can only be an indication that we are lacking in one of the chief elements of national greatness, that we do not properly value the institutions under which we live, and that we are not willing to make the sacrifices that every free people must make if they are desirous of preserving them. The same argument applies to public works, in connection with which it might be said that great advantage would arise from large expenditure; but with limited resources and an undeveloped territory it might be impossible for any small country to undertake the necessary outlay. Many works of this kind are not directly productive of revenue, although indirectly of the utmost advantage, and if the resources of a country generally cannot be applied to that outlay, the absence of such expenditure ought to be a subject of regret in the community, and not of rejoicing. (Hear, hear.) In this view let us look at the immense extent of territory that stretches away west of Upper Canada. The reason why we have not been able to assume possession of that territory and open it up to the industry of the youth of this country who, in consequence of the want of some such field for the employment of their energies, have been obliged to go off to the States in thousands, especially to those states possessing the boundless resources of the great North-West, is because the resources of Canada – great as they have been, considering the disadvantages under which she has labored – have been inadequate for the development of this great district. Now, one of the resolutions of the scheme before the House refers to this same question, and I believe that one of the first acts of the General Government of the United Provinces will be to enter into public obligations for the purpose of opening up and developing that vast region, and of making it a source of strength instead of a burden to us and to the Mother Country also. (Hear, hear.) Looking, however, to the whole question of expense, I must say that if the benefits of Confederation are to be weighed against the loss of three or four hundred thousand dollars, the House had better carefully consider whether the people of this country will not accept the former at such comparatively trifling cost – whether they will not feel that a union with a million of their fellow colonists is worth much more to them than any small pecuniary question of this kind that may arise. (Hear, hear.) I trust the House will not permit the question to be judged of in a small, contracted manner. I trust it will keep in view the desire the country manifests for the utmost possible development of its resources. Let us endeavor by this measure to afford a better opening than we now possess for the industry and intelligence of the people. Let us seek by this scheme to give them higher and worthier objects of ambition. Let us not reject the scheme with the bright prospect it offers of a nobler future for our youth, and grander objects for the emulation of our public men. Let us not refuse it on small questions of detail, but judge it on its general merits. Let us not lose sight of the great advantages which union offers because there may be some small matters which, as individuals, we may not like. Let us trust that this machinery, however faulty it may be, will yet under Providence open up for this country a happy career; while at the same time the House must not forget that it will forever remove the great and crying evils and dissensions which have existed in Canada for the last ten years, and which have threatened to plunge the country into the most disastrous and lamentable state of discord and confusion. (Cheers.) Surely this last fact alone will commend the project to the House. It should induce the Legislature and the people to make every allowance for the men who have been engaged in the work, and lead them to approach the result of their labors as now submitted, not in a hypercritical spirit so that the public mind may be led astray on mere matters of detail. Let the House frankly and kindly look at it as a great measure brought down for the purpose of relieving the country from distress and depression, and give it that consideration which is due, not to the arguments of the Government, feeble as they may be in view of the great interests involved, but to the fact that the country desires and cries for, at the hands of the House, some measure whereby its internal prosperity, peace and happiness may be developed and maintained. (Loud cheers.)

On motion of HON. MR. BROWN, the debate was then adjourned.

WEDNESDAY / FEBRUARY 8, 1865.

Hon. George Brown (President of the Council) [South Oxford]:

MR. SPEAKER, it is with no ordinary gratification I rise to address the House on this occasion. I cannot help feeling that the struggle of half a life-time for constitutional reform – the agitations in the country, and the fierce contests in this chamber – the strife and the discord and the abuse of many years, – are all compensated by the great scheme of reform which is now in your hands. (Cheers.) . . . Here is a people composed of two distinct races, speaking different languages, with religious and social and municipal and educational institutions totally different; with sectional hostilities of such a character as to render government for many years well-nigh impossible; with a Constitution so unjust in the view of one section as to justify any resort to enforce a remedy. And yet, sir, here we sit, patiently and temperately discussing how these great evils and hostilities may justly and amicably be swept away forever. (Hear, hear.) We are endeavoring to adjust harmoniously greater difficulties than have plunged other countries into all the horrors of civil war. We are striving to do peacefully and satisfactorily what Holland and Belgium, after years of strife, were unable to accomplish. We are seeking by calm discussion to settle questions that Austria and Hungary, that Denmark and Germany, that Russia and Poland, could only crush by the iron heel of armed force. We are seeking to do without foreign intervention that which deluged in blood the sunny plains of Italy. We are striving to settle forever issues hardly less momentous than those that have rent the neighboring republic and are now exposing it to all the horrors of civil war. (Hear, hear.) Have we not then, MR. SPEAKER, great cause of thankfulness that we have found a better way for the solution of our troubles than that which has entailed on other countries such deplorable results? And should not every one of us endeavor to rise to the magnitude of the occasion, and earnestly seek to deal with this question to the end in the same candid and conciliatory spirit in which, so far, it has been discussed? (Loud cries of hear, hear.) [Would the House and his hon. friend opposite – (MR. HOLTON) pardon him if he asked – Could the pages of history find a parallel to this?

Hon. Mr. Holton [Chateauguay] – We can't do it. (Loud laughter, cheers and counter-cheers.)]*

Hon. Mr. Brown – One hundred years have passed away since these provinces became by conquest part of the British Empire. I speak in no boastful spirit – I desire not for a moment to excite a painful thought – what was then the fortune of war of the brave French nation, might have been ours on that well-fought field. I recall those olden times merely to mark the fact that here sit to-day the descendants of the victors and the vanquished in the fight of 1759, with all the differences of language, religion, civil law, and social habit, nearly as distinctly marked as they were a century ago. (Hear, hear.) Here we sit to-day seeking amicably to find

* From Quebec *Morning Chronicle*, Feb. 9, 1865, report of Feb. 8.

a remedy for constitutional evils and injustice complained of – by the vanquished? No, sir – but complained of by the conquerors! (Cheers by the French Canadians.) Here sit the representatives of the British population claiming justice – only justice; and here sit the representatives of the French population, discussing in the French tongue whether we shall have it. One hundred years have passed away since the conquest of Quebec, but here sit the children of the victor and the vanquished, all avowing hearty attachment to the British Crown – all earnestly deliberating how we shall best extend the blessings of British institutions – how a great people may be established on this continent in close and hearty connection with Great Britain. (Cheers.) Where, sir, in the page of history, shall we find a parallel to this? Will it not stand as an imperishable monument to the generosity of British rule? And it is not in Canada alone that this scene is being witnessed. Four other colonies are at this moment occupied as we are – declaring their hearty love for the parent State, and deliberating with us how they may best discharge the great duty entrusted to their hands, and give their aid in developing the teeming resources of these vast possessions. And well, MR. SPEAKER, may the work we have unitedly proposed rouse the ambition and energy of every true man in British America. Look, sir, at the map of the continent of America, and mark that island (Newfoundland) commanding the mouth of the noble river that almost cuts our continent in twain. Well, sir, that island is equal in extent to the kingdom of Portugal. Cross the straits to the main land, and you touch the hospitable shores of Nova Scotia, a country as large as the kingdom of Greece. Then mark the sister province of New Brunswick – equal in extent to Denmark and Switzerland combined. Pass up the river St. Lawrence to Lower Canada – a country as large as France. Pass on to Upper Canada, – twenty thousand square miles larger than Great Britain and Ireland put together. Cross over the continent to the shores of the Pacific, and you are in British Columbia, the land of golden promise, – equal in extent to the Austrian Empire. I speak not now of the vast Indian Territories that lie between – greater in extent than the whole soil of Russia – and that will ere long, I trust, be opened up to civilization under the auspices of the British American Confederation. (Cheers.) Well, sir, the bold scheme in your hands is nothing less than to gather all these countries into one – to organize them all under one government, with the protection of the British flag, and in heartiest sympathy and affection with our fellow-subjects in the land that gave us birth. (Cheers.) Our scheme is to establish a government that will seek to turn the tide of European emigration into this northern half of the American continent – that will strive to develop its great natural resources – and that will endeavor to maintain liberty, and justice, and Christianity throughout the land.

Mr. T.C. Wallbridge – When?

Hon. Mr. Cartier – Very soon!

Hon. Mr. Brown – The hon. member for North Hastings asks when all this can be done? Sir, the whole great ends of this Confederation may not be realized in the lifetime of many who now hear me. We imagine not that such a structure can be built in a month or in a year. What we propose now is but to lay the foundations of the structure – to set in motion the governmental machinery that will one day, we trust, extend from the Atlantic to the Pacific. And we take especial credit to ourselves that the system we have devised, while admirably adapted to our present situation, is capable of gradual and efficient expansion in future years to meet all the great purposes contemplated by our scheme. But if the honorable gentleman will only recall to mind that when the United States seceded from the Mother Country, and for many years afterwards their population was not nearly equal to ours at this moment; that their internal improvements did not then approach to what we have already attained; and that their trade and commerce was not then a third of what ours has already reached; I think he will see that the fulfilment of our hopes may not be so very remote as at first sight might be imagined – (hear, hear). And he will be strengthened in that conviction if he remembers that what we propose to do is to be done with the cordial sympathy and assistance of that great Power of which it is our happiness to form a part. (Hear, hear.) Such, MR. SPEAKER, are the objects of attainment to which the British American Conference pledged itself in October. And said I not rightly that such a scheme is well fitted to fire the ambition and rouse the energies of every member of this House? Does it not lift us above the petty politics of the past, and present to us high purposes and great interests that may well call forth all the intellectual ability and all the energy and enterprise to be found among us? (Cheers.) I readily admit all the gravity of the question – and that it ought to be considered cautiously and thoroughly before adoption. Far be it from me to deprecate the closest criticism, or to doubt for a moment the sincerity or patriotism of those who feel it their duty to oppose the measure. But in considering a question on which hangs the future destiny of half a continent, ought not the spirit of mere faultfinding to be hushed? – ought not the voice of partisanship to be banished from our debates? – ought we not to sit down and discuss the arguments presented in the earnest and candid spirit of men, bound by the same interests, seeking a common end, and loving the same country? (Hear, hear, and cheers.) Some honorable gentlemen seem to imagine that the members of Government have a deeper interest in this scheme than others – but what possible interest can any of us have except that which we share with every citizen of the land?

What risk does anyone run from this measure in which all of us do not fully participate? What possible inducement could we have to urge this scheme, except our earnest and heartfelt conviction that it will inure to the solid and lasting advantage of our country? (Hear, hear.) There is one consideration, MR. SPEAKER, that cannot be banished from this discussion, and that ought, I think, to be remembered in every word we utter; it is that the constitutional system of Canada cannot remain as it is now. (Loud cries of hear, hear.) Something must be done. We cannot stand still. We cannot go back to chronic, sectional hostility and discord – to a state of perpetual Ministerial crises. The events of the last eight months cannot be obliterated; the solemn admissions of men of all parties can never be erased. The claims of Upper Canada for justice must be met, and met now. I say, then, that every one who raises his voice in hostility to this measure is bound to keep before him, when he speaks, all the perilous consequences of its rejection, – I say that no man who has a true regard for the well-being of Canada, can give a vote against this scheme, unless he is prepared to offer, in amendment, some better remedy for the evils and injustice that have so long threatened the peace of our country. (Hear, hear.) And not only must the scheme proposed in amendment be a better scheme – it must be something that can be carried. (Hear, hear.) I see an honorable friend now before me, for whose opinions I have the very highest respect, who says to me: "MR. BROWN, you should not have settled this part of the plan as you have done; here is the way you should have framed it." "Well, my dear sir," is my reply, "I perfectly agree with you, but it could not be done. Whether we ask for parliamentary reform for Canada alone or in union with the Maritime Provinces, the French Canadians must have their views consulted as well as us. This scheme can be carried, and no scheme can be that has not the support of both sections of the province."

Hon. Mr. Cartier – Hear, hear! there is the question!

Hon. Mr. Brown – Yes, that is the question and the whole question. No constitution ever framed was without defect; no act of human wisdom was ever free from imperfection; no amount of talent and wisdom and integrity combined in preparing such a scheme could have placed it beyond the reach of criticism. And the framers of this scheme had immense special difficulties to overcome. We had the prejudices of race and language and religion to deal with; and we had to encounter all the rivalries of trade and commerce, and all the jealousies of diversified local interests. To assert, then, that our scheme is without fault, would be folly. It was necessarily the work of concession; not one of the thirty-three framers but had, on some points, to yield his opinions; and, for myself, I freely admit that I struggled earnestly, for days together, to have portions of the scheme amended. But, MR. SPEAKER, admitting all this – admitting all the difficulties that beset us – admitting frankly that defects in the measure exist – I say that, taking the scheme as a whole, it has my cordial, enthusiastic support, without hesitation or reservation. (Hear, hear.) I believe it will accomplish all, and more than all, that we, who have so long fought the battle of parliamentary reform, ever hoped to see accomplished. I believe that, while granting security for local interests, it will give free scope for carrying out the will of the whole people in general matters – that it will draw closer the bonds that unite us to Great Britain and that it will lay the foundations deep and strong of a powerful and prosperous people. (Cheers.) . . .

But I am told by Upper Canadians – the constitution of the Lower House is all well enough, it is in the Upper House arrangements that the scheme is objectionable. And first, it is said that Upper Canada should have had in the Legislative Council a greater number of members than Lower Canada. –

Mr. T. C. Wallbridge – Hear, hear!

Hon. Mr. Brown – The honorable mem ber for North Hastings is of that opinion; but that honorable gentleman is in favor of a Legislative union, and had we been forming a Legislative union, there might have been some force in the demand. But the very essence of our compact is that the union shall be Federal and not Legislative. Our Lower Canada friends have agreed to give us representation by population in the Lower House, on the express condition that they shall have equality in the Upper House. On no other condition could we have advanced a step; and, for my part, I am quite willing they should have it. . . .

Now, MR. SPEAKER, I believe I have answered every objection that has come from any quarter against the proposed constitution of the Federal Legislature. I am persuaded there is not one well-founded objection that can be urged against it. It is just to all parties; it remedies the gross injustice of the existing system; and I am convinced it will not only work easily and safely, but be entirely satisfactory to the great mass of our people. But I go further; I say that were all the objections urged against this scheme sound and cogent, they sink into utter insignificance in view of all the miseries this scheme will relieve us from, – in view of all the difficulties that must surround any measure of parliamentary reform for Canada that could possibly be devised. (Cheers.) Will honorable gentlemen who spend their energies in hunting out blemishes in this scheme, remember for a moment the utter injustice of the one we have at present? Public opinion has made rapid strides in the last six months on the representation question, – but think what it was a week before the present coalition was formed! Remember how short a time has elapsed since the member for Peel (HON. MR. J. HILLYARD CAMERON) proposed to grant one additional member to Upper Canada, and could not carry even that. Remember that but a few weeks ago the hon. member for Hochelaga (HON. MR. DORION), who now leads the crusade against this measure, publicly declared that five or six additional members was all Upper Canada was entitled to, and that with these the Upper Canadians would be content for many years to come. (Hear, hear.) And when he has reflected on this, let the man who is disposed to carp at this great measure of representative reform, justify his conduct, if he can, to the thousands of disfranchised freeholders of Upper Canada demanding justice at our hands. (Cheers.) For myself, sir, I unhesitatingly say, that the complete justice which this measure secures, to the people of Upper Canada in the vital matter of parliamentary representation alone, renders all the blemishes averred against it utterly contemptible in the balance. – (Continued cheers.)

But, MR. SPEAKER, the second feature of this scheme as a remedial measure is, that it removes, to a large extent, the injustice of which Upper Canada has complained in financial matters. We in Upper Canada have complained that though we paid into the public treasury more than three-fourths of the whole revenue, we had less control over the system of taxation and the expenditure of the public moneys than the people of Lower Canada. Well, sir, the scheme in your hand remedies that. The absurd line of separation between the provinces is swept way for general matters; we are to have seventeen additional members in the house that holds the purse; and the taxpayers of the country, wherever they reside, will have their just share of influence over revenue and expenditure. (Hear, hear.) We have also complained that immense sums of public money have been systematically taken from the public chest for local purposes of Lower Canada, in which the people of Upper Canada had no interest whatever, though compelled to contribute three-fourths of the cash. Well sir, this scheme remedies that. All local matters are to be banished from the General Legislature; local governments are to have control over local affairs, and if our friends in Lower Canada choose to be extravagant, they will have to bear the burden of it themselves. (Hear, hear.) No longer shall we have to complain that one section pays the cash while the other spends it; hereafter, they who pay will spend, and they who spend more than they ought will have to bear the brunt. (Hear, hear.) It was a great thing to accomplish this, if we had accomplished nothing more, – for if we look back on our doings of the last fifteen years, I think it will be acknowledged that the greatest jobs perpetrated were of a local character – that our fiercest contests were about local matters that stirred up sectional jealousies and indignation to its deepest depth. (Hear, hear.) We have further complained that if a sum was properly demanded for some legitimate local purpose in one section, an equivalent sum had to be appropriated to the other as an off-set, – thereby entailing prodigal expenditure, and unnecessarily increasing the public debt. Well, sir, this scheme puts an end to that. Each province is to determine for itself its own wants, and to find the money to meet them from its own resources. (Hear, hear.) But, sir, I am told that, though true it is that local matters are to be separated and the burden of local expenditure placed upon local shoulders, we have made an exception from that principle in providing that a subsidy of eighty cents per head shall be taken from the federal chest and granted to the local governments for local purposes. Undoubtedly this is the fact – and I do not hesitate to admit that it would have been better if this had been otherwise. I trust I commit no breach of discretion in stating that in Conference I was one of the strongest advocates for defraying the whole of the local expenditures of the local governments by means of direct taxation, and that there were liberal men in all sections of the provinces who would gladly have had it so arranged. But, MR. SPEAKER, there was one difficulty in the way – a difficulty which has often before been encountered in this world – and that difficulty was simply this, it could not be done. (Hear, and laughter.) We could neither have carried it in Conference nor yet in any one of the existing provincial legislatures. Our friends in Lower Canada, I am afraid, have a constitutional disinclination to direct taxation, and it was obvious that if the Confederation scheme had had attached to it a provision for the imposition of such a system of taxation, my honorable friends opposite would have had a much better chance of success in blowing the bellows of agitation than they now have. (Laughter, and cheers.) The objection, moreover, was not confined to Lower Canada – all the Lower Provinces stood in exactly the same position. They have not a municipal system such as we have, discharging many of the functions of government; but their General Government performs all the duties which in Upper Canada devolve upon our municipal councils, as well as upon Parliament. If then the Lower Provinces had been asked to maintain their customs duties for federal purposes, and to impose on themselves by the same act direct taxation for all their local purposes, the chances of carrying the scheme of union would have been greatly lessened. (Hear, hear.) But I apprehend that if we did not succeed in putting this matter on the footing that would have been the best, at least we did the next best thing. Two courses were open to us – either to surrender to the local governments some source of indirect revenue, some tax which the General Government proposed to retain, – or collect the money by the federal machinery, and distribute it to the local governments for local purposes. And we decided in favor of the latter. We asked the representatives of the different governments to estimate how much they would require after the inauguration of the federal system to carry on their local machinery. As at first presented to us, the annual sum required for all the provinces was something like five millions of dollars – an amount that could not possibly have been allotted. The great trouble was that some of the governments are vastly more expensive than others – extensive countries, with sparse populations, necessarily requiring more money per head for local government than countries more densely populated. But as any grant given from the common chest, for local purposes, to one province, must be extended to all, on the basis of population, it follows that for every $1,000 given, for example, to New Brunswick, we must give over $1,300 to Nova Scotia, $4,000 to Lower Canada, and $6,000 to Upper Canada – thereby drawing from the federal exchequer much larger sums than these provinces needed for local purposes. The course we adopted then was this: We formed a committee of Finance Ministers and made each of them go over his list of expenditures, lopping off all unnecessary services and cutting down every item to the lowest possible figure. By this means we succeeded in reducing the total annual subsidy required for local government to the sum of $2,630,000 – of which Lower Canada will receive annually $880,000, and Upper Canada $1,120,000. But it is said that in addition to her eighty cents per head under this arrangement, New Brunswick is to receive an extra grant from the federal chest of $63,000 annually for ten years. Well, this is perfectly true. After cutting down as I have explained the local expenditures to the lowest mark, it was found that New Brunswick and Newfoundland could not possibly carry on their local governments with the sum per head that would suffice for all the rest. New Brunswick imperatively required $63,000 per annum beyond her share, and we had either to find that sum for her or give up the hope of union. The question then arose, would it not be better to give New Brunswick a special grant of $63,000 for a limited number of years, so that her local revenues might have time to be developed, rather than increase the subsidy to all the local governments, thereby placing an additional burden on the federal exchequer of over eight hundred thousand dollars per annum? We came unanimously to the conclusion that the extra sum needed by New Brunswick was too small to be allowed to stand in the way of union – we also determined that it would be the height of absurdity to impose a permanent burden on the country of $800,000 a year, simply to escape a payment of $63,000 for ten years – and so it came about that New Brunswick got this extra grant – an arrangement which received and receives now my hearty approval. (Hear, hear.) . . .

I am persuaded that this union will inspire new confidence in our stability, and exercise the most beneficial influence on all our affairs. I believe it will raise the value of our public securities, that it will draw capital to our shores, and secure the prosecution of all legitimate enterprises; and what I saw, while in England, a few weeks ago, would alone have convinced me of this. Wherever you went you encountered the most marked evidence of the gratification with which the Confederation scheme was received by all classes of the people, and the deep interest taken in its success. Let me state one fact in illustration. For some time previous to November last our securities had gone very low down in the market, in consequence, as my honorable friend the Finance Minister explained the other night, of the war raging on our borders, the uncertainty which hung over the future of this province, and the fear that we might be involved in trouble with our neighbors. Our five per cent. debentures went down in the market so low as 71, but they recovered from 71 to 75, I think, upon the day the resolutions for Confederation, which we are now discussing, reached London. Well, sir, the resolutions were published in the London papers, with eulogistic editorial articles, and the immediate effect of the scheme upon the public mind was such that our five per cents. rose from 75 to 92. (Hear, hear.)

Hon. Mr. Holton – What has put them down since?

Hon. Mr. Brown – I will presently tell the honorable gentleman what has put them down since. But I say that, if anything could show more clearly than another the effect this union is to have on our position over the world, it is a fact like this, that our securities went up 17 per cent. in consequence of the publication of the details of our scheme. (Hear, hear.) The honorable member for Chateauguay asks, "What put them down again?" I will tell him. They remained at 91 or 92 until the news came that a raid had been made from Canada into the United States, that the raiders had been arrested and brought before a Canadian Court, and that upon technical legal grounds, not only had they been set free, but the money of which they had robbed the banks had been handed over to the robbers. The effect of this news, coupled with General DIX's order, was to drive down our securities 11 per cent. almost in one day. (Hear, hear.) But, as my honorable friend the Finance Minister suggests, this is but an additional proof of the accuracy of the argument I have been sustaining – for this would not have happened, at all events to the same extent, if all the provinces had been united and prepared, as we are now proposing, not only for purposes of commerce but for purpose of defence. (Hear, hear.)

But secondly, MR. SPEAKER, I go heartily for the union, because it will throw down the barriers of trade and give us the control of a market of four millions of people. (Hear, hear.) What one thing has contributed so much to the wondrous material progress of the United States as the free passage of their products from one State to another? What has tended so much to the rapid advance of all branches of their industry, as the vast extent of their home market, creating an unlimited demand for all the commodities of daily use, and stimulating the energy and ingenuity of producers? Sir, I confess to you that in my mind this one view of the union – the addition of nearly a million of people to our home consumers – sweeps aside all the petty objections that are averred against the scheme. What, in comparison with this great gain to our farmers and manufacturers, are even the fallacious money objections which the imaginations of honorable gentlemen opposite have summoned up? All over the world we find nations eagerly longing to extend their domains, spending large sums and waging protracted wars to possess themselves of more territory, untilled and uninhabited. (Hear, hear.) Other countries offer large inducements to foreigners to emigrate to their shores – free passages, free lands, and free food and implements to start them in the world. We, ourselves, support costly establishments to attract immigrants to our country, and are satisfied when our annual outlay brings us fifteen or twenty thousand souls. But here, sir, is a proposal which is to add, in one day, near a million of souls to our population – to add valuable territories to our domain, and secure to us all the advantages of a large and profitable commerce, now existing. And because some of us would have liked certain of the little details otherwise arranged, we are to hesitate in accepting this alliance! (Hear, hear.) Have honorable gentlemen forgotten that the United States gladly paid twenty millions in hard cash to have Louisiana incorporated in the Republic? But what was Louisiana then to the Americans, in comparison with what the Maritime Provinces are at this moment to Canada? I put it to honorable gentlemen opposite – if the United States were now to offer us the State of Maine, what possible sum could be named within the compass of our ability that we would not be prepared to pay for that addition to our country? (Hear, hear.) If we were offered Michigan, Iowa or Minnesota, I would like to know what sum, within the compass of Canada, we would not be prepared to pay? These are portions of a foreign country, but here is a people owning the same allegiance as ourselves, loving the same old sod, enjoying the same laws and institutions, actuated by the same impulses and social customs, and yet when it is proposed that they shall unite with us for purposes of commerce, for the defence of our common country, and to develop the vast natural resources of our united domains, we hesitate to adopt it! If a Canadian goes now to Nova Scotia or New Brunswick, or if a citizen of these provinces comes here, it is like going to a foreign country. The customs officer meets you at the frontier, arrests your progress, and levies his imposts on your effects. But the proposal now before us is to throw down all barriers between the provinces – to make a citizen of one, citizen of the whole; the proposal is, that our farmers and manufacturers and mechanics shall carry their wares unquestioned into every village of the Maritime Provinces; and that they shall with equal freedom bring their fish, and their coal, and their West India produce to our three millions of inhabitants. The proposal is, that the law courts, and the schools, and the professional and industrial walks of life, throughout all the provinces, shall be thrown equally open to us all. (Hear, hear.)

But, thirdly, MR. SPEAKER, I am in favor of a union of the provinces because – and I call the attention of honorable gentlemen opposite to it – because it will make us the third maritime state of the world. (Hear, hear.) When this union is accomplished, but two countries in the world will be superior in maritime influence to British America – and those are Great Britain and the United States. (Hear, hear.)... On the 31st December, –

	Vessels	*Tons*
1864, Canada owned	2,311	287,187
1863, Nova Scotia	3,539	309,554
1863, New Brunswick	891	211,680
1863, Prince Edward Island	360	34,222
1863, Newfoundland	1,429	89,603
Total	8,530	932,246

. . . When recently in England, I was charged to negotiate with the Imperial Government of the opening up of the North-West territories. In a few days the papers will be laid before the House, and it will then be seen whether or not this Government is in earnest in that matter. Sir, the gentlemen who formed the Conference at Quebec did not enter upon their work with the miserable idea of getting the advantage of each other, but with a due sense of the greatness of the work they had on hand, with an earnest desire to do justice to all, and keeping always in mind that what would benefit one section in such a union must necessarily benefit the whole. (Cheers.) It has always appeared to me that the opening up of the North-West ought to be one of the most cherished projects of my honorable friends from Lower Canada. During the discussion on the question for some years back I had occasion to dip deep in North-West lore – into those singularly interesting narratives of life and travels in the North-West in the olden time, and into the history of the struggles for commercial domainancy in the great fur-bearing regions, – and it has always struck me that the French-Canadian people have cause to look back with pride to the bold and successful part they played in the adventures of those days. Nothing perhaps has tended more to create their present national character than the vigorous habits, the power of endurance, the aptitude for out-door life, acquired in their prosecution of the North-West fur-trade. (Hear, hear.) Well may they look forward with anxiety to the realization of this part of our scheme, in confident hope that the great north-western traffic shall be once more opened up to the hardy French-Canadian traders and *voyageurs*. (Hear, hear.) Last year furs to the value of £280,000 stg. ($1,400,000) were carried from that territory by the Hudson's Bay Company – smuggled off through the ice-bound regions of James' Bay, that the pretence of the barrenness of the country and the difficulty of conveying merchandise by the natural route of the St. Lawrence may be kept up a little longer. Sir, the carrying of merchandise into that country, and bringing down the bales of pelts ought to be ours, and must ere long be ours, as in the days of yore – (hear, hear) – and when the fertile plains of that great Saskatchewan territory are opened up for settlement and cultivation, I am confident that it will not only add immensely to our annual agricultural products, but bring us sources of mineral and other wealth on which at present we do not reckon. (Hear, hear.) . . .

But, sixthly, MR. SPEAKER, I am in favor of the union of the provinces, because, in the event of war, it will enable all the colonies to defend themselves better, and give more efficient aid to the Empire, than they could do separately. I am not one of those who ever had the war-fever; I have not believed in getting up large armaments in this country; I have never doubted that a military spirit, to a certain extent, did necessarily form part of the character of a great people; but I felt that Canada had not yet reached that stage in her progress when she could safely assume the duty of defence; and that, so long as peace continued and the Mother Country threw her shield around us, it was well for us to cultivate our fields and grow in numbers and material strength, until we could look our enemies fearlessly in the face. But it must be admitted – and there is no use of closing our eyes to the fact – that this question of defence has been placed, within the last two years, in a totally different position from what it ever occupied before. The time has come – it matters not what political party may be in power in England – when Britain will insist on a reconsideration of the military relations which a great colony, such as Canada, ought to hold to the Empire. And I am free to admit that it is a fair and just demand. We may doubt whether some of the demands that have been made upon us, without regard to our peculiar position at the moment, and without any attempt to discuss the question with us in all its breadth, were either just or well-considered. But of this I think there can be no doubt, that when the time comes in the history of any colony that it has overcome the burdens and embarrassments of early settlement, and has entered on a career of permanent progress and prosperity, it is only fair and right that it should contribute its quota to the defence of the Empire. What that quota ought to be, I think, is a matter for grave deliberation and discussion, as well as the measure of assistance the colony may look for, in time of war, from the parent state – and, assuredly, it is in this spirit that the present Imperial Government is desirous of approaching the question. (Hear, hear.) I am persuaded that nothing more than that which is fairly due at our hands will be demanded from us, and anything less than this, I am sure, the people of Canada do not desire. (Hear, hear.) In the conversations I had, while in England, with public men of different politics – while I found many who considered that the connection between Canada and England involved the Mother Country in some danger of war with the powerful state upon our borders, and that the colonial system devolved heavy and unreasonable burdens upon the Mother Country – and while a still larger number thought we had not acted as cordially and energetically as we ought in organizing our militia for the defence of the province, still I did not meet one public man, of any stripe of politics, who did not readily and heartily declare that, in case of the invasion of Canada, the honor of Great Britain would be at stake, and the whole strength of the Empire would be unhesitatingly marshalled in our defence. (Hear, hear.) But, coupled with this, was the invariable and most reasonable declaration that a share of the burden of defence, in peace and in war, we must contribute. And this stipulation applies not only to Canada, but to every one of the colonies. Already the Indian Empire has been made to pay the whole expense of her military establishment. The Australian Colonies have agreed to pay £40 sterling per man for every soldier sent there. This system is being gradually extended – and union or no union, assuredly every one of these British American Colonies will be called upon to bear her fair share towards the defence of the Empire. And who will deny that it is a just demand, and that great colonies such as these, should be proud to meet it in a frank and earnest spirit. (Cheers.) Nothing, I am persuaded, could be more foreign to the ideas of the people of Canada, than that the people of England should be unfairly taxed for service rendered to this province. Now, the question presented to us is simply this: will these contributions which Canada and the other provinces must hereafter make to the defence of the Empire, be better rendered by a hardy, energetic population, acting as one people, than as five or six separate communities? (Hear, hear.) There is no doubt about it. But not only do our changed relations towards the Mother Country call on us to assume the new duty of military defence – our changed relations towards the neighboring republic compel us to do so. For myself, I have no belief that the Americans have the slightest thought of attacking us. I cannot believe that the first use of their new-found liberty will be the invasion, totally unprovoked, of a peaceful province. I fancy that they have had quite enough of war for a good many years to come – and that such a war as one with England would certainly be, is the last they are likely to provoke. But, MR. SPEAKER, there is no better mode of warding off war when it is threatened, than to be prepared for it if it comes. The Americans are now a warlike people. They have large armies, a powerful navy, an unlimited supply of warlike munitions, and the carnage of war has to them been stript of its horrors. The American side of our lines already bristles with works of defence, and unless we are willing to live at the mercy of our neighbors, we, too, must put our country in a state of efficient preparation. War or no war – the necessity of placing these provinces in a thorough state of defence can no longer be postponed. Our country is coming to be regarded as undefended and indefensible. . . .

MR. SPEAKER, I could go on for many hours piling up arguments in favor of this scheme, but already I have detained the House too long – (cries of "no, no;" "go on!") – and must draw to a close. But I think I have given reasons enough to satisfy every candid man who desires the advancement of his country, why this House should go unanimously and enthusiastically for "the union, the whole union, and nothing but the union!" Before sitting down, however, there are one or two general objections urged against the scheme which I am desirous of meeting, and I will try to do so as briefly as possible. And first, sir, I am told that we should have made the union Legislative and not Federal. Undoubtedly this is a point on which different opinions may be honestly held by men sincerely seeking the same ends – but, speaking my own views, I think we came to a most wise conclusion. Had we continued the present Legislative union, we must have continued with it the unjust system of taxation for local purposes that now exists – and the sectional bickering would have gone on as before. And can any honorable gentleman really believe that it would have been possible for a body of men sitting at Ottawa to administer efficiently and wisely the parish business of Red River and Newfoundland, and all the country between? Only think of bringing suitors and witnesses such distances to promote a bill for closing a side-line or incorporating a club! And if such a thing were desirable, would it be possible for any body of men to go through such a mass of work? Why, sir, the Imperial Parliament with 650 members sits for eight months in the year, and even our Parliament sits three or four months, – how then would it be possible for the Legislature of all the provinces with a thousand or twelve hundred bills before it, to accomplish it all? The whole year would not suffice for it – and who in these colonies is able to sacrifice his whole time to the duties of public life? But there is another reason why the union was not made legislative – it could not be carried. (Hear, hear.) We had either to take a Federal union or drop the negotiation. Not only were our friends from Lower Canada against it, but so were most of the delegates from the Maritime Provinces. There was but one choice open to us – Federal union or nothing. But in truth the scheme now before us has all the advantages of a Legislative union and a Federal one as well. We have thrown over on the localities all the questions which experience has shown lead directly to local jealousy and discord, and we have retained in the hands of the General Government all the powers necessary to secure a strong and efficient administration of public affairs. (Hear, hear.) By placing the appointment of the judges in the hands of the General Government, and the establishment of a central Court of Appeal, we have secured uniformity of justice over the whole land. (Hear, hear.) By vesting the appointment of the lieutenant governors in the General Government, and giving a veto for all local measures, we have secured that no injustice shall be done without appeal in local legislation. (Hear, hear.) For all dealings with the Imperial Government and foreign countries we have clothed the General Government with the most ample powers. And finally, all matters of trade and commerce, banking and currency, and all questions common to the whole people, we have vested fully and unrestrictedly in the General Government. The measure, in fact, shuns the faults of the federal and legislative systems and adopts the best parts of both, and I am well persuaded it will work efficiently and satisfactorily. (Hear, hear.) . . .

A general election was ordered in 1861 – there was a fierce contest at the polls – and the main question at every hustings, was the demand for constitutional changes. The result of that contest was the overthrow of the CARTIER-MACDONALD Ministry and the formation of the MACDONALD-SICOTTE Administration in its room. But so bitter had been the struggle for and against constitutional changes, and so clearly defined were party-lines upon it, that it was found impossible to construct that Government without a distinct pledge that it would resist every motion made upon the subject –

Hon. Mr. Holton – Did you recognize the propriety of that course?

Hon. Mr. Brown – No, indeed, I did not. I but cite the fact to show how thoroughly the whole question has been agitated, and how perfectly its bearings have, for years past, been understood. Well, sir, mark what followed. One short year had not passed over the heads of the

MACDONALD-SICOTTE Ministry before they tottered to their fall – and so repugnant to the House and to the country was their conduct on the constitutional question, that they dared not appeal to the country until they had changed their avowed policy upon it, and replaced the men who had forced upon them the narrow policy of the year before, by gentlemen understood to be more in favor of constitutional changes. The Government (MACDONALD-DORION), so reconstructed, went to the country in 1863, but in the year following it, too, fell in its turn, simply because it did not deal boldly with the constitutional question –

Hon. Mr. Dorion – We had the support of all who were in favor of the question.

Hon. Mr. Brown – Indeed, you had not.

Hon. Mr. Holton – We should have fallen if we had attempted to deal with it.

Hon. Mr. Brown – I entirely deny that; had you pursued a bold policy upon it you might have been in office up to this hour. (Hear, hear.) Well, sir, the MACDONALD-DORION made way for the TACHÉ-MACDONALD Administration – but it, too, soon fell by a majority of two, simply because it did not deal with the constitutional question

A Voice – Oh, oh!

Hon. Mr. Brown – My honorable friend cries "oh, oh," and I am perfectly amazed at his doing so. I am about to offer my honorable friend the most complete proof of the correctness of my statement – proof so conclusive that if he does not accept of it as such, I do not know how he can be convinced of anything. In one single day the TACHÉ-MACDONALD Administration, by taking up the constitutional question boldly, turned their minority of two into a majority of seventy. (Loud cries of hear, hear.) Could anything prove more unanswerably than this the deep hold this question has on the public mind, and the assured confidence of the members of this House that their constituents understand its whole merits, when, in one day, such a startling political revolution was brought about? Was it, think you, a doubtful consideration that could have induced the Upper Canada Opposition, almost as one man, to cast down their party intrenchments and make common cause with their opponents? Could there have been the slightest doubt as to the sentiments of our people and the imperative necessity of immediate action, when such men as now sit on the treasury benches, were forced, by their supporters, to unite for the settlement of this question? And could there be a more conclusive proof of the ripeness of public opinion than the unanimous and cordial manner in which our so uniting has been sustained by the press of all parties, and by the electors at the polls? (Hear, hear.) Never, I venture to assert, was any great measure so thoroughly understood, and so cordially endorsed by the people of Canada, as this measure now under consideration. (Hear, hear.) – The British Government approves of it – the Legislative Council approves of it – this House almost unanimously approves of it – the press of all parties approves of it – and though the scheme has already been directly submitted to fifty out of the one hundred constituencies into which Canada is divided, only four candidates ventured to appear at the hustings in opposition to it – all of them in Lower Canada – and but two of them were elected. (Cheers.) And yet, sir, we are to be told that we are stealing a march upon the country; that it is not understood by the people; and that we must dissolve the House upon it, at a vast cost to the exchequer, and at the risk of allowing political partisanship to dash the fruit from our hands at the very moment we are about to grasp it! (Hear, hear.) Sir, I have no fears whatever of an appeal to the people. I cannot pretend to speak as to the popular feeling in Lower Canada, but I think I thoroughly understand the popular mind of the western province, and I hesitate not to say that there are not five gentlemen in this chamber (if so many) who could go before their constituents in Upper Canada in opposition to this scheme, with the slightest chance of being returned. (Hear, hear.) It is because I thoroughly comprehend the feelings of the people upon it, that I urge the adoption of this measure at the earliest possible moment. The most gross injustice is to be rectified by it; the taxpayer is to be clothed with his rightful influence by it; new commercial relations are to be opened up by it; a new impulse to the industrial pursuits of the country will be given by it – and I for one would feel myself false to the cause I have so long sustained, and false to the best interests of my constituents, if I permitted one hour unnecessarily to pass without bringing it to a final issue. (Cheers.)

It was only by the concurrence of most propitious circumstances that the wonderful progress this movement has made could have been accomplished. Most peculiar were the circumstances that enabled such a coalition to be formed as that now existing for the settlement of this question – and who shall say at what hour it may not be rent asunder? And yet, who will venture to affirm that if party spirit in all its fierceness were once more to be let loose amongst us, there would be the slightest hope that this great question could be approached with that candor and harmony necessary to its satisfactory solution? (Hear, hear.) Then, sir, at the very moment we resolved to deal with this question of constitutional change, the Maritime Provinces were about to assemble in joint conference to consider whether they ought not to form a union among themselves and the way was thus most propitiously opened up for the consideration of a union of all British America. The civil war too, in the neighboring republic; the possibility of war between Great Britain and the United States; the threatened repeal of the Reciprocity Treaty; the threatened abolition of the American bonding system for goods *in transitu* to and from these provinces; the unsettled position of the Hudson's Bay Company; and the changed feeling of England as to the relations of great colonies to the parent state; – all combine at this moment to arrest earnest attention to the gravity of the situation, and unite us all in one vigorous effort to meet the emergency like men. (Hear, hear.) The interests to be affected by this scheme of union are very large and varied – but the pressure of circumstances upon all the colonies is so serious at this moment, that if we cannot now banish partisanship and sectionalism and petty objections, and look at the matter on its broad intrinsic merits, what hope is there of our ever being able to do so? An appeal to the people of Canada on this measure simply means postponement of the question for a year – and who can tell how changed ere then may be the circumstances surrounding us? Sir, the man who strives for the postponement of this measure on any ground, is doing what he can to kill it almost as effectually as if he voted against it. (Hear, hear.) Let there be no mistake as to the manner in which the Government presents this measure to the House. We do not present it as free from fault, but we do present it as a measure so advantageous to the people of Canada, that all the blemishes, real or imaginary, averred against it, sink into utter insignificance in presence of its merits. (Hear, hear.) We present it, not in the precise shape we in Canada would desire it, but as in the best shape the five colonies to be united could agree upon it. We present it in the form in which the five governments have severally adopted it – in the form the Imperial Government has endorsed it – and in the form in which we believe all the legislatures of the provinces will accept it. (Hear, hear.) We ask the House to pass it in the exact form in which we have presented it, for we know not how alterations may affect its safety in other places, and the process of alteration once commenced in four different legislatures who can tell where that would end? Every member of this House is free as air to criticise it if he so wills, and amend it if he is able – but we warn him of the danger of amendment, and throw on him all the responsibility of the consequences. (Hear, hear.) We feel confident of carrying this scheme as it stands – but we cannot tell what we can do if it be amended. (Hear, hear.) Let not honorable gentlemen approach this measure as a sharp critic deals with an abstract question, striving to point out blemishes and display his ingenuity; but let us approach it as men having but one consideration before us – the establishment of the future peace and prosperity of our country. (Hear, hear.) Let us look at it in the light of a few months back – in the light of the evils and injustice to which it applies a remedy – in the light of the years of discord and strife we have spent in seeking for that remedy – in the light with which the people of Canada would regard this measure were it to be lost, and all the evils of past years to be brought back upon us again. (Hear, hear.) Let honorable gentlemen look at the question in this view – and what one of them will take the responsibility of casting his vote against the measure? Sir, the future destiny of these great provinces may be affected by the decision we are about to give to an extent which at this moment we may be unable to estimate – but assuredly the welfare for many years of four millions of people hangs on our decision. (Hear, hear.) Shall we then rise equal to the occasion? – shall we approach this discussion without partisanship, and free from every personal feeling but the earnest resolution to discharge conscientiously the duty which an over-ruling Providence has placed upon us? Sir, it may be that some among us will live to see the day when, as the result of this measure, a great and powerful people may have grown up in these lands – when the boundless forests all around us shall have given way to smiling fields and thriving towns – and when one united government, under the British flag, shall extend from shore to shore: – but who would desire to see that day if he could not recall with satisfaction the part he took in this discussion? MR. SPEAKER I have done. I leave the subject to the conscientious judgment of the House, in the confident expectation and belief that the decision it will render will be worthy of the Parliament of Canada. (The honorable gentleman resumed his seat amid loud and continued applause.) [*Alexander Morris* [South Lanark] – I would like to ask whether or not it was a distinct understanding, at the time of the formation of the existing Government, that steps should be taken by it to send delegates to the Lower Provinces to ascertain whether or not they were willing to join with us in a union of the British American Provinces?

Hon. Mr. Brown – Certainly it was.]*

On motion of the HON. MR. McGEE, the debate was further adjourned till Thursday evening.

THURSDAY / FEBRUARY 9, 1865.

Hon. Thomas D'Arcy McGee (Minister of Agriculture) [Montreal West]:

. . . Really, MR. SPEAKER, the attempt to fix the parentage of this child of many fathers is altogether absurd and futile. It is almost as ridiculous as the attempt to fix the name of this new Confederation, in advance of the decision of the Gracious Lady to whom the matter is to be referred. I have read in one newspaper published in a western city not less than

* From Quebec *Morning Chronicle*, Feb. 9, 1865, report of Feb. 8.

a dozen attempts of this nature. One individual chooses Tuponia and another Hochelaga, as a suitable name for the new nationality. Now I would ask any hon. member of this House how he would feel if he woke up some fine morning and found himself, instead of a Canadian, a Tuponian or Hochelagander. (Laughter.) I think, sir, we may safely leave for the present the discussion of the name as well as the origin of the new system proposed; when the Confederation has a place among the nations of the world, and opens a new page in history, it will be time enough to look into its antecedents, and when it has reached this stage there are a few men who, having struggled for it in its earlier difficulties, will then deserve to be honorably mentioned. I shall not be guilty of the bad taste of complimenting those with whom I have the honor to be associated; but when we reach the stage of research, which lies far beyond the stage of deliberation in these affairs, there are some names that ought not to be forgotten. (Hear, hear.) So far back as the year 1800, the Honorable MR. UNIACKE, a leading politician in Nova Scotia at that date, submitted a scheme of Colonial Union to the Imperial authorities. In 1815, CHIEF JUSTICE SEWELL, whose name will be well remembered as a leading lawyer of this city and a far-sighted politician, submitted a scheme. In 1822, SIR JOHN BEVERLEY ROBINSON, at the request of the Colonial Office, submitted a project of the same kind; and I need not refer to the report of LORD DURHAM on Colonial Union in 1839. These are all memorable, and some of them are great names. If we have dreamed a dream of union (as some hon. gentlemen say), it is at least worth while remarking that a dream which has been dreamed by such wise and good men, may, for aught we know or you know, have been a sort of vision – a vision foreshadowing forthcoming natural events in a clear intelligence. . . . But the immediate history of the measure is sufficiently wonderful without dwelling on the remoter predictions of so many wise men. Whoever, in 1862, or even in 1863, would have told us that we should see, even what we see in these seats by which I stand – such a representation of interests acting together, would be accounted, as our Scotch friends say, "half-daft"; – and whoever, in the Lower Provinces about the same time, would have ventured to foretell the composition of their delegations, which sat with us under this roof last October, would probably have been considered equally demented. (Laughter.) . . .

Events stronger than advocacy, events stronger than men, have come in at last like the fire behind the invisible writing to bring out the truth of these writings and to impress them upon the mind of every thoughtful man who has considered the position and probable future of these scattered provinces. (Cheers.) Before I go further into the details of my subject, I will take this opportunity of congratulating this House and the public of all the provinces upon the extraordinary activity which has been given to this subject since it has become a leading topic of public discussion in the maritime, and what I may call relatively to them, the inland provinces. It is astonishing how active has been the public mind in all those communities since the subject has been fairly launched. I have watched with great attention the expression of public opinion in the Lower Provinces as well as in our own, and I am rejoicing to find that even in the smallest of the provinces I have been able to read writings and speeches which would do no discredit to older and more cultivated communities – articles and speeches worthy of any press and of any audience. The provincial mind, it would seem, under the inspiration of a great question, leaped at a single bound out of the slough of mere mercenary struggles for office, and took post on the high and honorable ground from which alone this great subject can be taken in in all its dimensions. . . . [Men write and speak already, in the lower Provinces and in Canada, as if they were writing and speaking in the visible presence of all the Colonies; our orators and editors are no longer hole and corner celebrities. Poor MR. PALMER [Attorney General of Prince Edward Island], for example, finds himself discussed at Toronto, which must very much surprise him, and I find myself overhauled by a Halifax clipper, called the *Chronicle*, in a style which recompenses me for its hostility by giving another testimony, however unwillingly, that we are destined to be one people.]* . . . many men now speak with a dignity and carefulness which formerly did not characterize them, when they were watched only by their own narrow and struggling section, and weighed only according to a stunted local standard. (Hear, hear.) Federation, I hope, may supply to all our public men just ground for uniting in nobler and more profitable contests than those which have signalized the past. (Hear, hear.) . . . the policy of our neighbors to the south of us has always been aggressive. There has always been a desire amongst them for the acquisition of new territory, and the inexorable law of democratic existence seems to be its absorption. They coveted Florida, and seized it; they coveted Louisiana, and purchased it; they coveted Texas, and stole it; and then they picked a quarrel with Mexico, which ended by their getting California. (Hear, hear.) They sometimes pretend to despise these colonies as prizes beneath their ambition; but had we not had the strong arm of England over us, we should not now have had a separate existence. (Cheers.) The acquisition of Canada was the first ambition of the American Confederacy, and never ceased to be so, when her troops were a handful and her navy scarce a squadron. Is it likely to be

* From Quebec *Morning Chronicle*, Feb. 10, 1865, report of Feb. 9.

stopped now, when she counts her guns afloat by thousands and her troops by hundreds of thousands? ...

After the Coalition was formed an incident occurred, which, though not of national importance, it would be most ungrateful of me to forget. An intercolonial excursion was proposed and was rendered practicable through the public spirit of two gentlemen representing our great railway, of which so many hard things have been said that I feel it my duty to say this good thing – I refer to the HONORABLE MR. FERRIER and MR. BRYDGES. (Cheers.) Forty members of this House, twenty-five members of the other House, and forty gentlemen of the press and other professions, from Canada, joined in that excursion. So many Canadians have never seen so much of the Lower Provinces before, and the people of the Lower Provinces had never seen so many Canadians. Our reception was beyond all description kind and cordial. The general sentiment of union was everywhere cheered to the echo, though I am sorry to find that some of those who cheered then, when it was but a general sentiment, seem to act very differently now, that it has become a ripened project, and I fear that they do not intend to act up to the words they then uttered. They may, perhaps, intend to do so, but they have a very odd way of going about it. (Laughter.) Well, sir, this was in August; the Charlottetown Conference was called in September, the Quebec Conference in October, and the tour of the maritime delegates through Canada took place in November. Four months of the eight which have elapsed since we promised this House to deal with it have been almost wholly given up to this great enterprise. Let me bear my tribute, MR. SPEAKER, now that I refer to the Conference, to the gentlemen from the Lower Provinces, who sat so many days in council with us under this roof. (Cheers.) A very worthy citizen of Montreal, when I went up a day or two in advance of the Montreal banquet, asked me, with a curious sort of emphasis – "What sort of people are they?" – meaning the maritime delegates. I answered him then, as I repeat now, that they were, as a body, as able and accomplished a body as I thought any new country in the world could produce, – and that some among them would compare not unfavorably in ability and information with some of the leading commoners of England. As our Government included a representation both of the former Opposition, and the former Ministry, so their delegations were composed in about equal parts of the Opposition and Ministerial parties of their several provinces. A more hard-working set of men; men more tenacious of their own rights, yet more considerate for those of others; men of readier resources in debate; men of gentler manners; men more willing to bear and forbear, I never can hope to see together at one council table again. (Cheers.) But why need I dwell on this point? They were seen and heard in all our principal cities, and I am sure every Canadian who met them here was proud of them as fellow-subjects, and would be happy to feel that he could soon call them fellow-countrymen in fact as well as in name. (Cheers.) Sir, by this combination of great abilities – by this coalition of leaders who never before acted together – by this extraordinary armistice of party warfare, obtained in every colony at the same moment after all this labor and all this self-sacrifice – after all former impediments had been most fortunately overcome – the treaty was concluded and signed by us all – and there it lies on your table. . . .

THURSDAY / FEBRUARY 9, 1865.

Atty. Gen. Macdonald moved that the debate be adjourned till Thursday, 13th instant, and be then the first Order of the Day, after half-past seven.

Hon. Luther Hamilton Holton [Châteauguay]: MR. SPEAKER, we on this side had some doubt lest the Opposition might be placed at a disadvantage, by allowing the speeches of the Government to go to the country, without any comment on them. But if these five speeches, to which we have now listened, contain all that can be said in favor of this scheme, we have no fear of letting them go unanswered. I listened to the speech of the Attorney General West with great disappointment. The cause of that disappointment was simple enough. The hon. gentleman was, in that speech, giving the lie to twenty years of his political life. He was offering to the cause he is now advocating one speech against his continuous voice and vote for twenty years. He was struggling, all through that speech, against the consciousness of the falseness of his political position, and what everyone conceived would be the brightest effort of his life was the feeblest address he ever delivered on any important question, during the twenty years he has sat in this House. The Attorney General West was followed by the Attorney General East. I know not how to characterize the speech of that hon. gentleman, further than to say that it was quite characteristic. It was perfectly characteristic. I doubt whether any attorney general who ever existed, since attorneys general were first invented, besides that hon. gentleman, could have delivered, on an occasion like this, the speech which he delivered. It may be said of that hon. gentleman, as the poet said of a very different style of man – one who was not an hon. gentleman in the sense in which we are now speaking – "None but himself can be his parallel." (Laughter.) No attorney general, I repeat, since attorneys general were first invented, could have delivered a speech at all like that pronounced by the Attorney General East, in opening his side of the great question now submitted to the consideration of Parliament. Then followed the singularly able speech of my hon. friend the Finance Minister, which was delivered with all that ease and grace that mark all his efforts in this House, and with that fluency of diction which we all admire, and which I am always ready to acknowledge. But I think it will also be admitted by that hon. gentleman's own friends, that his speech was chiefly remarkable for an adroit avoidance of the very topics on which he was expected, or might have been expected, to address the House, and for a very adroit assumption of those very things which he might have been expected to prove. Such, at least, was the impression which that speech made upon my mind. Then came the speech – the herculean effort – of my hon. friend, the President of the Council, who, I am sorry to see, is not in his seat, and with reference, therefore, to whose speech I shall not make the remarks I might have done, if he were in his place. I must say, however, that that speech was a disappointing speech. (Cries of "oh! oh!" and "hear, hear.") I did expect, from the conspicuous part which that hon. gentleman has so long played in the politics of the country – from the leading part he has had in all the proceedings which have conducted to the project now before the House – that we should have had from him, at all events, some vindication of the steps which he has seen fit to take – some vindication of the principles of the proposed union, so contrary to all those principles which he has hitherto advocated. I say, we did expect that we would have had something of that kind from that hon. gentleman. But, instead of that, his whole speech was mainly an apology for his abandonment of all those objects for which he has contended through his political life, saving only the shadow of representation by population, to attain which shadow he seems to have sacrificed all the material objects, all the real objects, for the attainment of which the agitation for that change has proceeded on his part. Then we have had, to-night, the speech of my hon. friend, the Minister of Agriculture, a speech which I admit was one of very great interest, as a historical essay – one which will read very nicely in those reports which we are to get in a few days – one which does very great credit to his literary research and literary taste – but one, which I do venture to say, had very little practical bearing on the question that is now before us. Well, I repeat, I am not afraid that these speeches should go to the country unanswered. The country will see that these hon. gentlemen have utterly failed to establish a cause for revolution. They are proposing revolution, and it was incumbent upon them to establish a necessity for revolution. . . .

THURSDAY / FEBRUARY 16, 1865.

Hon. Antoine Aimé Dorion [Hochelaga]:

I should have desired to make my remarks to the House in French, but considering the large number of honorable members who are not familiar with that language, I think it my duty to speak at the present time in English. In rising on this occasion to address the House on the important question submitted to us, I must say I do so with an unusual degree of embarrassment, not only on account of the importance of the subject of our deliberations, but also because I have to differ from many of those with whom I have been in the habit of acting ever since I first entered into political life. . . .

I trust I shall be permitted to go a little into the history of the agitation of representation by population, for I owe it to myself, to my constituents and the country. My name has been used in various ways. It has sometimes been said that I was entirely favorable to representation by population – at other times that I was entirely favorable to the Confederation of the provinces, and I will now endeavor, once more, to state as clearly as possible what my real views have been and still are. (Hear.) The first time representation by population was mooted in this House, on behalf of Upper Canada, was, I believe, in the session of 1852, when the Conservative party took it up, and the HON. SIR ALLAN MACNAB moved resolutions in favor of the principle. We then found the conservatives arrayed in support of this constitutional change. It had been mooted before on behalf of Lower Canada, but the Upper Canadians had all opposed it. I think two votes were taken in 1852, and on one of these occasions the Hon. Attorney General West (HON. J.A. MACDONALD) voted for it; it came up incidentally. In 1854 the MACNAB-MORIN coalition took place, and we heard no more of representation by population from that quarter – that is, as mooted by the Conservative party, who from that moment uniformly opposed it on every occasion. It was, however, taken up by the present Hon. President of the Council, the member for South Oxford, and with the energy and vigor he brings to bear on every question he takes in hand, he caused such an agitation in its behalf as almost threatened a revolution. As the agitation in the country increased, so did the vote for it in this House increase, and on several occasions I expressed my views upon the subject. I never shirked the question – I never hesitated to say that something ought to be done to meet the just claims of Upper Canada, and that representation based on population was in the abstract a just and correct principle. I held, at the same time, there were reasons why Lower Canada could not grant it; I entreated Lower Canadian representatives to show themselves disposed to meet the views of Upper Canada by making, at any rate, a counter proposition; and in 1856, when Parliament was sitting in Toronto, I, for the first time, suggested that one means of getting over the difficulty would be to substitute for the present Legislative union a Confederation of the two Canadas, by means of which all local questions could be consigned to the deliberations of local legislatures, with a central government having control of commercial and other questions of common or general interest. I stated that, considering the different religious faith, the different language, the different laws that prevailed in the two sections of the country, this was the best way to meet the difficulty; to leave to a general government questions of trade, currency, banking, public works of a general character, &c., and to commit to the decision of local legislatures all matters of a local bearing. At the same time I stated that, if these views should not prevail, I would certainly go for representation by population, and such checks and guarantees as would secure the interests of each section of the country, and preserve to Lower Canada its cherished institutions. (Hear, hear.) This speech, sir, has been twisted in all sorts of ways. I have heard it quoted to prove that I was in favor of representation by population, pure and simple; that I was in favor of a Confederation of the provinces and for several other purposes, just as it suited the occasion or the purpose of those who quoted it. (Hear and laughter.)

The first time the matter was put to a practical test was in 1858. On the resignation of the MACDONALD-CARTIER Administration, the BROWN-DORION Government was formed, and one of the agreements made between its members was that the constitutional question should be taken up and settled, either by a Confederation of the two provinces or by representation according to population, with such checks and guarantees as would secure the religious faith, the laws, the language, and the peculiar institutions of each section of the country from encroachments on the part of the other. The subject came up again in the latter part of 1859, when the Toronto Convention took place. I should, however, first say that, when the BROWN-DORION Administration was formed, the Hon. the President of the Council urged very strongly that representation by population should be taken up as the method by which to settle the constitutional question; while, on the contrary, I saw the difficulty of so taking it up, even with such checks and guarantees as were spoken of, and made the counter-proposition that a Confederation of the two provinces should be formed. Of course as our Administration was so short-lived, the subject was not discussed in all its bearings. . . . In 1862 I was not in Parliament; the CARTIER-MACDONALD Administration was dismissed, and my hon. friend, the member for Cornwall (HON JOHN SANDFIELD

MACDONALD), was called upon to form a new one. He applied to MR. SICOTTE to form the Lower Canada section while he himself undertook the formation of the Upper Canada portion. The question of representation by population then necessarily came up for settlement – this time at the hands of the Liberal party who had voted for it year after year – and when I came down to Quebec, summoned by telegraph, I found the arrangements made, the policy of the new government was settled, representation by population was excluded. (Hear, hear.) The Liberal party from Upper Canada, sir, to my surprise, had decided that it was not to be taken up – that they were going into office just as the Conservative party had done before on a similar occasion in 1854; they decided that they would sustain an Administration which made it a closed question, and whose members all pledged themselves to vote against it (Hear, hear.)

Mr. Arthur Rankin [Essex] – No, no.

Hon. Mr. Dorion – If not, I was misinformed. I certainly understood that the Administration was formed on the understanding that every member of it should vote against the question of representation by population whenever it came up, and that the Upper Canada party would support the Administration so formed. At any rate the Upper Canada Liberal party supported, for eleven months, a government pledged to exclude representation by population from the category of open questions, and agreed to lay that question aside.

Mr. Alexander Mackenzie [Lambton] – No, no.

Hon. Mr. Dorion – I hear an honorable gentleman say it was not so, that he did not agree to lay aside representation by population then, but if he did not then has he not done so since? He declared at a public meeting the other day that representation by population was no cure for the evils afflicting Upper Canada. The members from Upper Canada who had joined the MACDONALD-SICOTTE Government had certainly abandoned representation by population, by entering into an Administration which bound every one of them to vote against it. . . . With these views on the question of representation, I pronounced in favor of a Confederation of the two provinces of Upper and Lower Canada, as the best means of protecting the varied interests of the two sections. But the Confederation I advocated was a real confederation, giving the largest powers to the local governments, and merely a delegated authority to the General Government – in that respect differing *in toto* from the one now proposed which gives all the powers to the Central Government, and reserves for the local governments the smallest possible amount of freedom of action. There is nothing besides in what I have ever written or said that can be interpreted as favoring a Confederation of all the provinces. This I always opposed. . . .

There was then another cause for this Confederation scheme of which representation by population was made the pretext. It is not so well known, but far more powerful. In the year 1861, MR. WATKIN was sent from England by the Grand Trunk Railway Company. He came with the distinct view of making a large claim on the country for aid, but in the then temper of the people, he soon found that he could not expect to obtain that. Thinking that if he only could put some new scheme afloat which would give a decent pretext to a well disposed Government, he would quietly get the assistance required, he immediately started for the Lower Provinces, and came back after inducing people there to resuscitate the question of the Intercolonial Railway. Parties were readily found to advocate it, if Canada would only pay the piper. (Hear, and a laugh.) A meeting of delegates took place, resolutions were adopted, and an application was made to the Imperial Government for a large contribution to its costs, in the shape of an indemnity for carrying the troops over the road. MR. WATKIN and HON. MR. VANKOUGHNET, who was then a member of the Government, went to England about this scheme, but the Imperial authorities were unwilling to grant the required assistance, and rejected their propositions. MR. WATKIN, although baffled in his expectations, did not give up his project. He returned again to Canada, and by dint of perseverance, induced my honorable friend on my right (HON JOHN SANDFIELD MACDONALD) and other honorable members of his Cabinet to enter into his views. As to the advantages of the Intercolonial Railway, I have not the slightest idea that my hon. friend had any suspicion whatsoever of the motives which animated these Grand Trunk officials, and that their object was to have another haul at the public purse for the Grand Trunk – (laughter) – but this was the origin of the revival of the scheme for constructing the Intercolonial Railway.

Hon. John Sandfield Macdonald [Cornwall] – We found the project then left to us as a legacy by the CARTIER-MACDONALD Administration.

Hon. Mr. Dorion – So it was. The MACDONALD-SICOTTE Government found the matter so far advanced that an arrangement had been made for a meeting of delegates of the several provinces to consider again this railway scheme, the other project having failed. At this meeting of delegates, which took place in September, 1862, a new scheme for building the Intercolonial was adopted, by which Canada was to pay five-twelfths and the Lower Provinces seven-twelfths. So unpopular was this arrangement that when its terms were made known, if a vote of the people had been taken upon it, not ten out of every hundred, from Sandwich to Gaspé, would have declared in its favor, although Canada was only to pay five-twelfths of its cost. (Hear,

hear.) This project having failed, some other scheme had to be concocted for bringing aid and relief to the unfortunate Grand Trunk – and the Confederation of all the British North American Provinces naturally suggested itself to the Grand Trunk officials as the surest means of bringing with it the construction of the Intercolonial Railway. (Hear, hear, and laughter.) Such was the origin of this Confederation scheme. The Grand Trunk people are at the bottom of it; and I find that at the last meeting of the Grand Trunk Railway Company, MR. WATKIN did in advance congratulate the shareholders and bondholders on the bright prospects opening before them, by the enhanced value which will be given to their shares and bonds, by the adoption of the Confederation scheme and the construction of the Intercolonial as part of the scheme. (Hear, hear.) I repeat, sir, that representation by population had very little to do with bringing about this measure. The TACHÉ-MACDONALD Government were defeated because the House condemned them for taking without authority $100,000 out of the public chest for the Grand Trunk Railway, at a time when there had not been a party vote on representation by population for one or two sessions. Those who had been the loudest in their advocacy of it, had let it drop. I was tracked through Lower Canada as being willing to sell Lower Canada, grant representation by population, and destroy Lower Canadian institutions. I thank God, sir, I never insulted Upper Canada, like some of those who reviled me. I never compared the people of Upper Canada to so many codfish. I shewed on the contrary that I was always willing to meet the just claims of Upper Canada. (Hear, hear.) Well, without any demand whatever for the agitation of this question, the moment the Government was defeated and there was necessity for resigning or going before the people, these gentlemen opposite prepared to embrace their greatest opponents and said to themselves, "We will make everything smooth, we will forget past difficulties, provided we can but keep our seats."

Hon. Atty. Gen. John Alexander Macdonald – (Ironically) Hear, hear.

Hon. Mr. Dorion – I hear a voice, sir, which is well known in this House, the voice of the Attorney General West, saying "hear, hear." But what was the course of that hon. gentleman last year, when the hon. member for South Oxford had a committee appointed to whom was referred the despatch written by his three colleagues, the Minister of Finance, the Attorney General East and the HON. MR. ROSS, who is now no longer a minister. He voted against the appointment of the committee, and, after it was named, as a member of it, he voted against the principle of Confederation. (Hear, hear.)

Hon. Atty Gen. Macdonald – Hear, hear.

Hon. Mr. Dorion – The last vote taken in that committee was about the middle of June, the very day of the crisis, and the hon. gentleman voted against the principle of Confederation of all the provinces, in accordance with the opinions he again and again expressed in this House, as being opposed to all Confederation whatever. (Hear.) When I state that these gentlemen only found out that Confederation was a panacea for all evils, a remedy for all ills, when their seats as ministers were in danger, I come to this conclusion quite legitimately, from facts which are well known to this House. (Hear, hear.) But, sir, it would probably be of very little moment whether I was formerly in favor of Confederation or against it, or whether the Hon. Attorney General West was in favor of Confederation or opposed to it, if the scheme proposed to us were an equitable one, or one calculated to meet the wishes of the people of this country; but, as I said a minute ago, the scheme was not called for by any considerable proportion of the population. It is not laid before the House as one which was demanded by any number of the people; it is not brought down in response to any call from the people; it is a device of men who are in difficulties, for the purpose of getting out of them. (Hear, hear.) The members of the TACHÉ-MACDONALD Government could not appeal to the country after their defeat upon the question, whether they were justified in taking $100,000 out of the public chest, in addition to the millions they had previously taken, without the consent of Parliament; so, having either to give up their seats or evade that particular issue, they abandoned all their previous opinions, and joined the hon. member for South Oxford in carrying out this Confederation scheme. (Hear.) I come now to another point, viz., is the scheme presented to us the same one that was promised to us by the Administration when it was formed? This, sir, might be but of slight importance if the manner in which this proposed Constitution was framed had not a most unfortunate bearing on the scheme itself; but it is a grave matter, since the scheme is so objectionable, especially as we are gravely told that it cannot be amended in the least, but that it is brought down as a compact made between the Government of this country and delegates from the governments of Nova Scotia, New Brunswick, Newfoundland, and Prince Edward Island – as a treaty which cannot be altered or amended in any particular. (Hear.) The plain meaning of this is, sir, that the Lower Provinces have made out a Constitution for us and we are to adopt it. . . .

The whole scheme, sir, is absurd from beginning to end. It is but natural that gentlemen with the views of honorable gentlemen opposite want to keep as much power as possible in the hands of the

Government – that is the doctrine of the Conservative party everywhere – that is the line which distinguishes the tories from the whigs – the tories always side with the Crown, and the Liberals always want to give more power and influence to the people. The instincts of honorable gentlemen opposite, whether you take the Hon. Attorney General East or the Hon. Attorney General West, lead them to this – they think the hands of the Crown should be strengthened and the influence of the people, if possible, diminished – and this Constitution is a specimen of their handiwork, with a Governor General appointed by the Crown, with local governors also appointed by the Crown; with legislative councils, in the General Legislature, and in all the provinces, nominated by the Crown; we shall have the most illiberal Constitution ever heard of in any country where constitutional government prevails. (Hear.) The Speaker of the Legislative Council is also to be appointed by the Crown, this is another step backwards, and a little piece of patronage for the Government. We have heard in a speech lately delivered in Prince Edward Island or New Brunswick, I forget which, of the allurements offered to the delegates while here in the shape of prospective appointments as judges of the Court of Appeal, Speaker of the Legislative Council, and local governors – (hear, hear) – as one of the reasons assigned for the great unanimity which prevailed in the Conference.

Hon. Mr. Holton – They will divide all these nice things amongst them. (Laughter.)

Hon. Mr. Dorion – . . . Now, sir, when I look into the provisions of this scheme, I find another most objectionable one. It is that which gives the General Government control over all the acts of the local legislatures. What difficulties may not arise under this system? Now, knowing that the General Government will be party in its character, may it not for party purposes reject laws passed by the local legislatures and demanded by a majority of the people of that locality. This power conferred upon the General Government has been compared to the veto power that exists in England in respect to our legislation; but we know that the statesmen of England are not actuated by the local feelings and prejudices, and do not partake of the local jealousies, that prevail in the colonies. The local governments have therefore confidence in them, and respect for their decisions; and generally, when a law adopted by a colonial legislature is sent to them, if it does not clash with the policy of the Empire at large, it is not disallowed, and more especially of late has it been the policy of the Imperial Government to do whatever the colonies desire in this respect, when their wishes are constitutionally expressed. The axiom on which they seem to act is that the less they hear of the colonies the better. (Hear, hear.) But how different will be the result in this case, when the General Government exercises the veto power over the acts of local legislatures. Do you not see that it is quite possible for a majority in a local government to be opposed to the General Government; and in such a case the minority would call upon the General Government to disallow the laws enacted by the majority? The men who shall compose the General Government will be dependent for their support upon their political friends in the local legislatures, and it may so happen that, in order to secure this support, or in order to serve their own purposes or that of their supporters, they will veto laws which the majority of a local legislature find necessary and good. (Hear, hear.) We know how high party feeling runs sometimes upon local matters even of trivial importance, and we may find parties so hotly opposed to each other in the local legislatures, that the whole power of the minority may be brought to bear upon their friends who have a majority in the General Legislature, for the purpose of preventing the passage of some law objectionable to them but desired by the majority of their own section. What will be the result of such a state of things but bitterness of feeling, strong political acrimony and dangerous agitation? (Hear, hear.)

. . . this scheme proposes a union not only with Nova Scotia, New Brunswick, Prince Edward Island, and Newfoundland, but also with British Columbia and Vancouver's Island.... I must confess, MR. SPEAKER, that it looks like a burlesque to speak as a means of defence of a scheme of Confederation to unite the whole country extending from Newfoundland to Vancouver's Island, thousands of miles intervening without any communication, except through the United States or around Cape Horn. (Oh!)

Hon. Atty. Gen. Cartier – There is an Interoceanic Railway to be built.

Hon. Mr. Dorion – Yes, I suppose that is another necessity of Confederation, to which we may soon look forward. Some western extension of this Grand Trunk scheme for the benefit of MESSRS. WATKIN & CO, of the new Hudson's Bay Company. So far as Lower Canada is concerned, I need hardly stop to point out the objections to the scheme. It is evident, from what has transpired, that it is intended eventually to form a legislative union of all the provinces. The local governments, in addition to the General Government, will be found so burdensome, that a majority of the people will appeal to the Imperial Government for the formation of a Legislative union. (Hear, hear.) I may well ask if there is any member from Lower Canada, of French extraction, who is ready to vote for a Legislative union. What do I find in connection with the agitation of this scheme? The honorable member for Sherbrooke stated at the dinner to the delegates given at

Toronto, after endorsing everything that had been said by the Honorable President of the Council: –

We may hope that, at no far distant day, we may become willing to enter into a Legislative Union instead of a federal union, as now proposed. We would have all have desired a legislative union, and to see the power concentrated in the Central Government as it exists in England, spreading the ægis of its protection over all the institutions of the land, but we found it was impossible to do that at first. We found that there were difficulties in the way which could not be overcome.

Honorable members from Lower Canada are made aware that the delegates all desired a Legislative union, but it could not be accomplished at once. This Confederation is the first necessary step towards it. The British Government is ready to grant a Federal union at once, and when that is accomplished the French element will be completely overwhelmed by the majority of British representatives. What then would prevent the Federal Government from passing a set of resolutions in a similar way to those we are called upon to pass, without submitting them to the people, calling upon the Imperial Government to set aside the Federal form of government and give a Legislative union instead of it? (Hear, hear.) Perhaps the people of Upper Canada think a Legislative union a most desirable thing. I can tell those gentlemen that the people of Lower Canada are attached to their institutions in a manner that defies any attempt to change them in that way. They will not change their religious institutions, their laws and their language, for any consideration whatever. A million of inhabitants may seem a small affair to the mind of a philosopher who sits down to write out a constitution. He may think it would be better that there should be but one religion, one language and one system of laws, and he goes to work to frame institutions that will bring all to that desirable state; but I can tell honorable gentlemen that the history of every country goes to show that not even by the power of the sword can such changes be accomplished. (Hear, hear.) . . .

There is no hurrry in regard to the scheme. We are now legislating for the future as well as for the present, and feeling that we ought to make a Constitution as perfect as possible, and as far as possible in harmony with the views of the people, I maintain that we ought not to pass this measure now, but leave it to another year, in order to ascertain in the meantime what the views and sentiments of the people actually are. (The honorable gentleman was loudly cheered on resuming his seat.)

MONDAY / FEBRUARY 20, 1865.

Henri Gustave Joly [Lotbinière]:

. . . But who are those two men who now pitch their voices in harmony (formerly so discordant) to predict civil war, if we do not vote for Confederation? They are the Attorney General for Lower Canada, and the President of the Council (HON. MESSRS. CARTIER AND BROWN!) – the one demanding representation by population, the other refusing it: both took their stand as the champions of their sections, and became their chieftains respectively. When they found out that that game was unprofitable to both, as the President of the Council seemed to be excluded for ever from the ministerial benches, and the Attorney General could not maintain himself in his position on them, the Attorney General gave way: he agreed to representation by population, trying to disguise it under the name of Confederation; and to reward him for this complaisance, the President of the Council saved him – him and his colleagues – and condescended to take a seat among them. They hold over us a threat of civil war to force us to ratify their bargain. There is only one man in Canada who could have done what the Attorney General for Lower Canada has done, and that man is himself. Thanks to his energy, to his intimate acquaintance with the strong and the weak points of his fellow-countrymen, the Attorney General for Lower Canada has succeeded in attaining an elevation which no one can dispute with him – that of chief of the French Canadian nationality. To attain this eminence, he has crushed the weak, cajoled the strong, deceived the credulous, bought up the venal, and exalted the ambitious; by turns he has called in the accents of religion and stimulated the clamor of interest – he has gained his end. When Lower Canada heard of his alliance with the President of the Council, there arose from all quarters one universal cry of indignation. He managed to convert the cry of anger into a shout of admiration. When his scheme of Confederation became public, a feeling of uneasiness pervaded all minds; that instinct forewarned them of the danger which impended. He has hushed that feeling to a sleep of profound security. I shall compare him to a man who has gained the unbounded confidence of the public, who takes advantage of it to set up a Savings Bank, in which the rich man deposits his wealth, and the day laborer the small amount which he has squeezed out of his wages, against a day of need – both without a voucher. When that man has gathered all into his strong box, he finds an opportunity to purchase, at the cost of all he holds in trust, the article on which he has long set his ambitious eye; and he buys it, unhesitatingly, without a thought of the wretches who are doomed to ruin by his conduct. The deposit committed to the keeping of the Attorney General is the fortune of the French Canadians – their nationality. That fortune had not been made in a day; it was the accumulation of the toil and the savings of a whole people in a whole century. To prolong the ephemeral existence of his administration for a few months, the Attorney General has sacrificed, without a scruple, this precious trust, which the unbounded confidence of his fellow-countrymen had confided to his keeping.

Hon. Mr. Cartier – And what have I received in payment for that?

Mr. Joly – A salary of five thousand dollars per annum, and the honor of the position.

Hon. Mr. Cartier – That is not enough for me.

Mr. Joly – I am well aware of it; that is why the honorable member is desirous of extending the circle of his operations. But he will not long enjoy the fruits of his treason; by crushing the power of the French Canadians he has crushed his own, for upon them his existence depends. Does he believe in the sincerity of the friendship of the Liberals of Upper Canada? They fought with him for too long a time to allow of the existence of any sympathy between them and him, and now he has lost even their respect. They consented to ally themselves with him in order to obtain their object – representation by population; but when they no longer stand in need of him, they will throw him aside like a worn-out tool. . . .

WEDNESDAY / FEBRUARY 22, 1865.

Hon. John Rose [Montreal Centre]:

. . . I will now say a few words in reference to the objections which have been urged against its character, viz., because it embraces those elements of disruption which are to be found in every Federal union. That is the objection of many who, while they would be willing to go for a purely Legislative union, object to one of a Federal character. They see in it that which tends to a disruption, and collision with the Central Government. Now, sir, I do not deny that if a Legislative union, pure and simple, had been practicable, I, for one, would have preferred it; but I cannot disguise from myself that it was. and is at present, utterly impracticable, and I cannot help expressing my astonishment and extreme gratification, that five colonies which had been for so many years separate from each other, had so many separate and distinct interests and local differences, should come together and agree upon such a scheme. Remembering the difficulties that had to be encountered in the shape of local interests, personal ambition, and separate governments, I certainly am surprised at the result, and I cannot withhold from the gentlemen who conducted these negotiations, the highest praise for the manner in which they overcame the difficulties that met them at every step, and for tbe spirit in which they sunk their own personal differences and interests in preparing this scheme of Confederation. (Hear, hear.) It is remarkable that a proposition having so few of the objections of a Federal system, should have been assented to by the representatives of five distinct colonies, which had heretofore been alien, practically independent, not only of each other, but almost of England, and almost hostile to eacb other. (Hear, hear.) There had been very much to keep these colonies apart, and very little to bring them together, and the success which has attended their efforts speaks well for those statesmen who applied their minds earnestly to the work of union. (Hear, hear.) . . .

Let us forget the past; let us forget former differences; do not let us revive former animosities! Let us consider that we are starting fresh in life, or as the term has been used, that we are entering upon a new era of national existence. (Hear, hear.) Let us cast aside past recriminations and look at the merits of this scheme. I have only to say that a man who does not change his opinions is a very unsafe man indeed to guide the affairs of a nation. Such a man is like an old sign-post on a road that is no longer used for travel. The sign-post is consistent enough, it remains where it had been placed, but though a type of consistency it is an emblem of error. (Hear, hear.) The hon. member for Hochelaga [HON. H.A. DORION] spoke of his consistency and the inconsistency of others, but he was like the sign-post which pointed out a road that existed twenty years ago, but which no one could now pass over. (Hear, hear, and laughter.) I think, therefore, that instead of endeavoring to find objections to this scheme because it does not give us a Legislative instead of a Federal union, we ought to acknowledge the sacrifices of those men who came together and prepared it. (Hear, hear.) Whatever may be said of our desire to get out of our own constitutional difficulties in Canada, that objection cannot be urged against the public men of the Lower Provinces. Newfoundland has not been in a state of crisis like us, and New Brunswick has been tolerably faithful to MR. TILLEY for the last ten years; a short time ago the Premier of Nova Scotia had a majority of thirty in a very small house – everything went on swimmingly there, and even Prince Edward Island was not much embarrassed.

A Voice – It wanted a railway.

Hon. Mr. Rose – Let us attribute no motives, but rather give to every man who has had anything to do with this measure the credit of being actuated by the utmost patriotism and singleness of purpose. Such, I believe, is the feeling of nine-tenths – yes, ninety-nine hundredths of the people of this country. What inducement, except those of a public kind, had my hon. friend the President of the Council, or the Attorney General West to enter the same Government, if it was not with a view to bring about a union of the colonies? And even if they had only in view to heal the constitutional difficulties of the past, we ought to be deeply thankful to them. (Hear, hear.) . . .

Now we, the English Protestant minority of Lower Canada, cannot forget that whatever right of separate education we have was accorded to us in the most unrestricted way before the union of the provinces, when we were in a minority and entirely in the hands of the French population. We cannot forget that in no way was there any attempt to prevent us educating our children in the manner we saw fit and deemed best; and I would be untrue to what is just if I forgot to state that the distribution of State funds for educational purposes was made in such a way as to cause no complaint on the part of the minority. I believe we have always had our fair share of the public grants in so far as the French element could control them, and not only the liberty, but every facility, for the establishment of separate dissentient schools wherever they were deemed desirable. A single person has the right, under the law, of establishing a dissentient school and obtaining a fair share of the educational grant, if he can gather together fifteen children who desire instruction in it. Now, we cannot forget that in the past this liberality has been shown to us, and that whatever we desired of the French majority in respect to education, they were, if it was at all reasonable, willing to concede. (Hear, hear.) We have thus, in this also, the guarantee of the past that nothing will be done in the future unduly to interfere with our rights and interests as regards education, and I believe that everything we desire will be as freely given by the Local Legislature as it was before the union of the Canadas. (Hear, hear.) But from whence comes the practical difficulty of dealing with the question at the present moment? We should not forget that it does not come from our French-Canadian brethren in Lower Canada, but that it arises in this way – and I speak as one who has watched the course of events and the opinion of the country upon the subject – that the Protestant majority in Upper Canada are indisposed to disturb the settlement made a couple of years ago, with regard to separate schools, and rather to hope that the French majority in Lower Canada should concede to the English Protestant minority there, nothing more than is given to the minority in the other section of the province. But still it must be conceded that there are certain points where the present educational system demands modification – points in which the English

Protestant minority of Lower Canada expect a modification. I would ask my honorable friend the Attorney General East, whether the system of education which is in force in Lower Canada at the time of the proclamation is to remain and be the system of education for all time to come; and that whatever rights are given to either of the religious sections shall continue to be guaranteed to them? We are called upon to vote for the resolutions in ignorance, to some extent, of the guarantees to be given by subsequent legislation, and therefore my honorable friend will not take it amiss if I point out to him where the Protestant minority desire a change, with a view of ascertaining how far the Government is disposed to meet their views by coming down with a measure in which they may be embodied. . . .

I would, however, ask the attention of the House to another statement made the other evening by the hon. member from Hochelaga. He said that we were making a mistake in supposing that we were discussing a question of colonial union. Confederation, he said, was simply tacked on to the Intercolonial Railway at the suggestion of MR. WATKIN, and that the whole arrangement was merely a nicely planned scheme for the benefit of the Grand Trunk Railway.

Mr. Wallbridge [North Hastings] – That was the very motive.

Hon. Mr. Rose – Well, does anyone suppose that my hon. friend the President of the Council could be duped in that way? Is it possible that my hon. friend from Hochelaga believes he has so little astuteness as not to see through such an attempt as that? The argument was used to get the support of the opponents of railways in this House against the Federation. Sir, it would appear that the hon. President of the Council, and the hon. Provincial Secretary and the other members of the Government, who are anti-railway in their views, have been altogether mistaken, and that we are merely going to build up another gigantic railway monopoly for fraudulent purposes. They may all be deceived by this imaginary project, and it would seem too, sir, that MR. WATKIN, possessing the wiles of MEPHISTOPHELES, had hoodwinked the Governor General, and the Colonial Secretary, and caused them to fall into the trap also. Nay, further, it would appear that his wiles had reached the Throne itself, for Her Majesty has expressed herself in the speech to Parliament in favor of the scheme. (Hear, hear.) . . .

Those who say that the people throughout the country are opposed to this measure, I am satisfied, know very little what the sentiment of the country is. I believe there is a deep-rooted sentiment of approbation of the steps that have been taken. I know that those who are perhaps most fearful with reference to it, and whose interests are perhaps most in jeopardy – the English speaking minority in Lower Canada – have considered it carefully, and with all their prejudices against it at the outset, are now warmly in its favor. I speak particularly of those who have great interests at stake in the community which I represent – the great and varied interests of commerce, trade, banking, manufactures and material progress generally, which are supposed to centre in the city of Montreal. These men – and there are none more competent in the province – have considered the scheme in a calm and business-like way, and have deliberately come to the conclusion that it is calculated to promote the best interests and greatly enhance the prosperity of this country. (Hear, hear.) . . .

THURSDAY / FEBRUARY 23, 1865.

Alexander Mackenzie [Lambton):

. . . I am free to confess that, when I first came into this House, I labored under some slight misapprehension of the position which the Lower Canadians occupied towards us of Western Canada. There is, or there was then, a popular opinion that the Lower Canadians were only afraid of representation by population, because they dreaded that the people of Canada West would use the larger power they would thereby obtain for the injury, if not the destruction, of their religious institutions. That is entirely an error. I am convinced that the people of Lower Canada have no such opinion and no such fear. In speaking the other day on that subject, the honorable member for Hochelaga (HON. MR. DORION) quoted from a speech of mine delivered in Toronto a few days before this session commenced; and I do not think the hon. gentleman shewed his usual candor or fairness in making the representation he did. He represented me as having stated at that meeting, that I had abandoned representation by population, as a thing that was not advisable, or possible, or something of that sort. Now what I did say was this: –

Having taken some part in public affairs, he (MR. MACKENZIE) *had long felt it would be almost impossible, by representation by population, to obtain to the full extent the justice that Upper Canada should receive with a legislative union as the basis of our power.*

Hon. Mr. Brown – Hear, hear!

Mr. A. Mackenzie – . . . *There was one element, however, which always entered largely into the discussion of all our national questions, and that was that the French people were a people entirely different from ourselves in origin, and largely in feeling. We all had a certain pride in our native country, and gloried in the deeds of our ancestors.*

The French people had that feeling quite as strongly as any of us; for this reason, and also because they were a conquered people, they felt it necessary to maintain a strong national spirit, and to resist all attempts to procure justice by the people of the west, lest that national existence should be broken down. He (MR. MACKENZIE) *felt for one that mere representation by population, under such circumstances, would perhaps scarcely meet the expectations formed of it, because although Upper Canada would have seventeen more members than Lower Canada, it would be an easy thing for the fifty or fifty-five members representing French constituencies to unite with a minority from Upper Canada, and thus secure an Administration subservient to their views.*

These were the sentiments that I uttered at that meeting, and the sentiments to which I am prepared now to give utterance again. (Hear, hear.) I believe that that feeling of nationality has been our sole difficulty, in working our present political system. But I do not believe for one moment that it would be possible or perhaps desirable to extinguish that strong feeling of nationality. Break down that feeling and all patriotism will be broken down with it. (Hear, hear.) I do not think it would be fair, or kind, or honorable, to attempt to do so. . . .

At the time of the formation of the MACDONALD-SICOTTE Government, I was; with many others, strongly blamed, because we allowed that Government to come into existence at all. It is quite possible we were wrong, but I think after all it was fortunate that the hon. member for Cornwall (HON. J.S. MACDONALD) had a fair opportunity to try his favorite remedy for our constitutional difficulties – the "double majority principle." That principle had been pressed on the attention of the country for ten years as one amply sufficient as a remedial measure, under which the existing political system could be harmoniously worked. In the MACDONALD-SICOTTE Government it had a fair trial and a speedy death. (Hear, hear, and laughter.) The existence of that Government, if it served no other purpose, showed the utter impracticability of the one means, by which my hon. friend hoped to accomplish what he, in common with ourselves, had long aimed at. . . .

One of the objections urged by the opponents of the measure is, that it is being hurried through too fast – that in a matter of so much importance to present and future generations, more time for consideration should be given. We have been discussing this question for many years in Canada West. Since the Toronto Convention of 1859, the question has been continuously before the people. It is now nearly a year since it was proposed in something like its present shape in this House, and since that time the whole of our newspapers have been writing upon it continually. We have nearly 300 newspapers in the country – and they have been carrying on a constant argument for or against the scheme, until I do not think it is possible to say or write much more upon the subject with any advantage. If the question is not now fully understood, I fear it will not be much better understood by any delay that can be now accorded. (Hear, hear.) . . .

FRIDAY / FEBRUARY 24, 1865.

William McGiverin [Lincoln]:

. . . The honorable member for North Ontario (MR. M.C. CAMERON) has stated, that while he is an advocate of union, he believed that a Legislative would be preferable to a Federal union. It is easy for honourable members to make that assertion. There are few, at least, of the English-speaking of this country who would not also be favorable to the principle of a legislative union. But can we get it? We have tried year after year to obtain representation by population, with a view to bettering our condition in the western section of the province, by getting a fair and equal distribution of the public moneys of the country, according to our wealth and population, and the measure in which we contribute to the public revenue. . . . The honorable member for North Ontario favors a kind of union which, though desirable in many respects, most people believe to be impracticable. Are the French population, who are entitled to claim just and equal rights, willing to concede it? I believe not. Even the Liberal section of Lower Canada refused to concede to us a fair legislative union. The honorable member for Hochelaga – a gentleman for whom I entertain the highest respect – I believe a more liberal or high-minded man does not sit in this House – even he, whilst we were acting with him politically, when appealed to time after time to join with the Liberal section of Upper Canada in some policy that would remove these unfortunate difficulties, constantly refused to do so, and told us it was impossible for him and his friends to meet us on that ground. Therefore, when at the close of last session, the people of Upper Canada were met, as they were met, by the other political party of Lower Canada, telling us – "Here, we are willing to yield you what you desire, only instead of conceding representation by population pure and simple, we believe a Confederation of the whole British North American Provinces, with that principle recognised in the General Government, would be preferable; or, failing that, we are willing to have a Federation of the two provinces of Canada," – when that was offered us, would we have been justified in rejecting it, simply because in accepting it we were compelled for the time to allow party feelings to remain in abeyance, or because we had to work in harmony for a time with the men to whom we had been opposed politically, whom perhaps in time past we had strongly denounced? Should we, when offered that for which we, as a party and as a people, had worked and agitated year after year, have refused it, simply because it was not offered by those with whom we had hitherto acted politically? (Hear, hear.) I for one felt – whatever opinions any might entertain of my conduct – I felt that, as an Upper Canadian and in justice to my country, I was bound to set aside party feeling and take that course which was for the best interests of our common country. (Hear, hear.) . . .

MONDAY / FEBRUARY 27, 1865.

Christopher Dunkin [Brome]:

MR. SPEAKER, almost everyone who has yet spoken in this debate has begun with some expression of his feeling of embarrassment. For my part, I should be glad if I could begin in some other way, but I confess that I cannot. For I certainly never did rise to address this House, or any other public body, under a feeling of such oppressive embarrassment as I experience at this moment. It is impossible for me, occupying the position in which I now stand, not to feel that I am opposed to powerful odds, and that there is a sort of foregone conclusion, here, against the views I desire to impress upon the House. It is impossible for me not to feel that the considerations to which I have to ask the attention of the House, are so many and so complex, that no sort of justice can possibly be done them within the limits of my capacity to speak, or of yours to listen. The interests at stake, too, are so large – so much larger than ever were at stake in any question which has yet been brought under the notice of this House, and the difficulties arising out of the question are so formidable owing in no small measure to what I must call the many reticences with which this scheme has been laid before us, and the ambiguities of expression which everywhere characterize it, as to tax seriously the courage of those who may attempt to discuss it. I feel, besides, that I am entirely cut off from that description of remark which most of all tends to make one's speech pleasant to listen to; for I cannot prophesy smooth things, or dilate on the marvels of progress to result from Confederation in the future. There is a character of hurry, too, impressed on the whole style of this debate; everybody feels so impatient, that one can scarcely hope to express his views fully, as he would wish and ought, on this vast scheme. I have even the feeling that my capacity for exertion is not up to its ordinary standard. I address the House in a state of health that renders me less capable than usual of physical exertions. I must, therefore, beg honorable members to make allowance for these circumstances surrounding my position; believing me that what I wish to do is to present as briefly as I can, and as truthfully as I can, my own deep seated convictions on the question now before the House. (Hear, hear.) . . .

I freely admit and sincerely maintain that it ought not to be discussed otherwise than as a great question, to be considered entirely on a large view of its merits. It is not a question of party, it is not a question of persons, it is not a question of merely local, or class, or passing interest, and it is not to be met by any of those passing appeals which are too often resorted to. It is not to be settled upon any ground of mere theory, or by any criticism of mere details. It requires indeed to be taken up at once as a question of principle, and also as a question of detail, involving a multitude of details; and there must necessarily be a careful criticism of such details. The question really presented is this: on the whole, viewing them collectively, are the details involved in this great scheme such as to commend the scheme itself to our approbation, or are they not? (Hear, hear.) I pledge myself that I will discuss the question from that point of view. I will do my utmost to avoid mere passing or personal allusions. I will try to tread the dangerous ground before me without arousing dangerous feelings. I do not know that I can succeed, but at least I will make the effort. This, however, I am bound to repeat at the outset, that no one can do justice to a question like this, and start with the idea of at all ignoring details. Here is a measure proposed for our acceptance, embodied in seventy-two resolutions, and which resolutions affirm a great many more than seventy-two propositions, connected with almost every principle known to have reference to the theory and practice of popular government. I say it is a scheme which is as complex and as vast as one can well imagine, and declamation about first principles can be of no real use in its discussion – can avail only to mislead in reference to it. We have to deal with no mere abstract question of a nationality, or of union or disunion, or of a Federal as opposed to a Legislative union. It is idle to talk vaguely about the maintenance of British connection, or to go into magnificent speculations about the probable results of independence, or blindly to urge this scheme as a sure preventative of annexation to the United States. These cheap and easy generalities are thoroughly unreliable. The only question is, how is this plan, in its entirety, going to work? And this question is one which is not easy to answer; it is one requiring much patience, and a close examination of details. It is the question which, if the House will lend me its attention, I will endeavor to discuss to the extent of my ability. (Hear, hear.) I may further take leave to say at starting, that I do not approach this question from any new point of view whatever. Always I have been, and now I am, a unionist in the strictest and largest sense of the term. I desire to perpetuate the union between Upper and Lower Canada. I desire to see developed, the largest union that can possibly be developed (I care not by what name you call it) between all the colonies, provinces, and dependencies of the British Crown. I desire to maintain that intimate union which ought to subsist, but which unfortunately does not subsist as it ought, between the Imperial Government and all those dependencies. I am a unionist, who especially does not desire to see the provinces of Upper and Lower Canada disunited. To my mind, this scheme does not at all present itself as one of union; and if hon. gentlemen opposite will admit the truth, they will acknowledge that, practically, it amounts to a disunion between Upper and Lower Canada. (Hear, hear.) I confess that I am irreconcilably opposed to that portion of the scheme. . . .

If I could be astonished at anything in politics, MR. SPEAKER, I should be astonished at the attempt which has been made by some honorable gentlemen on the Treasury benches to represent the state of the public feeling on this subject as not having that mere sudden, sensational, unreliable character which I have ascribed to it. Long forgotten expressions of individual opinion; clauses said to have formed part of bills not to be found, and not known to have been even drawn; motions threatened but never made, the small party fencings of past times, from before the days of the Canada Trade Act downwards, have been pressed into service to meet the exigencies of a hard case. Well, I shall not follow out that line of argument: it is not worth while. We all know that, from the time of the union of Canada, at all events, until very lately indeed, nothing like serious discussion of the propriety or impropriety of a Federal union, or of any union at all, of the aggregate of these British American Provinces, has ever so little occupied the public mind. I will here go back merely to 1858, when the sixth Parliament was elected, and from that time bring under review, as rapidly as I can, such few points of our political history as are relevant to shew that this is the fact; although, indeed, argument to establish it is scarcely necessary. At the election of 1857–58, what really were the issues before the country? They can be easily stated. I take the *résumé*, in fact, from the announcements of the *Globe*, the organ of the great popular party of Upper Canada at that time; mentioning not everything, but everything at all material. The great demand of the then Upper Canada

Opposition, which gave the key-note to the whole political controversies of the time, was representation according to population, irrespectively of the dividing line between Upper and Lower Canada. That was urged as involving everything. It was urged for the sake of all the rest, and as sure to bring about all the rest, that was demanded by the party. It was to enable them to carry out their opposition to what were called sectarian grants, their opposition to the holding of land in mortmain for sectarian uses, their opposition to separate schools on a sectarian basis. It was urged for the avowed purpose of obtaining uniform legislation in the future for the two sections of the province, and also what was spoken of as the assimilation of the existing institutions of the two sections of the province, but which was meant to be an assimilation of those of Lower Canada to those of Upper Canada much more than of those of Upper Canada to those of Lower Canada. (Hear, hear.) It was urged with the view of obtaining what was called free-trade, that is, an anti-Lower Canadian commercial policy. It was urged with the view of obtaining the settlement of the North-West; in other words, the relative aggrandizement of Upper Canada. It was urged, also, no doubt, with the view of obtaining what was called administrative reform – the driving from power of a set of men who were alleged, for various reasons, to be unworthy of holding it. But the great questions of measures above alluded to came first; those as to the mere men, second. (Hear, hear.) The grand object was declared to be to obtain an Upper Canadian preponderance of representation on the floor of this House, in order to put an end to everything like sectarian grants, the holding of lands in mortmain and separate schools, to render uniform our legislation, to assimilate our institutions, to carry out an anti-Lower Canadian commercial policy, and to secure the North-West for the aggrandizement of Upper Canada. In this way the question of Upper Canada against Lower Canada was unmistakably raised. What must have been, what could not fail to be, the result of an appeal of that kind? It was easy to foresee that there would be returned in Upper Canada a majority in favor of these demands, and in Lower Canada an overwhelming majority against them. I do not go into this to raise the ghost of past animosities; I am merely showing what cannot be denied – that no one at that time spoke of or cared for this magnificent idea of the union of the provinces, by Confederation or otherwise. (Hear, hear.) The session [of 1858] commenced. Those who had the advantage or disadvantage of sitting in that Parliament that session will remember the tremendous contrast there was between all those debates which had reference to this class of subjects, and the one single debate which was attempted, but could not be made to take place, on the question of the Confederation of the provinces. With all his ability – and there are few abler men than the hon. gentleman [A.T. GALT (Sherbrooke)] who undertook at that time to bring that question before the House – with all his ability, and the most earnest effort on his part to press it on the attention of the House, he could scarcely obtain a hearing. No one cared for the matter; and it was felt by everyone that such was the case. Soon after, a ministerial crisis took place. A new government came in for a few hours, and started a policy. But that policy, again, was not this policy. It did not touch this question. (Hear, hear.) It was proposed, indeed, to deal with that question of representation, by population by applying some system of checks or guarantees, doing or trying to do something that might lessen the objection of Lower Canada to a change urged forward as that had been. But that was all. That government fell – fell instantly – and another was formed in its place. And the present Finance Minister, the honorable member for Sherbrooke, who, with all his ability, had not been able to obtain a serious hearing for his proposal of Confederation of provinces, going into the new government, induced his colleagues to come before the House and the country, with that as a professed portion of their policy. I may be pardoned, perhaps, for a single word here of personal reference, for saying, *en passant*, that when that idea was thus broached (as it was by a Government of which I was as firm a supporter as any man in the House), I did not fail to make it known, that if ever it should be presented to the House as a practical measure by that Government, I should cease to be (so far as it was concerned) one of such supporters. (Hear, hear.) That was not the first time I had thought of it. It had long before been a matter of study with me; and all the anxious reflection I have ever been able to give it, has only had the result of strengthening my convictions against it every day. But how was this idea then brought forward? Tentatively, and just to neutralize the scheme which the BROWN-DORION Administration had hinted to the country. The one fire was to burn out another's burning. (Hear, hear.) The plan of that Government was to make propositions to the Imperial Government and to the governments of the Lower Provinces. But how? If you want to gain an object, you put that object before those to whom you propose it in the way most likely to induce them to say yes. This scheme was suggested to the Imperial Government, and to the people and governments of the Lower Provinces, precisely in the way most calculated to induce them to say no. We went and told them, "We are in such a state of embarrassment, we have political questions which so trouble and bother us, that we do not know if we can get along at all, unless you will be so kind as to come into this union with us." (Hear, hear.) It was just as though I were in business, and went round to half a dozen capitalists, telling them, "I have got into debt; my business is gone to the dogs; I have no business capacity; help me by going into partnership with me, or I am ruined." (Hear, hear.) If the object had been not to carry it, it does appear to me that those gentlemen could not have taken a better method of accomplishing that object. And we saw this – that just so soon as it was found that the Lower Provinces did not, as under the circumstances they could not, say yes to a proposal of this kind, and that the Imperial Government let the matter drop, our Administration let it drop too. We never heard another word about it. The despatches were laid on our table in 1859, but nobody asked a question about them. The child was still-born, and no one troubled himself about its want of baptism. We went on with our old questions – representation by population; Upper Canada against Lower Canada; measures, to a great extent; men also, to a great and increasing extent. And we quarrelled and fought about almost everything, but did not waste a thought or word upon this gigantic question of the Confederation of these provinces. (Hear, hear.) In a little while we drifted into another crisis – that of 1862. And from the time of that crisis, and the formation of the MACDONALD-SICOTTE Administration, down to the time when the present Administration was, last summer, brought into its present shape, the one prominent demand made upon political parties and political men everywhere was, to set aside the older questions of measures, and occupy ourselves very much more – not to say exclusively – with the question of men. (Hear, hear.) I am not blaming honorable gentlemen; I am not raising the question whether they were right or wrong in taking that course. They may have been the purest patriots, the most farseeing statesmen the world has known, for aught I care. What I say is merely this, that whether for good or evil, whether wisely or unwisely, the fact is, that the public mind was not occupied in the least with this Confederation question. After having fought a long time, mainly about measures, and secondarily about men, we were all suddenly called upon, in 1862, to consider nothing but the question of the men who were to do everything right, and to settle everything fairly and honestly, and so forth. Representation by population was unmistakably, for a time at least, laid upon the shelf, declared to be secondary, almost unimportant. It had been half shelved some time before; then, it was wholly shelved. It was hardly taken down from the shelf in 1863, when the MACDONALD-DORION Government merely put it back to the same place, which it had long occupied to no purpose of a practical character under the CARTIER-MACDONALD Administration. (Hear, hear.) Such, then, was the state of affairs – nobody thinking or caring about this great question, until last session of Parliament, when the hon. member for South Oxford, the present President of the Council, moved for and obtained a committee on the subject of constitutional changes generally. Certainly that hon. gentleman did a very clever thing, in embodying in his motion extracts from the unfortunate defunct despatch of MESSRS. CARTIER, GALT and ROSS.

Hon. Atty. Gen. Cartier – It was a fortunate despatch – unfortunate for you, but fortunate for us.

Mr. Dunkin – It is an old proverb that says "He laughs well who laughs last."

Hon. Atty. Gen. Cartier – I expect to laugh the last.

Mr. Dunkin – No doubt. But I do not care to joke in a matter which I think of a very serious character; and, seriously speaking, I think the hon. gentleman is very wrong. We have yet to see, in the first place, whether the thing is done, and then, if it is done, whether it succeeds.

Hon. Mr. McGee – "If 'twere done, 'twere well 'twere done quickly."

Mr. Dunkin – The Minister of Agriculture is too good a Shakespearian to need to be reminded that the thing to be done in that case was a something very bad. The hon. gentleman is welcome to all he can make of his quotation, – "If 'twere done when 'tis done, then 'twere well it were done quickly." To return, however. It was clever, undoubtedly clever, in the hon. member for South Oxford to quote from the despatch of these hon. gentlemen – then, by the way, in opposition to the then Government and to himself – an expression of opinion almost coinciding with his own. He carried his committee. No one made any great objection to it. I have been told that I am guilty of some sort of inconsistency, after having voted for that committee, in now opposing this measure. The *sequitur* is hard to see. I did certainly speak and vote for it, but on the express ground that I believed it would do no sort of harm, and that, on the contrary, it might have the good effect of leading other hon. gentlemen to the sober conclusion at which I had long before arrived myself. I therefore had no objection to the committee, and I sat on it. I am not going to reveal what have been called the secrets of the committee. As in many other like cases, there was mighty little in them. Owing to accidents, wholly aside from this question of Confederation, the report of the committee was presented on the very night that vote happened to be given, indirectly adverse to the TACHÉ-MACDONALD Administration. The report itself was an accident. All the allusion there was in it to Federation of any sort, found its way there at the last moment and unexpectedly. It is no violation of confidence to say that it was even voted against by the leader of this House, the Attorney General for Upper Canada, the now leading advocate of the present scheme. That fact is on the printed record. It was voted against, also, by the members for Cornwall [HON. J.S. MACDONALD] and West Elgin [JOHN SCOBLE]. There were five other members, of whom I am sorry I was one, who were absent; had I been there, unquestionably my vote would have been against it. (Hear, hear.) And, MR. SPEAKER, those who were in this House at the time that report was made, will remember pretty well the more than cool indifference with which it was here received, little or nothing, after all, as it amounted to. Well, this vote in the House thus following, the opportunity suddenly offered to honorable gentlemen opposite of starting on a tack which, up to that moment, I believe no two men in the House had ever thought of as possible. And from that day to this, a series of accidents, each one more extraordinary than its predecessor, has led to a state of things about as extraordinary as the accidents themselves were. (Laughter.)

Hon. Atty. Gen. Cartier – It is said the world was made by a series of accidents.

Mr. Dunkin – I dare say some people think so; and it may be so according to the theology of my hon. friend, but not according to mine. . . .

And now what have we? Why, the cry that the whole thing must be passed, "now or never." It will never pass, we are told, if it does not pass now! (Hear, hear.) Was there ever a measure of this magnitude before, on which the heart of a country was set, the whole of which was so wise and good as this scheme is said to be – and yet, that had to be passed (the whole of it) at once, or never? (Hear, hear.) We are even told that it is a positive treaty – made however, by the way, by parties who were never authorized to make any treaty at all. I must say, for one, that I cannot but see in all this precipitancy the unmistakable admission *de facto*, that the Government themselves know and feel that the feeling they have got up in favor of this scheme is a passing feeling of momentary duration, that they cannot themselves in the least rely upon. (Hear, hear.) MR. SPEAKER, it is rather curious that hon. gentlemen, in recommending this scheme of theirs, seem never to be tired of speaking of its excellences in general, and of modestly eulogizing the wisdom, and foresight, and statesmanship of those who got it up. I cannot wonder that their judgment in this behalf should be a little led astray by their surprise at the success which has so far attended their project. Their "officious" visit to Prince Edward Island took but a very few days, and it resulted in the scheme of a legislative union for the Lower Provinces being (as I think, unfortunately) laid aside; and then followed the Conference at Quebec, where these twelve honorable gentlemen representing Canada, and twenty-one other gentlemen representing the Lower Provinces, sat together for the long period of nineteen days – seventeen working days and two Sundays – and as the result of these seventeen days of but partial work by the way, we have from these thirty-three gentlemen a scheme of a Constitution which they vaunt of as being altogether better than that of the model republic of the United States, and even than that of the model kingdom of Great Britain. Neither the model republic nor yet the model kingdom of whose glorious traditions and associations we are all so proud, is for a moment to be compared with this work of theirs. (Hear, hear.) So perfect do they seem to regard their pet measure, that they tell us we must not take time to discuss it. . . .

Surely, MR. SPEAKER, this Legislative Council, constituted so differently from the Senate of the United States, presided over by a functionary to be nominated by the General Government; having no such functions of a judicial or executive character as attached to that body, and cut off from that minute oversight of the finances which attaches to the Senate of the United States; although it may be a first-rate deadlock; although it may be able to interpose an absolute veto, for no one can say how long, on all legislation, would be no Federal check at all. I believe it to be a very near approach to the worst system which could be devised in legislation. While the Senate of the United States is nearly perfect in the one way, our Legislative Council is to be as nearly perfect in the other way. (Laughter.) The Hon. Attorney General for Upper Canada, the other night, devised and stated just the cleverest defence he could, of this constitution of the Legislative Council. But what did it amount to? Nothing. He undertook to tell us, that from the ordinary course of events, the deaths to be counted on in a body numbering its certain proportion of elderly men, and so forth, the personal composition of this Council would not change so slowly as many feared. He also urged that those who thus found their way into it would be but men after all – perhaps politicians a little or more than a little given to complaisance – but at any rate men, who would know they had no great personal hold on public confidence; and so, that they might sometimes even yield to pressure too easily, in place of resisting it too much. Well, sir, I have heard it said that every government in the world is in a certain sense a constitutional government – a government, that is to say, tempered by check of some kind. The despotism of the Grand Turk has been said to have its constitutional check in a salutary fear of the bow-string; and there may prove to be something of the same sort here. But I confess I do not like the quasi-despotism of this Legislative Council, even though so tempered. Representing no public opinion or real power of any kind, it may hurt the less; but it can never tend to good, and it can never last. It is satisfactory for one to find that in this view I do not stand alone. This plan is condemned, not simply by the Colonial Secretary, but by the Imperial Government, as one which cannot be carried out. The Imperial authorities cannot but see that a body appointed for life and limited in numbers, is just the worst body that could be contrived – ridiculously the worst.

Hon. Atty. Gen. Cartier – Do they say it is the worst?

Mr. Dunkin – I say it is the worst. They say it is bad. It is condemned by Her Majesty's Government, in diplomatic terms it may be, but in sufficiently emphatic terms. I believe Her Majesty's Government regard it as I do – as pretty nonsensical. I know it may be said that Her Majesty's Government, perhaps, may apply a remedy by leaving out the provision about a limited number of members.

Hon. Atty. Gen. Cartier – That is our security.

Mr. Dunkin – Security it is none, but the very contrary. . . .

I have to ask honorable gentlemen opposite how they are going to organize their Cabinet, for these provinces, according to this so called Federal scheme? (Hear, hear.) I think I may defy them to shew that the Cabinet can be formed on any other principle than that of a representation of the several provinces in that Cabinet. It is admitted that the provinces are not really represented to any Federal intent in the Legislative Council. The Cabinet here must discharge all that kind of function, which in the United States is performed, in the Federal sense, by the Senate. . . . With us, as at home, the Constitution makes the whole Ministry, collectively, responsible for all the acts it performs; but it is well known that here, for all practical purposes, we have for years had our Ministry acting by two sections – each section with a chief of its own, to a large extent a policy of its own, and the responsibility of leading and governing a section of this House of its own. (Hear, hear.) We have been federalising our Constitution after a very new and anomalous fashion ever since 1848, and by that, more than by anything else, having been getting ourselves into that sort of difficulty in which we have latterly found ourselves. (Hear, hear.) And now, MR. SPEAKER, I just want to know how this proposed scheme is going to work in this respect? . . .

Hon. Atty. Gen. Cartier – There will be no difficulty.

Mr. Dunkin – The hon. gentleman never sees a difficulty in anything he is going to do.

Hon. Atty. Gen. Cartier – And I have been generally pretty correct in that. I have been pretty successful. (Hear, hear.)

Mr. Dunkin – Pretty successful in some things – not so very successful in some others. The hon. gentleman has been a good deal favored by accident. But I am not quite certain that I believe in the absolute omniscience of anybody. (Hear, hear.) But now, if this Executive Council is to have in it, as I am sure it must have, in order to work at all, a representation of the different provinces, all or nearly all of them, let us look for a moment at what will have to be its number. There are two ways of calculating this – two sets of *data* on which to go. Either we must go upon what I may call the wants of the component parts, or we may start from the wants of the country as a whole. Suppose, then, we start from the wants of the different provinces. I take it that no section of the Confederation can well have less than one representative in the Cabinet. Prince Edward Island will want one; Newfoundland, one. A difficulty presents itself with regard to Lower Canada. On just the same principle upon which Lower Canada wants, for Federal ends, to have a proper representation in the Executive Council, on that same principle the minority populations in Lower Canada will each want, and reasonably want, the same thing. We have three populations in Lower Canada – the French Canadians, the Irish Catholics, and the British Protestants. In other words, there are the Catholics, and the non-Catholics, and the English speaking and the non-English-speaking, and these two crosslines of division cut our people into the three divisions I have just indicated. Well, if in a government of this Federal kind the different populations of Lower Canada are to feel that justice is done them, none of them are to be there ignored. The consequences of ignoring them might not be very comfortable. Heretofore, according to general usage, the normal amount of representation for Lower Canada in the Executive Council has been six seats out of twelve. Of those, four may be said legitimately to belong to the French Canadians, one to the Irish Catholics, and one to the British Protestant class. Everyone is satisfied that that is about the fairest thing that can be done. There have been times when these proportions have varied. There have been exceptional times when the British Protestant population has had to put up with a Solicitor-General out of the Cabinet, and has done so with no very loud complaint. There has never been a time, I think, when there was not an Irish Catholic in the Cabinet. There have been times when the number of French Canadians has been less than four, and there was then much complaint. Six members – four, one and one – are just about what you must give to please each section of Lower Canada. Well, sir, if there are to be six for Lower Canada, there must be six or seven for Upper Canada, and you cannot very well leave less than three each for Nova Scotia and New Brunswick, and, as I have said, one each for Newfoundland and Prince Edward Island; and thus you have an Executive Council of twenty or twenty-one members, besides all we might have to add for other provinces; and this, I rather think, is a little too many. The thing could not be done; for so large a Cabinet could never work. Suppose then, on the other hand, that we start with the idea of limiting the number of our Executive Council to meet what I may call the exigencies of the country as a whole. Eleven, twelve or thirteen – the latter, as an hon. member observes, is an unlucky number – will be as many as we can possibly allow. Of this number one, as before, will be wanted for Newfoundland and one for Prince Edward Island. If one is wanted for each of the little provinces, New Brunswick and Nova Scotia will be sorely discontented unless they get, at least, two apiece; and neither Lower Canada nor Upper Canada will be contented with the three left for each of them. And for Lower Canada, in particular, how will anyone divide this intractable figure between her French, Irish and British? Shall we give them one apiece, and ask the French-Canadian element to be content with one voice in a cabinet of a dozen? – or, give that element two, without satisfying it – so leaving out either the Irish or the British, to its intense disgust? – or, give the preponderating element the whole, to the intense disgust of both the others? It will be none too easy a task, sir, I think, to form an Executive Council with its three members for Lower Canada, and satisfy the somewhat pressing exigencies of her creeds and races.

Hon. Atty. Gen. Cartier – Hear! hear!

Mr. Dunkin – The Hon. Attorney General East probably thinks he will be able to do it.

Hon. Atty. Gen. Cartier – I have no doubt I can. (Laughter.) . . .

Mr. Dunkin – SIDNEY SMITH once said of a leading Cabinet minister at home, that he would be willing at the shortest notice, either to undertake the duties of the Archbishop of Canterbury or to assume command of the Channel fleet. (Laughter.) We have some public men in this country who, in their own judgment, have ample capacity for assuming the responsibility and discharging the functions of those two high posts, and perhaps of a field marshal or commander-in-chief besides. (Renewed laughter.)

Hon. Atty. Gen. Cartier – I would say, that although I do not feel equal to the task of commanding the Channel fleet or filling the office of Archbishop of Canterbury, I do feel equal to the work of forming an Executive Council that will be satisfactory to Upper and Lower Canada, as well as to the Lower Provinces. (Hear, hear, and laughter.)

Mr. Dunkin – Well, it will require, in my opinion, something more than bold assertion, and capacity for a hearty laugh, to overcome the difficulty that will some day or other be presented. (Hear, hear.). . .

But now, sir, what is the system we are going to adopt according to these resolutions? What are the relations to be established between our general and local governments? We are told to take for granted that no clashing of interest or feeling need be feared; that the Federal union offered us in name will be a Legislative union in reality. Yet, whoever dislikes the notion of a Legislative union is assured it will be nothing of the sort. Now, sir, I do not believe that you can have all the advantages of these two systems combined in one. (Hear, hear.) A Legislative union is one thing; a Federal union is another. The same system cannot be both at once. You cannot devise a system that shall have all the advantages of the one and of the other; but it is quite possible that you may devise one that will combine the chief disadvantages of both, and that is, I fear, pretty much what this system does. (Hear, hear.). . .

To be sure there is the grand power of disallowance by the Federal Government, which we are told, in one and the same breath, is to be possessed by it, but never exercised.

Hon. Atty. Gen. Cartier – The presumption is, it will be exercised in case of unjust or unwise legislation.

Mr. Dunkin – The hon. gentleman's presumption reminds me of one, perhaps as conclusive, but which DICKENS tells us failed to satisfy his MR. BUMBLE. That hen-pecked beadle is said to have said, on hearing of the legal presumption that a man's wife acts under his control: – "If the law presumes anything of the sort, the law's a fool – a natural fool!" (Laughter.) If this permission of disallowance rests on a presumption that the legislation of our provinces is going to be unjust or unwise, it may be needed; but under that idea, one might have done better either not to allow, or else to restrict within narrower limits, such legislation. If the promised non-exercise of the power to disallow rests on a presumption that all will be done justly and wisely in the provincial legislatures, the legislative power is well given; but then there is no need, on the other hand, for the permission to disallow. (Hear, hear.)...

Well, MR. SPEAKER, undoubtedly, before the union, Lower Canada, as I have said, was the place where the war of races was at its height; and that war of races did not nearly cease for a number of years after. But the strife did very gradually lessen, and a better and more friendly feeling has for some time prevailed, in both camps. Indeed, there has been a more tolerant state of feeling in both camps, than in any other community so divided as to race and creed, that I know of. But the moment you tell Lower Canada that the large-sounding powers of your General Government are going to be handed over to a British-American majority, decidedly not of the race and faith of her majority, that moment you wake up the old jealousies and hostility in their strongest form. By the very provisions you talk of for the protection of the non-French and non-Catholic interests, you unfortunately countenance the idea that the French are going to be more unfair than I believe they wish to be. For that matter, what else can they well be? They will find themselves a minority in the General Legislature, and their power in the General Government will depend upon their power within their own province and over their provincial delegations in the Federal Parliament. They will thus be compelled to be practically aggressive, to secure and retain that power. They may not, perhaps, wish to be; they may not, perhaps, be aggressive in the worst sense of the term. – I do not say that they certainly will be; but whether they are or not, there will certainly be in this system the very strongest tendencies to make them practically aggressive upon the rights of the minority in language and faith, and at the same time to make the minority most suspicious and resentful of aggression. The same sort of alienation, as between the two faiths, will be going on in Upper Canada. Note of warning is already given by this scheme, to both parties, that they prepare for fight; and the indications, I regret to say, are that such note of warning is not to be given in vain. (Hear, hear.) The prejudices of the two camps are once more stirred to their depths; and if this scheme goes into operation, they will separate more and more widely, and finally break out into open war, unless, indeed, it shall work very differently from what anyone can now imagine. . . .

TUESDAY / FEBRUARY 28, 1865.

Christopher Dunkin (continued);

. . . But I have to turn now, MR. SPEAKER, to another branch of my comparison – the financial; and here, I may at once give the House an assurance, which I am sure it will be glad to have, that I will not trouble it with more figures than are absolutely necessary to my explanation of the views I have to present, and that I will not give a single figure as to which there can be the possibility of a controversy. The contrast between the financial system as a whole, with which the framers of the United States Constitution started, and the financial system with which it is proposed we shall start, is as salient as it is possible for the human intellect to conceive; and further the contrast between this proposed financial system, and the financial system of England, is just as salient too. The framers of the United States Constitution started with the principle, that between the United States and the several states there should be no financial dealings at all. They were to have separate financial systems, separate treasuries, separate debts – all absolutely distinct. And ever since the time when the unhappy attempt on the part of Great Britain to tax the colonies was given up, almost as absolute a line of demarcation between the Imperial finances and treasury and the colonial finances and treasuries, has been maintained. We have had our own separate finances and our own separate treasury, with which the Imperial Government has had nothing to do. The Imperial Government may have gone, and may still go, to some expense on provincial behalf; but the British principle is, that Imperial finance is as distinct from the provincial, as in the United States Federal finance is from that of any state. Now, the system proposed here for our adoption is not this of entire and simple separation of the federal from the provincial treasuries, but a system of the most entire and complex confusion between them. One has to think a good deal upon the subject, and to study it pretty closely to see precisely how the confusion is going to operate; but there it is, unmistakably, at every turn. I do not mean to say that under all the circumstances of the case something of this sort was not unavoidable. In the course of debate the other day, I remember a remark was thrown across the floor of the House upon this point and the Hon. Minister of Finance in effect said: "Yes, indeed, and it would have been a very pleasant thing for gentlemen opposed to the scheme, if it had thrown upon the provinces a necessity of resorting to direct taxation." Of course, in the mere view of making the scheme palatable, it was clever to make the Federal treasury pay for provincial expenditure; but the system that had need be established should bear testimony, not to cleverness, but to wisdom. . . .

But for all this part of the plan, sir, it is like the rest, framed on the mere idea of making things pleasant – the politician idea of anyhow winning over interests or parties for to-day – not on any statesmanlike thought as to its future working and effects. (Hear, hear.) . . .

But there is another result, about which there can be no question. With one accord, not in Newfoundland merely – I was hinting a little while ago at what would be the case of Newfoundland, as to its lands, mines and minerals – not there only, but in the all provinces – the provincial governments will, in a quiet way, want money, and the provincial legislators and people will want it yet more; grants for roads and bridges, for schools, for charities, for salaries, for contingencies of the legislative body – for all manner of ends they will be wanting money, and where is it to come from? Whether the constitution of the Provincial Executive savors at all of responsible government or not, be sure it will not be anxious to bring itself more under the control of the legislature, or to make itself more odious than it can help, and the easiest way for it to get money will be from the General Government. I am not sure, either, but that most members of the provincial legislatures will like it that way the best. (Hear, hear.) It will not be at all unpopular, the getting of money so. Quite the contrary. Gentlemen will go to their constituents with an easy conscience, telling them: 'True, we had not much to do in the Provincial Legislature, and you need not ask very closely what else we did; but I tell you what, we got the Federal Government to increase the subvention to our province by five cents a head, and see what this gives you – $500 to that road – $1000 to that charity – so much here, so much there. That we have done; and have we not done well?" (Hear, hear.) I am afraid in many constituencies the answer would be: "Yes, you have done well; go and do it again." I am afraid the provincial constituencies, legislatures and executives will all show a most calf-like appetite for the milking of this one most magnificent government cow. . . .

I am at last very near the close of the remarks I have to offer to the House; but I must say a few words as to the domestic consideration urged to force us into this scheme. We are asked, "What are you going to do? You must do something. Are you going back to our old state of dead-lock?" At the risk of falling into an unparliamentary expression, I cannot help saying that I am reminded of a paragraph I read the other day in a Lower [i.e., Maritime] Province paper, in which the editor was dealing with this same cry, which seems to be raised in Nova Scotia as well as here – the cry that something must be done, that things cannot go on as they are. I have not his words here, but their general effect was this – "Whenever," says he, "I hear this cry raised, that something must be done, I suspect there is a plan on foot to get something very bad done. Things are in a bad way – desperate, may be. But the remedy proposed is sure to be desperate. I am put in mind of a story of two boys who couldn't swim, but by ill luck had upset their canoe in deep water, and by good luck had got on the bottom of it. Says the big boy to the little one, 'Tom, can you pray?' Tom confessed he could not call to mind a prayer suited to the occasion. 'No, Bill,' says he, 'I don't know how.' Bill's answer was earnest, but not parliamentary. It contained a past participle passive which I won't repeat. It was, 'Well, something must be done – and that – soon!'" (Laughter.) Now, seriously, what do honorable gentlemen mean when they raise here this cry that "something must be done"? Is it seriously meant that our past is so bad that positively, on pain of political annihilation, of utter and hopeless ruin, of the last, worst consequences, we must this instant adopt just precisely this scheme? If that is so, if really and truly those political institutions which we were in the habit of saying we enjoyed, which, at all events, we have been living under and, for that matter, are living under now, if they have worked so ill as all that comes to, or rather if we have worked them so ill, I think we hold out poor encouragement to those whom we call upon to take part with us in trying this new experiment. We Canadians have had a legislative union and worked it close upon five-and-twenty years, and under it have got, it is said, into such a position of embarrassment among ourselves, are working our political institutions so very badly, are in such a frightful fix, that, never mind what the prospects of this particular step may be, it must positively be taken; we cannot help it, we cannot stay as we are, nor yet go back, nor yet go forward, in any course but just this one. (Hear, hear.) If this thing is really this last desperate remedy for a disease past praying for, then indeed I am desperately afraid, sir, that it will not succeed. The hot haste with which gentlemen are pressing it is of ill omen to the deceived Mother Country, to our deceived sister provinces, and to our most miserably deceived selves. But the truth is that we are in no such sad case; there is no fear of our having to go back to this bugbear past; we could not do it if we would. Things done cannot be undone. In a certain sense, whatever is past is irrevocable, and it is well it should be. True we are told by some of the honorable gentlemen on the Treasury benches that their present harmony is not peace, but only a sort of armed truce, that old party lines are not effaced, nor going to be. Well, sir, if so, suppose that this scheme should be ever so well dropped, and then that some day soon after these gentlemen should set themselves to the job of finding out who is cuckoo and who hedge-sparrow in the government nest that now shelters them all in such warm quiet, suppose there should thus soon be every effort made to revive old cries and feuds – what then? Would it be the old game over again, or a variation of it amounting to a new one? For a time at least, sir, a breathing time that happily cannot be got over, those old cries and old feuds will not be found to be revivable as of old. Even representation by population will be no such spell to conjure with – will fall on ears far less excitable. It has been adopted by any number of those who might otherwise be the likeliest to run it down. It will be found there might be a worse thing in the minds of many. Give it a new name and couple it with sufficient safeguard against legislation of the local stamp being put through against the vote of the local majority – the principle tacitly held so, and found to answer in the case of Scotland – and parliamentary reform may be found no such bugbear to speak of after all. And as for the bugbears of the personal kind, why, sir, after seeing all we have seen of the extent to which gentlemen can set aside or overcome them when occasion may require, it is too much to think they will for some little time go for so very much. Like it or not, honorable gentlemen, for a time, will have to be to some extent busy with a game that shall be not quite the old one. The friends of this project, MR. SPEAKER, never seem to tire of prophesying to us smooth things, if only it is once first adopted. To every criticism on its many and manifest defects, the ready answer is, that we do not enough count upon men's good sense, good feeling, forbearance, and all that sort of thing. But, sir, if the adoption of this scheme is so to improve our position, is to make everything so smooth, to make all our public men so wise, so prudent, and so conscientious, I should like to know why a something of the same kind may not by possibility be hoped for, even though this project should be set aside. If we are to be capable of the far harder task of working out these projected unworkable political institutions, why is it that we must be incapable of the easier task of going on without them? I know well that in all time the temper of those who do not think has been to put faith rather in the great thing one cannot do, than in the smaller thing one can. "If the prophet had bid thee do some great thing, wouldest thou not have done it?" And here too, sir, as so often before, if the truth must be told, the one thing truly needed is what one may call the smaller thing – not perhaps easy, but one must hope not impossible – the exercise by our public men and by our people of that amount of discretion, good temper and forbearance which sees something larger and higher in public life than mere party struggles and crises without end; of that political sagacity or capacity, call it which you will, with which they will surely find the institutions they have to be quite good enough for them to use and quietly make better, without which they will as surely find any that may anyhow be given them, to be quite bad enough for them to fight over and make worse. . . .

THURSDAY / MARCH 2, 1865.

Joseph Goderic Blanchet [Lévis]:

MR. SPEAKER, as no one is disposed to take the floor just now, and it would seem as if all who intend to discuss this question are bent on having a large audience in the galleries, I shall take upon me to say a few words. Those who moved to have the speeches of this House printed in official form certainly did no good service to the country; for all are trying which shall make the longest speech, and I do not think it is altogether just to the public purse. Each one would speak at a particular hour, and to the ears of a certain audience; but the history of the Parliament of England shews that her great statesmen and orators did not concern themselves about that. The greatest and most important speeches were delivered in the House of Commons at a very late hour of the night; thus FOX delivered his great speech on the East India Bill at two o'clock in the morning; PITT his on the abolition of the slave trade at four o'clock in the morning; and we should lose nothing by speaking before half-past seven in the evening. . . .

THURSDAY / MARCH 2, 1865.

Joseph Dufresne [Montcalm]:

MR. SPEAKER, I do not rise to speak on the question now before the House, but simply to express my surprise that after six weeks of discussion the Opposition pretend that we refuse them time to discuss the measure, and that nevertheless they refuse to discuss it during the afternoon sittings, and will only take it up in the evening. For my part, I am prepared to vote at once upon this matter, and I believe that the question is perfectly mastered and well understood by every member of this House. Why are the Opposition unwilling to speak during the afternoon sittings? Their object in speaking is to kill time, rather than to discuss the merits of the question. And why is this? Is it because they are waiting for a few more petitions, a few more names, in order to protest against Confederation? But we know the value of these petitions – we know what the *Rouges* are, and that they will sign any and every petition, provided it be against the Government and its policy. The Opposition is like a sulky child; if you refuse him a plaything he cries for it, and then if you offer it to him he refuses to take it. The Confederation is in reality the plan of those gentlemen themselves, and yet to-day they will not hear of it; they reject it as something horrible. . . .

THURSDAY / MARCH 2, 1865.

Hon. Joseph Cauchon [Montmorency]:

. . . when I myself have, elsewhere, at such considerable length and so completely developed, with the feeble abilities which Providence has conferred upon me, the considerations which militate for or against the entirety and the details of the work of the Quebec Conference, I might – perhaps I should – have remained a simple spectator of these solemn debates, while awaiting the hour at which I should be permitted to record my vote in accordance with my convictions. I considered, however, that as one of the oldest representatives of the people, after having spoken elsewhere, I should speak again within the parliamentary precinct, in order to accomplish to the letter my trust, and in order to obey that voice which has a right to command me. I have therefore come this evening in order to bring my feeble tribute of ideas to the decisive ordeal which is being accomplished. . . .

Mr. Joseph Perrault [Richelieu] – I rise to a question of order. We have listened with much pleasure to the excellent pamphlet which the honorable member has been reading out to us for half an hour past. I can understand that the honorable member having written a pamphlet in 1858 against Confederation, and another in 1865 in favor of Confederation, now feels the necessity of writing a third pamphlet to make the two others agree. But, as the honorable member for Montmorency possesses great powers of improvisation, the House, I think, ought not to be more indulgent to him than to other members, who are compelled to speak under all the disadvantages of improvisation, which is always difficult. I have, therefore, to ask whether the honorable member for Montmorency is in order in reading his magnificent speech from beginning to end?

Hon. Atty. Gen. Cartier – I see nothing extraordinary in this particular case. I see that my honorable friend the member for Montmorency has notes before him to which he refers, but I do not see any speech. The honorable member for Richelieu, with his eccentric genius, requires no notes when he makes those splendid speeches with which he regales us from time to time. I can easily understand that for such lucubrations no very lengthy preparation is necessary. (Laughter.)

Hon. Mr. Cauchon – Everyone has not the genius of the honorable member for Richelieu. I know also that he is one of those who can talk a long time, because they do not always know what they are saying. (Laughter.) The honorable member may talk as long as he likes, without being afraid of my interrupting him, for his speeches can do no harm except to the person who utters them. (Laughter.)

The Speaker said it was not exactly in order for an honorable member to read a speech quite through, but he might make use of notes.

Hon. Mr. Cauchon – . . . In the present day, parties disappear and become fused with others, while others arise from passing events. In New Brunswick, Conservatives join the Liberal government to carry Confederation, and we see no parties there but the partisans and the opponents of the union. . . . We see the same thing in Nova Scotia. This is true patriotism and the real dignity of public men. It is unfortunate for us that we do not follow their example here.

Mr. Geoffrion – Hear!

Hon. Mr. Cauchon – The honorable member from Verchères says "Hear!" Is it not a fact that the Opposition vote as a party on the present question? If it is not so, will he name a single member of the Opposition who does not vote against Confederation?

Hon. J.S. Macdonald – Hear! hear!

Hon. Mr. Cauchon – The honorable member for Cornwall says "Hear! hear." He may well say so – he who never had a party. He came into power, nobody expected he would. He will never get it again, everybody expects that. (Continued laughter.) . . .

FRIDAY / MARCH 3, 1865.

Joseph Xavier Perrault [Richelieu]:

... I say, MR. SPEAKER, that the scheme of Confederation is not expedient. But even if the scheme of Confederation was expedient, I maintain that the object of it is hostile. I gave an historical sketch of the encroaching spirit of the English race on the two continents. I pointed out the incessant antagonism existing between it and the French race. Our past recalled to us the constant struggle which we had to keep up in order to resist the aggression and the exclusiveness of the English element in Canada. It was only through heroic resistance and a happy combination of circumstances that we succeeded in obtaining the political rights which are secured to us by the present Constitution. The scheme of Confederation has no other object than to deprive us of the most precious of those rights, by substituting for them a political organization which is eminently hostile to us. . . .

FRIDAY / MARCH 3, 1865.

Col. Frederick W. Haultain [Peterborough]:

. . . Hon. gentlemen from Lower Canada, who have expressed an opinion that this question had ceased to be considered as of importance in the west, manifest a very great ignorance of the character, the feelings and the intentions of the men they had to deal with. My hon. friend from Brome [C. DUNKIN] was one of those who wished to make light of our present difficulties. He said, towards the close of his speech, that it only needed a little patience, that very little was wanted to make everything quite smooth. But, sir, even he was obliged to admit that a slight measure of parliamentary reform was necessary in order to remove the difficulties by which we were surrounded, and he evidently intimated his willingness to concede it. And there have been hints thrown out by certain Liberal members from Lower Canada that it would not be such an impossible thing, if we would give up this scheme of union, for Upper Canada to obtain her right position, and what she has so justly claimed. But if this be their feeling, I ask them why they did not come boldly out before and avow it? I would ask my hon. friend from Brome – and I regret extremely that he is not in his place – why did he not, in 1862, speak of concessions to Upper Canada, instead of, by vote and by argument, do his best to convince us that we could expect no relief from him and from those acting with him, from the same section. Very different language is now used by Lower Canada members of all shades of opinion, to that we have been accustomed to hear. Those who now admit the justice of the demands of Upper Canada, and yet in time past have resisted them, ought to be the last to oppose this scheme, which settles the difficulty on a basis accepted by all. The honorable member for Brome and the British members from Lower Canada, who resisted the reform asked for, ought to be foremost in supporting the scheme before us; and I am sorry to find that my hon. friend appears to me to occupy a very inconsistent position. Had he always advocated parliamentary reform, he might with consistency have opposed the proposed union. In some such position, and even in a stronger point of view, do the French Liberal members appear to be. They were the professed allies of the Reform party in Upper Canada, and were, of course, aware that no reform government could stand that did not deal with the representation question. Now, it appears to me, sir, that the Liberal French party have been singularly untrue to their Upper Canada allies –

Hon. Mr. Holton (ironically) – Hear! hear!

Col. Haultain – I repeat, sir, that the Liberal French members have pursued a course that if continued in, could only have terminated as it has done. . . .

It seemed to me that he [MR. DUNKIN] looked at everything relating to this question through a distorted medium. I listened with the greatest pleasure to the dissection the hon. gentleman made of these resolutions, and to the microscopic analysis to which he subjected the smallest part of their provisions. It shewed the great acuteness of his observation, as well as the large and extended information of his mind. But I could not help feeling that he was looking at this subject through the discolored lens of a powerfully miscroscopic mind. (Laughter.) I have no doubt whatever that this also was the impression made by his speech on other hon. gentlemen. His talents and his ability I fully recognize, and I have no doubt that every hon. gentleman listened, equally with myself, with pleasure to what I may call the excruciating dissection to which he submitted these important resolutions. (Hear, hear, and laughter.) But I must at the same time say that the result of all his analysis, and the summing up of all his observations, only proved to me that the ground on which the advocates of this scheme stand is well nigh immovable and unassailable, and convinced me of the smallness of the objections which have yet been urged against it. . . .

MONDAY / MARCH 6, 1865.

Hon. Atty. Gen. Macdonald:

Before the debate on the resolutions in your hands, MR. SPEAKER, is continued, I wish to say a few words. The Government is well aware that the House must naturally feel anxious and desirous of information – and that no doubt questions will be asked – as to the course which the Government will pursue in consequence of the news that has been received from the Province of New Brunswick, with reference to the result of the elections in that province. (Hear, hear.) . . . The Government will, therefore, at once state, that it is our design to press, by all proper and parliamentary modes of procedure within our power, for an early decision of the House – yes or no – whether they approve of this scheme or do not. (Hear, hear.) One great reason, among others, calling for promptness, is to provide as much as possible against the reaction which will take place in England from the disappointment that will pervade the minds of the people of England, if they get the impression that the project of the union of the provinces is abandoned. (Hear, hear.) I believe that if one thing more than another has raised British America, or the Province of Canada, its chief component part, in the estimation of the people and Government of England, it is that by this scheme there was offered to the Mother Country a means by which these colonies should cease to be a source of embarrassment, and become, in fact, a source of strength. This feeling pervades the public mind of England. Every writer and speaker of note in the United Kingdom, who has treated of the subject, says a new era of colonial existence has been inaugurated, and that if these colonies, feeble while disunited, were a source of weakness, they will, by forming this friendly alliance, become a strong support to England. . . .

Another reason why this question must be dealt with promptly and an early decision obtained, is, that it is more or less intimately connected with the question of defence, and that is a question of the most imminent necessity. (Hear, hear.) No one can exaggerate the necessity which exists for the Legislature of this country considering at once the defences that are called for in the present position of affairs on this continent. I need not say that this subject has engaged our anxious attention as a Government. The Provincial Government has been in continued correspondence with the Home Government as to the best means of organizing an efficient defence against every hostile pressure, from whatever source it may come. And, as this House knows, the resolutions themselves speak of the defence question as one that must immediately engage the attention of the Confederation. We had hoped that the Confederation scheme would have assumed such an aspect that the question could have been adjudged of as a whole, and that one organized system of defence could have been arranged between the Federal Government and the Imperial Government at an early day. But we cannot disguise, nor can we close our eyes to the fact that the course of events in New Brunswick will prevent an early united action among the provinces on the subject of defence; and, therefore, that question comes up as between Canada and England, and we feel that it cannot be postponed. (Hear, hear.) In fact the subject has already been postponed quite too long. (Hear, hear.) It is time, high time, that it was taken up and dealt with in a vigorous manner. (Hear, hear.) These are two of the reasons which, the Government feel, press for a prompt decision of the House upon the resolutions before it. (Hear, hear.)...

MONDAY / MARCH 6, 1865.

Hon. John Sandfield Macdonald [Cornwall]:

. . . I come now, sir, to a matter personal perhaps more to myself than to anyone else. I would ask the House who was it that assailed the Government of Canada more by his speeches and letters than this same HON. MR. TILLEY? Who was it that charged the Government of this country with a breach of faith towards the Lower Provinces in reference to the construction of the Intercolonial Railway; and whose statement was it that was reëchoed on the floor of this House over and over again, that Canada had lowered its character and dignity by failing to go on with that undertaking? Was it not the HON. MR. TILLEY who made these false accusations, and were they not, on his authority, repeated here by an honorable gentleman now in the Government, at the head of the Bureau of Agriculture (HON. MR. MCGEE)? Recollecting these things, sir, I have a pleasure – a mischievous pleasure – (hear, hear, and laughter) – I have a mischievous pleasure, I say, in knowing that the HON. MR. TILLEY has been defeated. (Ironical cheers.) I repeat that I have experienced to-day a considerable degree of happiness in announcing that the man who, at the head of the Government of New Brunswick, betrayed the trust of the people, who failed to carry out their wishes in respect to the union of the Maritime Provinces, who exceeded the authority with which he was entrusted, who betrayed the interests of his province and abandoned everything that he was sent to Charlottetown to obtain – the man who went throughout the length and breadth of his province crying out against the good faith of the then Canadian Government – I say

I have happiness in announcing that he has been disposed of by the people. (Hear, hear.) HON. MR. TILLEY came to Quebec in 1863, with HON. MR. TUPPER, and although he made the charge of bad faith against the Canadian Government, he knew as well as HON. MR. TUPPER that the agreement of 1862 respecting the Intercolonial Railway was to be abandoned, except so far as the survey of the line was concerned.

Hon. Mr. McGee – Hear, hear.

Hon. J. S. Macdonald – The honorable gentleman cries "Hear, hear," but can he say that, while a member of the Government, he did not write a letter to a gentleman in this province, in which he said that the scheme of 1862 was abandoned by the Canadian Government.

Hon. Mr. McGee – The honorable gentleman has made that charge once before publicly, and I denied it publicly. If he can get any such letter of mine, he is fully authorized by me to make it public. HON. MR. TILLEY, so far from believing the scheme abandoned, went back to New Brunswick with a very different impression; and I ask the honorable gentleman whether he did not say to him while here: – "I declare to God, TILLEY, if I thought by resigning my office we could get the Intercolonial Railway, I would do it." The honorable gentleman is out of office now, and perhaps he will say whether he made this declaration or not. (Hear, hear.)

Hon. J. S. Macdonald – I do not deny that. I was then, and always have been, in favor of the Intercolonial Railway, and am desirous that it should be built. I think that an outlet to the ocean on British soil, at all seasons of the year, is a very desirable thing to be obtained, and upon that point I have never changed my opinion. But I do say that HON. MR. TUPPER and HON. MR. TILLEY understood that it was not to be proceeded with at that time, and a memorandum was drawn up by DR. TUPPER at the time (I am now speaking in the presence of my late colleagues, who are aware of all the facts), embodying the decision at which the Government arrived, but which was not signed, because HON. MR. TILLEY asked that MR. FLEMING might be considered as engaged to proceed with the survey, and wished to reserve it for the formal ratification of his colleagues when he went back to New Brunswick. When he did go back, his colleagues dissented from the views he had formed, and, in order to get himself out of the awkward position in which he was placed, he took the ground that the abandonment of the project was owing to the bad faith of the Canadian Government. Now I say it is a matter of great satisfaction to me that the honorable gentleman who circulated this charge, and gave ground for honorable gentlemen now on the Treasury benches to attack the Government of which I was a member, and accuse it of bad faith to the sister provinces, has for these bold and audacious statements met his just deserts. . . .

MONDAY / MARCH 6, 1865.

Hon. Antoine Aimé Dorion [Hochelaga]:

. . . Well, sir, I must say that if the honorable gentlemen opposite had not been untrue to their pledge – if they had brought to this House the measure they then promised [federation of the Canadas] – we in this country would, at all events, have been saved the humiliation of seeing the Government going on its knees and begging the little island of Prince Edward to come into this union, and then going to Nova Scotia and New Brunswick and supplicating them to relieve us of our difficulties; and saved the humiliation of seeing these supplications and the bribes in every direction with which they were accompanied, in the shape of subsidies to New Brunswick and Newfoundland, and of the Intercolonial Railway, rejected by those to whom they were offered. Canada would, at all events, have held a dignified position, and not suffered the humiliation of seeing all the offers of our Government indignantly rejected by the people of the Lower Provinces. The Hon. Attorney General West says that the scheme of Confederation has obtained the consent of the governments of all the provinces; but where are those governments now? Where is the Government of New Brunswick? Where is the Government of Prince Edward Island? (Hear, hear.) As for the Government of Nova Scotia, it pledged itself to bring the scheme before the Legislature; but it is well known that it care not press it, and still less appeal to the people upon it. The members of that Government were wiser than the Government of New Brunswick, and would not appeal to the people. . . .

TUESDAY / MARCH 7, 1865.

Hon. Atty. Gen. John A. Macdonald:

. . . Therefore, there should not be any loss of time whatever, and with that view the Government would ask this House – as the discussion has already gone on to a considerable length, and a great many honorable gentlemen have spoken on the subject – that it will offer no undue delay in coming to a conclusion in this matter. Of course the Government would not attempt to shut down the floodgates against all discussion; but they would merely ask and invite the House to consider the importance of as early a vote as the House can properly allow to be taken upon this question. It is for the House to determine whether the Federation scheme which has been proposed by the Government and laid before the House is one which, with all its faults, should be adopted, or whether we shall be thrown upon an uncertain future. In order that the House may at once come to an understanding in the matter, I shall, as I stated yesterday, take every possible step known to parliamentary usage to get a vote as soon as it can conveniently be got, and I have therefore now to move the previous question. (Ironical Opposition cheers and counter cheering.) I move, sir, that the main question be now put. (More cheering.) Honorable gentlemen opposite know very well that my making this motion does not in any way stop the debate. (Hear, hear.) . . .

The Speaker – If honorable gentlemen desire it, I will read the rule of the House as to the previous question. The 35th rule of the House is as follows: – "The previous question, until it is decided, shall preclude all amendments to the main question" – (ironical Opposition cheers) – "and shall be in the following words – 'That this question be now put.' If the previous question be resolved in the affirmative, the original question is put forthwith, without amendment or debate." (Hear, hear.)

Hon. Mr. Cartier – MR. SPEAKER, I second the motion. (Derisive Opposition cheers.)

TUESDAY / MARCH 7, 1865.

Hon. Luther Hamilton Holton [Châteauguay]:

I say it has always been a theory of my own, and facts are rapidly demonstrating the truth of that theory, that this Government was formed in consequence of the emergencies of certain gentlemen who were in office, and desired to retain office, and of certain other gentlemen who were out of office and who desired to come in. I believe that the whole constitutional difficulties, or alleged constitutional difficulties, of this country arose from the personal or rather the political emergencies in which certain hon. gentlemen found themselves, from causes to which I shall not now advert. (Hear, hear.) Well, sir, feeling that this scheme has failed – feeling that the pretext upon which they have held office for six or nine months is about to fail them, they devise other means, as a sort of lure to the country, whereby office may be kept for a further period. I admit the dexterity with which the thing is done – a dexterity for which the Hon. Attorney General West has long been famous in this country. His theory is: "Take care of to-day – when to-morrow comes we will see what can be done" – and by adhering to this maxim he has managed to lengthen out the term of his political existence. That, I believe, will be acknowledged to be the theory upon which the hon. gentleman acts.

Hon. Atty. Gen. Macdonald – And a very sensible theory it is. (Laughter.)

Hon. Mr. Holton – A sensible theory no doubt it is. I am glad to hear that the hon. gentleman does not deny the fact; but while admitting that he has achieved a considerable measure of success in this way, whether, after all that success, he has earned the highest kind of reward of a public life – whether there is anybody who speaks or thinks of the hon. gentleman as a statesman, may perhaps be doubted. It is admitted that he is an adroit manager – his management being based on the theory of doing to-day what must be done to-day, and of leaving till to-morrow whatever can be deferred. I doubt, however, after all, whether, when the hon. gentleman comes to review his career, he will be satisfied that that sort of policy brings with it the highest rewards of public life.

Hon. Atty. Gen. Macdonald – I shall be quite satisfied to allow the hon. member for Chateauguay to be my biographer. (Laughter.)

Hon. Mr. Holton – But while that has been his theory and his practice, and a certain degree of success has attended it, I would like to ask the Hon. President of the Council whether he has heretofore acted upon that theory, and whether he can quite afford to act upon it now? Most of us remember – those of us who have been for a few years in public life in this country, must remember a very striking speech delivered by the hon. member for South Oxford (HONORABLE MR. BROWN), in Toronto, in the session of 1856 or 1857 – he has delivered many striking speeches in his time, but this was one of the most striking – in which he described the path of the Hon. Attorney General West as being studded all along by the grave-stones of his slaughtered colleagues. (Hear, hear.) Well, there are not wanting those who think they descry in the not very remote distance, a yawning grave waiting for the noblest victim of them all. (Laughter.) And I very much fear, that unless the hon. gentleman [GEORGE BROWN] has the courage to assert his own original strength – and he has great strength – and to discard the blandishments and the sweets of office, and to plant himself where he stood formerly, in the affections and confidence of the people of this country, as the foremost defender of the rights of the people, as the foremost champion of the privileges of a free Parliament – unless he hastens to do that, I very much fear that he too may fall a victim – as I have said, the noblest victim of them all – to the arts, if not the arms, of the fell destroyer. (Laughter.) . . .

TUESDAY / MARCH 7, 1865.

Hon. François Evanturel [Quebec County]:

As one of the friends of the present Administration, I must say that I am surprised by the conduct of the Government and the extreme position in which they choose to place themselves. For my part, I am in favor of the principle of Confederation, and one of those who maintain that by means of that principle the rights and liberties of each of the contracting parties may be preserved; but, on the other hand, I am of opinion, and I do not disguise it from myself, that it may be so applied as to endanger and even destroy, or nearly so, the rights and privileges of a state which is a party to this Confederation. Everything, therefore, depends on the conditions of the contract. As a friend of the Administration I can understand, as well as anyone, that any Confederation and particularly such a one as this which is now laid before us, can only be brought about by means of a compromise; and, on this account, MR. SPEAKER – and it is probably needless to proclaim it here – I am ready and disposed to go to as great a length as it is possible for any man to go. I am also one of those who, when we are called upon to unite, under the ægis of a strong government, the different provinces of British North America, and when I see that the general interest calls for such a union, will give my cordial support to all who seek to establish such a government. I shall always be prepared to meet them halfway; but when the question assumes a different shape, as it now does, and when, in consequence of the events announced to this House yesterday, the Constitution proposed to us seems to concern none but the provinces of Upper and Lower Canada, I say, MR. SPEAKER, that the compromise between the different provinces no longer existing, we are no longer called upon to be so generous. I say that if we admit that New Brunswick, by its recent repudiation, and Nova Scotia and Prince Edward Island are no longer parties to the contracts agreed on between the provinces, and we have now to ask of England to modify the Constitution only in relation to the two Canadas, I say that the conditions are no longer the same as they concern us – (hear, hear) – and that I am on that account much less disposed to allow the Government to proceed to present in England, as the basis of our future Constitution, the resolutions which we have been compelled to accept in very unfavorable circumstances. I do not hesitate in saying that the position assumed by the Government is a very dangerous one for themselves, and for those who would gladly assist them to pass a good scheme of Confederation. If I understand aright, the intention of the Government, in moving the previous question, is to place their friends in the awkward position of not being able to move any modification of the plan. In our altered position we are going, therefore, to say to England that we were obliged to submit to such and such concessions in order to come to an understanding; that the other provinces have backed out of the bargain, notwithstanding these onerous concessions and the compromise which we were obliged to make, and which have not been accepted by the other parties; and that, in the face of all this, we come to pray that our Constitution may be altered so as to accord with those very same onerous conditions which we had accepted at the Quebec Conference. Why tie us down so strictly now? Why should we not avail ourselves of the retrogression of the provinces to make alterations in the scheme which will be less onerous for us? I think it my duty to declare that the Government, in acting as they have done, place their friends in a very awkward position. For my part, MR. SPEAKER, I am strongly in favor of Confederation, and am ready to support the Government in their efforts to release the chariot of the state from the position in which it now lies; but I wish, on the other hand – and I think it is but bare justice to say it – I wish that Ministers should place us in such a position before the country, that I and all others may be able to say that we have done our best to improve the situation. This is why I so deeply regret that the Government have thought fit to take their present arbitrary attitude. (Hear, hear.) I acknowledge, with the Administration, that time is precious; but we ought not, in avoiding one danger, to risk falling into another. . . .

TUESDAY / MARCH 7, 1865.

Hon. Mr. Luther Holton:

. . . I state – and I am sure I have only to state it to him [MR. MACDONALD] to convince him of the justice of it – that a persistence in moving the previous question will be simply a violation of the assurance the hon. gentleman gave to the House, and of the distinct understanding arrived at by the House at the opening of the debate, and stated by you, sir, from the chair. (Hear, hear.) Am I to understand that the hon. gentleman adheres to his motion?

Hon. Atty. Gen. Macdonald – I certainly do adhere to it.

Hon. Mr. Holton – And has the hon. gentleman nothing to say to my objections?

Hon. Atty. Gen. Macdonald – To what?

Hon. Mr. Holton – In reference to cutting off amendments by this motion. Hon. Atty. Gen. Macdonald – Why did not the hon. gentleman put them?

Hon. Mr. Holton – We relied upon the assurance given by the hon. gentleman that there would be no attempt to cut short discussion, no attempt to prevent a full and free expression of the opinion of the House upon every feature of the scheme. I ask him now again if he intends to adhere to that declaration? (Hear, hear.)

Hon. Atty. Gen. Macdonald – I will, MR. SPEAKER, on reflection, make a few remarks in answer to the hon. gentleman. He speaks as if it was a great concession to the majority of this House and to the Government that the arrangement was made at the opening of the debate. Why, sir, it was no concession whatever to the Government or to the majority of the House. (Hear, hear.) Acting on behalf of the Government, and with the full approbation of my colleagues, I made a motion that an Address should be presented to Her Majesty, praying Her sanction to the resolutions adopted at the Quebec Conference. That motion was quite parliamentary in its character, and there was no parliamentary reason whatever why it should be considered in Committee of the Whole. The hon. gentleman could not, by any rule known to parliamentary practice, force us to go into committee or require us to discuss anyone of these resolutions by itself. It was then quite open to me, according to the usage of the House, to make a motion for an Address to Her Majesty for the purpose stated, and it was not as a favor to the Government that the arrangement was made to discuss it as if the House were in Committee of the Whole. On the contrary, it was a concession of the Government to the minority in the House; for I stated, of my own mere motion, that although I had a right to proceed in the ordinary manner with the Speaker in the chair, and to restrict honorable gentlemen to a single speech in accordance with the rules that govern debate – that although this was my undoubted right according to parliamentary practice, yet, for the purpose of allowing the fullest and freest discussion, I suggested that the same rule should obtain as if the House were in Committee of the Whole, when every member could speak twenty times if he felt so disposed, and present his views fully on all the points of the scheme. That was the proposition made by the Government; it was a fair, liberal, even generous one. But how were we met by honorable gentlemen opposite? We were ready to proceed with the discussion at once, and to present the subject to the House without delay. But it was stated that that would be unfair – that the members of the Government should first make a statement, and allow it to go to the House and country, so that neither should be taken by surprise in a matter of so much importance, and that honorable gentlemen might have the fullest information upon which to make up their minds. We did make our statement, and when asked for a week's delay in order that these speeches might be fully considered, we consented to it. Supposing that after this postponement the debate would go on at once, we gave hon. gentlemen opposed to the scheme a whole week to consider our remarks, to prepare themselves for debate, to work out objections to our arguments, and pick out all the flaws they could find in the scheme itself. We did this because we thought it fair, and because we believed hon. gentlemen were sincere in their professed desire to have the fullest information upon the subject. Well, the debate began, it has gone on now for three weeks since that postponement, and as my hon. colleague the Hon. Provincial Secretary has said, it has dragged on wearily, with no prospect of an early termination. And how have we been met by hon. gentlemen opposite? Has it been in the same spirit that actuated the Government throughout the debate? We asked them to come forward, and honestly and fairly, in the presence of the House and country, to discuss the scheme; but instead of so doing, they have deliberately trifled with the question and wasted the time of the House. (Hear, hear.)

Hon. Mr. Holton – No, no!

Hon. Atty. Gen. Macdonald – The hon. gentleman as a man of honor cannot deny it, as a man of candor he cannot deny it; and if he should deny it, his character as a man of honor and candor would sink in the estimation of this House. (Hear, hear.) I say it distinctly that this was the plot of hon. gentlemen opposite, to delay the consideration of this subject. Their policy was to wait, like MICAWBER, for "something to turn up," to see what would happen favorable to them in New Brunswick, to learn what would be done in Nova Scotia, and to embrace every pretext of delay that presented itself. The hon. gentleman was playing, deliberately playing, a trick. He talked about a base trick having been played upon the Opposition, but was it not a base trick in him not to discuss this question, but to put it off upon every possible excuse, to interrupt hon. gentlemen when they discussed it, making innuendoes, suggesting motives for delay, trying to disparage the scheme and ourselves in the estimation of the House and country, and getting others to say what he would not dare to say himself. (Hear, hear.) That was the plan of the hon. gentleman. He complains of not being able to move an amendment, but the Opposition attempted to move none. It was friends of the Government who offered the only amendments yet presented. The policy of the Opposition was just this – they wished to spend the whole of March and the best part of April in the general discussion upon my motion; and then, when they could do nothing more to nauseate the House and disgust the country with the subject, when they had wearied the members and made the reporters sick with their talk – (laughter) – they were to spend the remainder of April, all May and June, and run the debate well into summer, upon the amendments they intended to propose one after another. (Hear, hear, and laughter.) It is because these honorable gentlemen have not endeavored honestly and candidly to discuss the question, but have played the game of prolonging the debate to midsummer and preventing the House coming to a final decision upon it, that the Government have taken the step now proposed, and have said to these hon. gentlemen: "Here, you have had a month to move amendments and make speeches. You have been allowed to sit here discussing the question every night during that time, and sometimes till one or two o'clock in the morning. You have not fairly discussed the scheme, nor moved any amendments to it. You appear, on the contrary, determined to obstruct the measure by every means in your power. You have deliberately laid a plot to throw it back with the view of defeating it in this underhand manner. We are not going to allow that, nor should be worthy of the position we hold as a Government if we did allow it"; and, sir, I should be unworthy of the character the hon. gentleman (HON. MR. HOLTON) gives me of being a good parliamentary strategist, if I allowed this plot of preventing the House coming to a vote to succeed. (Hear, hear.) Now, in resorting to measures to prevent the success of this game played by the Opposition, we have not taken hon. gentlemen opposite or the House by surprise. We gave them from the middle of winter almost to the beginning of spring, and the opening of navigation, to discuss the question and propose amendments; and when we saw they were determined to waste the time of the House and country indefinitely, I came down yesterday and, on behalf of the Government and with the full approbation of my colleagues, stated fairly and frankly that it was of the greatest consequence, the utmost consequence, to the best interests of this country, that this question should not be allowed to drag on before Parliament, but that a vote should be taken without delay, in order that we might be able to tell the sister provinces and inform Her Majesty that the contract we made with them, the arrangement we entered into with the governments of those provinces, had met the full approbation and consent of the Parliament and people of Canada. (Hear, hear.) And I gave fair notice that the Government considered the recent political events in New Brunswick, and the state of affairs in that province, called not only for action, but prompt action by this House; and that every proper and legitimate means known to parliamentary practice would be taken by the Government for the purpose of getting this House to come to a full and final decision upon the question. (Hear, hear.) We have never taken hon. gentlemen by surprise. On the contrary, we have allowed them every latitude in this debate, and have given them fair notice all through of what we intended to do. But how have we been met by them? Have we been met in the same spirit of frankness and sincerity? No – and I say it without hesitation, we have been met throughout in a spirit of obstruction and hostility; and, instead of discussing the question fairly on its merits, hon. gentlemen opposite are dragging on the debate slowly for months, in order to tire out the patience of the House and country. (Hear, hear.) I ask the House whether they will permit such a shabby, such a miserable game to be played successfully? Will they allow a question so closely identified with the best interests of Canada to be thrown across the floor of the House like a battledore between the hon. members for Cornwall and Chateauguay? Will they allow these hon. gentlemen to trifle with it, not so much because they are opposed to the scheme itself or disapprove of its general principles, as because of those by whom it is presented for the adoption of the House. (Hear, hear.) Sir, there has been some little misapprehension as to the effect of the motion I have proposed to the House, which it is as well should be removed. It has simply and only this effect – that it does not prevent hon. members expressing their views fully and freely upon the subject, but calls upon every hon. gentleman to give – if I may use an Americanism – a straight and square vote upon the question, and to state plainly whether or not he approves of the scheme of Confederation as a whole. (Hear, hear.) . . .

We have pledged ourselves as a Government to come down to the Canadian Parliament and say – "Here is a Constitution which we have agreed upon for the future government of these provinces. We have agreed to submit it to this House, just as the governments of the other provinces have agreed to submit it to their respective legislatures. We have a right to ask the members of this House whether in their judgment it is a scheme that, with all the faults and imperfections it may have, ought to be entered into by the Parliament of this country. We exercise this right, and ask you to declare by your votes, yes or no, whether we were right in framing this measure, and whether it is such an one as ought to be adopted by this House." (Hear, hear.) This, MR. SPEAKER, is the position of the Government; and what though amendments should be carried – what though the amendment of which the honorable member for North Ontario [M.C. CAMERON] has given notice should succeed, and the House should declare in favor of a Legislative instead of a Federal union (supposing the honorable gentleman did present and carry such a motion) – what good could it possibly do? The contract that we entered into with the other provinces would be broken; this Legislature would be violating the solemn engagement under which we are to the other colonies, and we would have a Constitution drawn up which none of the other provinces would adopt. We know that they would reject it – we know that Lower Canada would go as one man against it. (Hear, hear.)

Hon. Mr. Holton – Well, the other provinces go against this.

Hon. Atty. Gen. Macdonald – At all events the governments of the other provinces will submit the question to their legislatures and take their opinion upon it, and we have a right to ask this House – "Do you or do you not approve of it? If you disapprove of the scheme altogether because of its general principles, why vote it out. If you think that it ought to be a Legislative and not a Federal union, why vote it out. If you think it wrong to create a life peerage instead of an elective Legislative Council, why vote it out. Vote it out for any or all of these reasons if you like; but give us at once an honest, candid and fair vote one way or the other, and let the sister colonies know without delay whether you approve of the arrangement or not." (Hear, hear.) And, sir, amendments are a mere matter of folly and absurdity. (Hear, hear, and ironical cheers from the Opposition.) Honorable gentlemen opposite cry "Hear, hear." I do not of course speak of the merits of any proposition in amendment for a legislative union, or an elective Legislative Council, or for any other change in the provisions of the scheme; but I state this in all earnestness, that for all practical purposes the carrying of any amendment to this scheme is merely to lose the only chance of union we can ever hope to have with the Lower Provinces for the sake of some fancied superior Constitution which we cannot get any of the colonies to agree to. (Hear, hear.) All we ask this House to do is what the other branch of the Legislature has already candidly done, to discuss the matter fairly and honestly upon its merits, and then to come to a vote upon it. Those who think the Constitution likely to place the country in a worse position than it now occupies, will vote against it. Those who think, on the other hand, that it is an approximation at any rate to what is right, that it will bring the colonies together into closer communication, that it will form the basis of a powerful and enduring alliance with England, will vote for it with all its faults. (Hear, hear.) . . .

We cannot say how those [Maritime] legislatures will vote, but what we propose to do is to lay our action before the Imperial Government, and ask it to exercise its influence with the other colonies in securing the passage of the scheme. And I have no doubt that if the Mother Country gives friendly advice to the sister colonies in that kindly spirit in which she always gives it, if she points out that in her view this scheme is calculated to serve, not only our interests, but the general interests, welfare and prosperity of the Empire, I am quite satisfied that the people of those colonies, whatever may be their local feelings, will listen at all events with respect, and perhaps with conviction, to the advice so given by the Imperial Government. I have no doubt, indeed I am satisfied, that if the Imperial Government gives that advice, it will be in the spirit of kindness and maternal love and forbearance, and that if England points out what is due to ourselves as well as to the Empire, and shows what she, in her experience and wisdom, believes to be best for the future interests of British North America, her advice will be accepted in the spirit in which it is offered, and sooner or later with conviction. (Cheers.) For all these reasons I think the members of the Government would be wanting in their duty in this great strait, this great emergency in our affairs, if they did not press for the decision of this House as quickly as possible. (Hear, hear.) Why, there is the question of defence, which the honorable member for Cornwall admits to be of the most pressing importance, that requires immediate attention and demands that further delay in dealing with this scheme should not be allowed.

Hon. Mr. Holton – What has defence to do with this scheme of Confederation? The honorable gentleman has stated, over and over again, that it has nothing to do with it. (Hear, hear.)

Hon. Atty. Gen. Macdonald – The honorable gentleman is mistaken. The two questions are intimately connected. . . . When I say that there is an intimate connection between these two questions of defence and Confederation, I mean this: that the progress of recent events – events which have occurred since the commencement of this debate – has increased the necessity of immediate action, both with regard to defence and to this scheme. Honorable gentlemen opposite have been in the Government – they have been behind the scenes – and they know that the question of the defence of British North America is of great and pressing importance, and they know that the question of the defence of Canada cannot be separated from it. And honorable gentlemen have been informed, and will find by the scheme itself, that the subject was considered by the Conference, and that it was arranged that there should be one organized system of defence for the whole of the provinces and at the cost of the whole. Well, it is now of the greatest importance that some members of the Government should go home immediately, in order that England may know what the opinion of Canada is upon this question of Confederation, as well as upon the question of defence. (Hear, hear.)

Hon. J. S. Macdonald – Is that what you want them to go for?

Hon. Atty. Gen. Macdonald – Yes. The season is fast approaching when it will be necessary to commence these works – the only season during which they can be carried out at all; and that man is not true to his country, that man is not a true patriot, who, for the sake of a petty parliamentary triumph, for the sake of a little party annoyance – for the conduct of the Opposition amounts to nothing more – would endeavor to postpone some definite arrangement on this important question of defence. (Hear, hear.) Yes, MR. SPEAKER, this opposition is either one or the other of two things – it is either for the sake of party annoyance, or it is a deliberate desire to prevent anything being done to defend ourselves, in order that we may easily fall a prey to annexation. (Cheers.) I do not like to believe that honorable gentlemen opposite entertain any wish to become connected with the neighboring republic, and therefore I am forced to the conviction that they are actuated by the miserable motive of gaining a little parliamentary or party success. There are only two alternatives of belief, and one or the other of them must be correct. (Hear, hear.) I believe the honorable member for Chateauguay is in his heart strongly in favor of a Federal union of these colonies; but because it is proposed by honorable gentlemen on this side of the House, he cannot and will not support it. (Hear, hear.) So long as my honorable friend the Hon. Finance Minister sits here on these benches, so long as MORDECAI sits at the King's gate – (laughter) – and so long as the honorable gentleman sits on the opposite instead of this side of the House, so long will he find fault and object. Hit high or hit low, like the flogged soldier, nothing will please him. (Renewed laughter.) But I believe the House will not sanction such pitiful conduct as honorable gentlemen opposite exhibit. I believe we will have a large, an overwhelming majority, to sustain us in the course we have adopted; and that we should be highly blamable were we to exhaust the patience not only of ourselves, but of our supporters, by allowing this conduct to be pursued much longer unchecked. These, sir, are my answers to the questions of the honorable member for Chateauguay. (Cheers.)

Hon. Mr. Holton – I have the satisfaction of having provoked from the hon. gentleman altogether the best speech he has delivered during this debate. So much I freely admit, and I think his own followers will confess that this is the first time he has spoken with anything like his usual spirit and force during the whole debate. . . .

THURSDAY / MARCH 9, 1865.

Jean Baptiste Eric Dorion [Drummond and Arthabaska]:

. . . Why, MR. SPEAKER, are we engaged this evening in discussing a Confederation of the Provinces of British North America? Because we had, last year, a Ministerial crisis, from which arose a proposal for the union of the two political parties who divided public opinion. The MACDONALD-TACHÉ Ministry, who represented the Conservative party in the country, had just been defeated in the Legislative Assembly; they were obliged to resign. It will be recollected that the Government were beaten on a question of mal-administration of the public business. I allude to the advance of $100,000 made to the Grand Trunk Railway without authority of Parliament, for which act several members of the Cabinet were responsible. Could you inform me, MR. SPEAKER, what has become of the $100,000 question? Alas! it disappeared in the

Ministerial crisis, and left us the extraordinary Coalition which now governs us, composed of men who for ten years treated each other as men devoid of political principle! (Hear, hear.) . . .

They [Maritimers] seem to be afraid of us; and notwithstanding the offers of money made to them, they will have nothing to do with a union. Our reputation for extravagance must be very bad to frighten them to that degree; and, no doubt, when they saw us spend in the course of a month or two, for receptions, in traveling and in feasting, sums equaling in amount the whole of revenue of Prince Edward Island, they must have gone back with a sorry idea of our way of managing public business. (Hear, hear.) . . .

Now, let me justify my opposition to the projected change. I am opposed to the scheme of Confederation, because the first resolution is nonsense and repugnant to truth; it is not a Federal union which is offered to us, but a Legislative union in disguise. Federalism is completely eliminated from this scheme, which centres everything in the General Government. Federalism means the union of certain states, which retain their full sovereignty in everything that immediately concerns them, but submitting to the General Government questions of peace, of war, of foreign relations, foreign trade, customs and postal service. Is that what is proposed to us? Not at all. In the scheme we are now examining, all is strength and power, in the Federal Government; all is weakness, insignificance, annihilation in the Local Government! . . .

I am opposed to the scheme of Confederation, because by means of the right of *veto* vested in the Governor by the 51st resolution, local legislation will be nothing but a farce. They may try to make us believe that this power would be but rarely exercised, and that it differs in nowise from that exercised by the present Governor when he reserves bills for the Royal assent; but all the country knows that it would not be so. From the moment that you bring the exercise of the right of *veto* more nearly within the reach of interested parties, you increase the number of opportunities for the exercise of the right – you open the door to intrigues. As, for instance, a party will oppose the passing of a law, and not succeeding in his opposition in Parliament, he will approach the Ministers and the Governor General, intriguing to obtain as a favor that the law may be disallowed. Take an example. I suppose your Confederation to be established; that a bill is passed for the protection of settlers, such as we have seen pass the House six times in ten years without becoming law, on account of the opposition to it in the Legislative Council by the councillors from Upper Canada; what would happen? The few interested parties who were opposed to the measure would rush to the Governor General to induce him to disallow the law. By an appeal to the right of property, to the respect due to acquired rights, and to other sophistries, they would override the will of the people on a measure which is just in itself, and which is sought for and approved of by all legal men of Lower Canada in the present House. The people of Lower Canada will be prevented from obtaining a law similar to those now existing in thirteen different states of the American union, and which would in no way affect the principles of the existing law in Lower Canada. (Hear, hear.) This is one instance out of a thousand, and will serve to illustrate the effect of this right of *veto*. I am opposed to the scheme of Confederation, because I cannot see why, on the one hand, it has been agreed to give all the public lands to the Government of each province, and on the other hand that the Government should purchase the lands in the Island of Newfoundland. The General Government gives up the fertile lands of Upper and Lower Canada, but it purchases the barren lands of Newfoundland at the enormous price of $150,000 per annum, a sum representing a capital of $2,500,000. Is not this a grand speculation for the country? The Government at Ottawa will not possess a single inch of land in Canada, New Brunswick or Nova Scotia, but they will have a Land Department for the management of their superb possessions in Newfoundland? Is it imagined that if the public lands of that island had been of any value, they would have been given up to the General Government for any amount? No, the fact is that these lands are utterly useless for cultivation, that the whole island does not produce hay enough for the town. of St. John's, and that every year large quantities of it are imported. I know a farmer in Three Rivers who has sent cargoes of hay to Newfoundland, and who is now only waiting for the navigation to open to send more – and these are the lands which it is proposed to buy for a fabulous price, in order to induce that province to come into the Confederation. (Hear.) . . .

I say that the people of Lower Canada are alarmed at the scheme of Confederation, and the unknown changes which are on foot. I do not say that this feeling prevails in the district of Quebec, for in that locality everybody seems to be fast asleep; but it exists, beyond doubt, and very warmly, in that of Montreal, and even as far as Three Rivers, on both sides of the river. . . .

THURSDAY / MARCH 9, 1865.

Paul Denis [Beauharnois]:

. . . For several days past, MR. SPEAKER, we have listened to pompous speeches made by honorable members of the Opposition, appealing incessantly to the religious and national prejudices of the population of Lower Canada, with the view of defeating the Government scheme. These honorable gentlemen draw pictures which are really heartrending. They tell the Protestants that under Confederation they will lose all their rights in Lower Canada in respect of the education of their children; and, on the other hand, they tell the Catholics that their religion is in danger, because the Federal Government will have the right of *veto* in respect of all the measures of the Local Government. But this right of *veto* must of necessity exist somewhere, in order that the minority may be protected from any injustice which the majority might attempt to do them. We cannot hope to have the majority in the Federal Parliament, when we French Lower Canadians and Catholics have never had it under the existing union. And yet we cannot but congratulate ourselves upon the relations which have always existed between us and our fellow-countrymen of other origins and religions. . . .

It has been also said that the use of our language was in danger, and that the French laws would disappear when Confederation was accomplished. But is it not a well-known fact that we owe the protection of our French laws to the Hon. Attorney General for Lower Canada (HON. MR. CARTIER), and is not the *Code Civil*, which he has just laid before us, a sufficient answer to all that can be asserted on this head? The French laws will be maintained and respected in Lower Canada, and this we owe to the Hon. Attorney General (HON. MR. CARTIER). We shall have a statute to assimilate the law of evidence in commercial matters in Lower Canada; but the French laws will not be abolished. If there is a man in the whole country who possesses real legal judgment, and who is perfectly acquainted with the laws and statutes of Lower Canada, it is certainly the Hon. Attorney General for Lower Canada, MR. GEORGE ETIENNE CARTIER. No one will deny this, and there is not a man who can compete with him in this respect. Why come here and tell us that our language is about to disappear, and that its use is to be abolished in the Federal Legislature? Is it because lies must be told in order to oppose the scheme of the Government, and real reasons for opposition cannot be found? A drowning man catches at a straw, and that is what the Opposition are doing to-day. But they ought to be just, and to admit that we shall have our code, which will guarantee to us the maintenance of our laws in Lower Canada, just as the Imperial Act will guarantee to us the use of our language. . . .

FRIDAY / MARCH 10, 1865.

Walter Shanly [South Grenville]:

In rising to address the House on the great question under debate, it is not my intention to go minutely into the subject; for after all that has been said, and the great length to which the debate has dragged on, I cannot expect to be able to fix the attention of my hearers for very long, even were the subject one to which I could speak authoritatively, instead of being, as it is, one that the ablest and most statesmanlike among us must in a great measure accept upon faith – trusting to the future to develop the excellences claimed for it on the one hand, or to establish the faults that are charged on it on the other. But though I do not pretend to be able to say anything new on the subject, or to throw any light on the uncertain future that lies before us, still I would be unwilling that in, perhaps, the most important division ever taken in a Colonial Legislature, my vote should be recorded without my first stating some, at all events, of the reasons that actuate me in voting as I intend to vote. One feature has been strikingly observable in the debate, and that is, that from first to last, as far as it has yet gone, no new thing has been offered or suggested. The programme of Confederation stands now exactly as it was presented in a *quasi* private form to the representatives of the people of this country some four months ago. The promoters of the scheme have added nothing to, taken nothing from the original bill of fare, and they have as good as told us, frankly and squarely, that they would add nothing to, take nothing from it if they could. The opponents of the project on the other hand, while giving it a sweeping condemnation, offer nothing, suggest nothing to replace that which they so summarily reject. Nothing is easier than to find fault with other men's work; it is a talent that we all possess, and that few of us ever think to hide under a bushel. For myself, though in favor of the scheme, being equally at a loss with other honorable members to say anything new upon it, I, too, will have to turn to my fault-finding instincts in the first instance. The honorable member for Montreal Centre (HON. MR. ROSE) has said in his able speech that if we could not improve on the project, we should forbear to find fault with it. I do not agree with him. On the contrary, I conceive that even though approving of the resolutions as a whole, it is the duty of members speaking to the question to point out and place on record the faults that strike them as likely to require correction by and by. And first of all – coming to discuss Confederation from my own standpoint – I would say that I have long looked forward to the time when the whole of the British North American Provinces would be united under one stable government; believing, as I always have believed ever since I came to know this country well, that we possess all the elements, in natural resources and endowments, and in distinctive geographical position, to form the ground-work of a power on this continent. I feared, nevertheless, when the project was foreshadowed here last year, that the time was not yet full for bringing about the desired combination. I feared that the almost total separation, political and social, which had heretofore existed between ourselves and the provinces below, might possibly cause a premature union to result in permanent estrangement. It appeared to me that we should first have cultivated social and commercial relations with our kindred on the seaboard before uniting, for better or for worse, in a political alliance. These were the views which I took of the Confederation project when it was so suddenly sprung upon us at the close of last session; and I confess that I still entertain grave apprehensions that we may be about to come together upon too short an acquaintance, before we have an opportunity of knowing one another, and learning to adapt ourselves the one to the other. In this consists my broad and general objection, not to the principle of Confederation, but to the hastiness with which it is sought to be carried out – threatening, as I fear, to mar our destiny in striving to overtake it. . . .

It would be in vain to attempt to conceal from ourselves that Canada is at this moment approaching the most critical period of her hitherto existence. Threatened with aggression from without, we are not in a gratifying condition of prosperity within, let blue books and census returns say what they will to the contrary. Great and momentous events are transpiring just beyond our frontier – events which have already seriously and injuriously affected us commercially, and which must inevitably, in some way or other, affect us politically. A people until recently devoted only to industrial pursuits and the development of their country, have suddenly expanded into a great military power. To use their own expression, the Americans are "making history very fast," and it is impossible that that eventful history can be manufactured in a territory separated from our own by little more than an imaginary line, without our having eventually some part in its pages, for good or for evil. In fact we cannot conceal from ourselves that some great change is impending over the destinies of our country – a change that will present itself to us in some form or other, and that before long, without its being in our power to avert, though it may be in our power to shape it. There is fast growing up in England a feeling of want of confidence in Canada. We see it in the tone of the press, in the parliamentary debates and elsewhere. We are told that we are giving more trouble to the Mother Country than we are worth. A similar feeling of want of confidence, amounting almost to contempt, has always prevailed towards us in the United States. The ignorance of everything relating to Canada – of our political and social condition – of our resources and our commerce – our growth and our progress – that exists among our kindred across the border, cannot fail to have surprised those who have mingled much among them, and if not altogether creditable to them is certainly very humiliating to us; but, great as the ignorance is there, it is fully equalled by that which exists with respect to Canada, and all pertaining to Canada, among our nearer and dearer kindred in the old world. What can we do to remedy this unfortunate and humiliating state of things? What can we do to inspire confidence in us abroad; to command respect; to defy contempt? These appear to me to be the practical questions with which we have to deal. We are plainly told by England that we must rely more upon our own resources in the future than we have done in the past, and it is right and just we should do so. . . .

I wish to take this opportunity of saying that I never had more than a sort of a half-confidence in the Government as now constituted. When the leaders of the Conservative party, with whom I have always acted, saw fit last year to make certain political combinations which, even they must admit, astonished and startled the country – combinations resulting in the present Coalition Ministry – I claimed that I and every member of the Conservative party, in this House or out of it, who chose to dissent from the course adopted by our leaders, had a right to hold ourselves absolved from all party ties and obligations whatever. I claimed then as I claim now, that from thenceforward I owed no political allegiance, no party fealty, to any man or any body of men on the floor of this House. In electing to adopt for myself the anomalous and hybrid position of an "independent member," I knew full well that it was to "burn my ship" – to cast away from me all chances of political advancement; but I never had political aspirations that warred with my own notions of political honor and consistency, or with my love of personal independence. But when great changes in our political relations are taking place; when all feel, as I believe all do feel, that a great and momentous event is impending; when, under such circumstances, my hon. friend the Honorable Attorney General for Upper Canada announces, as he has done, in a frank, bold, manly and statesmanlike manner, prompt and vigorous policy on the part of the Government in dealing with an unlooked-for difficulty – I allude to the difficulty growing out of the New Brunswick elections – I will tell that hon. gentleman that he and his colleagues may now – and always when boldly grappling with the political emergencies of the country – count on a cordial, earnest and admiring support from me. (Hear, hear.) Without further discussion or debate, I cast my vote for and my lot with the Confederation, and this I do in the fullest confidence and belief that, however faulty may be certain of the details of the scheme, and however awkward it may be to work out some of its provisions successfully, the resources of the people of these provinces, their innate adaptation for self-government, will be found fully equal to overcoming all the difficulties and obstacles that may beset their path. I fully believe that the faults which I now object to in the plan of Confederation will, like the diseases incident to childhood, grow out of our system as we advance in political strength and stature, and that when another decade has passed over us we will be found a strong, united British people, ready and able, in peace or in war, to hold our own upon this continent. (Cheers.)

FRIDAY / MARCH 10, 1865.

Joseph Rymal [South Wentworth]:

. . . It has been contended that with a view to our security, it was necessary to combine our strength. Now the strength, in my humble judgment, which we would obtain by consummating this union, is just that kind of strength which a fishing rod would obtain by fastening to it some additional joints. (Hear, hear.) If you can, by some convulsion of nature, bring Nova Scotia, New Brunswick, Prince Edward Island and Newfoundland, and place them where the uninhabitable mountains, fifteen or twenty miles north of this place, now are, or leave a couple of them in the bosom of Lake Ontario, we might have additional strength. But, under our actual circumstances, you propose merely to add to us several hundred miles more of length, without any additional hands to defend them. (Hear, hear.) . . .

MONDAY / MARCH 13, 1865.

Hon. Attorney General John A. Macdonald:

. . . One thing connected with this subject I greatly regret. I very much regret that although the debate has been so long protracted, and although we have had an expression from almost every member of this House, we have hitherto failed in getting the arguments promised in the speech of my hon. friend from Chateauguay [LUTHER HOLTON]. (Hear, hear.) For some reason or other we cannot get that speech out. Just as MOSES went up to Pisgah's top and viewed the promised land in the distance, just so the hon. member gives us an occasional glimpse of the promised speech, but we have thus far been disappointed in our expectations of hearing it delivered. . . . The thing which so utterly destroys the hon. gentleman's utility is his extreme modesty. (Laughter.) Why, when he had to rush to the rescue of the disordered finances of this country, at great personal sacrifice, for the sake of saving the country from the ruin that hung over it through the lavish extravagance of my hon. friend the present Hon. Finance Minister, he looked, with the exercise of his great financial ability, down into the recesses of the public chest and speedily discovered the source of all the evils that had fallen upon the country, and yet the modesty of the hon. gentleman prevented him from making known the remedy. (Laughter.) And so it is even now. He has been promising to give us his views upon this great question; but four weeks have passed, and his speech yet hangs fire. . . .

The hon. gentleman has somehow or other become the guardian of my political reputation. He has, on two or three occasions, warned me that although the course I took was, perhaps, that of a practical man – that of one who desired merely to keep office and become famous for political acuteness – yet it would never secure for me the fame of being a great statesman. Well, sir, I am satisfied to confine myself to practical things – to the securing of such practical measures as the country really wants. I am satisfied not to have a reputation for indulging in imaginary schemes and harboring visionary ideas that may end sometimes in an annexation movement, sometimes in Federation and sometimes in a legislative union, but always utopian and never practical. I am satisfied to leave the imaginary, the poetic and the impossible to the hon. member for Chateauguay. The other day the honorable gentleman paused to say, in the course of one of his little, numerous, by the by speeches, that in taking the course I have done on this question – that of advocating a Federal instead of a Legislative union – I violated all the principles of my former life having a bearing on this subject. . . . The hon. gentleman will see, from this passage, what my sentiments were, in 1861, on the subject, while taking part in a debate on representation by population. I was replying to a speech made by my present colleague, the Hon. Minister of Agriculture. I said: –

The only feasible scheme which presented itself to his (my) mind, as a remedy for the evils complained of, was a Confederation of all the provinces. (Hear, hear.) But in speaking of a Confederation he must not be understood as alluding to it in the sense of the one on the other side of the line. For that had not been successful. . . . The fatal error which they had committed – and it was, perhaps, unavoidable from the state of the colonies at the time of the revolution – was in making each state a distinct sovereignty, and giving to each a distinct sovereign power, except in those instances where they were specially reserved by the Constitution and conferred upon the General Government. The true principle of a Confederation lay in giving to the General Government all the principles and powers of sovereignty, and that the subordinate or individual states should have no powers but those expressly bestowed on them. We should thus have a powerful Central Government, a powerful Central Legislature, and a decentralized system of minor legislatures for local purposes.

These, sir, were the opinions I uttered in a speech delivered in 1861; and I say that the Constitution which this House, by a majority of three to one, has carried out as far as it is concerned, is, in spirit and letter, that which I then pointed out; and that was not the result of my experience, my thought and my opinion alone, but of the experience, thought and opinion of every man who had studied and taken into consideration the character of the Constitution of the United States. I know that in making that quotation I am committing the error which I have charged upon other hon. members of the House of going back in the debate; but I thought that it was due to myself to read it to the House, because the hon. member for Chateauguay – not in that blunt, plain-spoken style which characterizes some hon. gentlemen, but with that soothing, soft language that is so grateful to one's feelings – (laughter) – stated that in proposing a Federal union of these provinces I belied the whole of my political life, and that it was for this reason I made so feeble and ineffectual a speech when I offered these resolutions to the House. As to the feebleness and ineffectiveness of my speech, that, sir, I admit; but as to my sentiments on Confederation, they were the sentiments of my life, my sentiments in Parliament years ago, my sentiments in the Conference, and my sentiments now. (Hear, hear.) . . .

Suggestions for Further Reading

The standard accounts of the coming of Confederation are to be found in three works from the Centennial decade. W.L. Morton, *The Critical Years: The Union of British North America 1857-1873* (Toronto: McClelland and Stewart, 1964) offers a broad overview. Donald Creighton, *The Road to Confederation: The Emergence of Canada 1863-1867* (Toronto, Macmillan of Canada, 1964) is more detailed, and written with a nationalist bias. P.B. Waite, *The Life and Times of Confederation 1864-1867: Politics, Newspapers and the Union of British North America* (Toronto: University of Toronto Press, 1962) is a lively picture of the coming of Confederation as seen through the press. In a preface to a new edition (Toronto: Robin Brass Studio, 2001), Waite confesses that he avoided secondary sources while conducting his research: "I was afraid of them; I wanted my history as naked as possible." In fact, *Life and Times* also provides an exceptionally detailed bibliography.

English-speaking historians often imply that French Canada was "noises off," unconnected to the main events. Waite's discussion of Lower Canadian opinion may be supplemented by A.I . Silver, *The French-Canadian Idea of Confederation 1864- 1900* (Toronto: University of Toronto Press, 2nd ed., 1997). Brian Young, *George-Etienne Cartier: Montreal Bourgeois* (Kingston: McGill-Queen's University Press, 1981) places Cartier's approach to Confederation in its business, political, and social contexts. Andrée Désilets, *Hector-Louis Langevin: un père de la confédération canadienne (1826-1906)* (Quebec: Les Presses de l'Université Laval, 1969) shows how a prominent Bleu had argued for British North American union as far back as 1847. Marcel Hamelin, *Les premières années du parlementarisme québécois (1867- 1878)* (Quebec: Les Presses de l'Université Laval, 1974) provides a useful sequel to the Confederation debates by showing what Quebecers did with provincial autonomy. Wary anglophones can be reassured that both Désilets and Hamelin write in flowing and accessible French. Unhappily, the same cannot be said for the linguistic Gothic of the major contemporary statement of the case for Confederation in French, Joseph Cauchon's *L'Union des Provinces de l'Amérique Britannique du Nord* (Quebec: A. Côté et Cie, 1865).

Biographies of two rival Fathers of Confederation stand out. They are Donald Creighton, *John A. Macdonald: The Young Politician* (Toronto: University of Toronto Press, 1952) and the two volumes by J.M.S. Careless: *Brown of the Globe: I, The Voice of Upper Canada 1818-1859* (Toronto: Macmillan of Canada, 1959) and *Brown of the Globe: 2, Statesman of Confederation 1860-1880* (Toronto: Macmillan of Canada, 1963). *Brown of the Globe* was reissued by Dundurn Press of Toronto in 1989, Creighton's *Macdonald* by the University of Toronto Press in 1998. For entries in the multi-volume *Dictionary of Canadian Biography*, see Introduction page xxxii, note 21.

Canada's modern constitutional upheavals have encouraged fresh perspectives on the events of the 1860s. Christopher Moore, *1867: How the Fathers Made a Deal* (Toronto: McClelland and Stewart, 1997) is a collection of breezy essays expressly overshadowed by the Meech Lake controversy. A broad and controversial challenge comes from Paul Romney in *Getting It Wrong: How Canadians Forgot Their Past and Imperilled Confederation* (Toronto: University of Toronto Press, 1999). Romney argues that by telling the story in terms of centralisation, a nationalist school of Canadian historians has obscured an equally important view of the country as a federal compact between centre and periphery. Another analysis that focuses upon the centrifugal elements in Canadian governance is Robert C. Vipond, *Liberty and Community: Canadian Federalism and the Failure of the Constitution* (Albany: State University of New York Press, 1991). In "The Ideological Origins of Canadian Confederation," in Janet Ajzenstat and Peter J. Smith, eds, *Canada's Origins: Liberal, Tory or Republican* (Ottawa: Carleton University Press, 1995), Peter J. Smith traces an alternative intellectual thread, seeing Confederation as the outcome of a Tory belief in strong government. Ged Martin, *Britain and the Origins of Canadian Confederation 1837-67* (Vancouver: University of British Columbia Press, 1995) argues that a consensus among opinion-formers in Britain in favour of British North American union provided a supportive context which provincial politicians exploited in 1864-67.

The full text of the debates was published as *Parliamentary Debates on the Subject of the Confederation of the British North American Provinces, 3rd Session, 8th Provincial Parliament of Canada* (Quebec: Hunter, Rose & Co, 1865). A facsimile edition was issued in 1951

(Ottawa: Edmond Cloutier, King's Printer). The arguments advanced in the Confederation debates may be compared with a compilation of speeches made in 1864 at public, mainly festive, occasions by the architects of the new constitution: Edward Whelan, *The Union of the British Provinces* (ed. D.C. Harvey: Gardenvale, Quebec: Garden City Press, 1927). G. P. Browne, ed., *Documents on the Confederation of British North America* (Toronto: McClelland and Stewart, 1969) samples a broader collection of source materials, including reports of discussions behind closed doors at the 1864 Quebec Conference. Janet Ajzenstat, Paul Romney, Ian Gentles, and William D. Gairdner, eds, *Canada's Founding Debates* (Toronto: Stoddart, 1999) gives extracts from debates on Confederation across the continent, organised thematically. The editors perceive an impressive intellectual discourse, even in communities as small as British Columbia and the Red River, and insist on the continuing relevance of views expressed then to the Canada of today.

Confederation remains a crossroads event in Canada's past, pointing to many aspects of the country's experience. *The Reader's Guide to Canadian History* (second edition, Toronto: University of Toronto Press, 1994) provides signposts for further exploration. Volume 1 (*Beginnings to Confederation*) is edited by M. Brook Taylor; Volume 2 (*Confederation to the Present*) by Doug Owram.

Index